FEELING NORMAL

DELETED

FEELING NORMAL

Sexuality and Media Criticism in the Digital Age

F. Hollis Griffin

Indiana University Press

Bloomington and Indianapolis

This book is a publication of

Indiana University Press
Office of Scholarly Publishing
Herman B Wells Library 350
1320 East 10th Street
Bloomington, Indiana 47405 USA

iupress.indiana.edu

The paper used in this publication meets the minimum requirements
of the American National Standard for Information Sciences—
Permanence of Paper for Printed Library Materials, ANSI
Z39.48-1992.

Manufactured in the United States of America

Cataloging information is available from the Library of Congress.

ISBN 978-0-253-02447-3 (cloth)
ISBN 978-0-253-02455-8 (paperback)
ISBN 978-0-253-02459-6 (ebook)

1   2   3   4   5   21   20   19   18   16

With love to my great-grandmother,
Rose Steinmuller,
1912–2009

Contents

Acknowledgments   *ix*

Introduction   *1*

1 Cities as Affective Convergences   *23*

2 The Aesthetics of Banality after New Queer Cinema   *53*

3 Cable TV, Commodity Activism, and Corporate Synergy (or Lack Thereof)   *82*

4 Toward a Queerer Criticism of Television   *112*

5 Wanting Something Online   *140*

Afterword: #LoveWins   *169*

Selected Bibliography   *175*

Index   *183*

Acknowledgments

ONE HEARS ABOUT it ahead of time, and then one learns it: when you finish writing a book, you want to thank everyone you have ever met. First, thanks to my editor, whose keen eye and gentle encouragement were exactly what this project needed. Raina Polivka knew the book I wanted to write and then she let me write it. It turns out that hers was no small act of faith. I felt lucky when she saw something worth paying attention to in a bunch of convoluted e-mails and messy initial pages, and I still feel that way now. Thanks also to Janice Frisch for her patience, kindness, and attention to detail in moving the manuscript through the production process—if only other first-time authors could be as lucky in this regard. Thanks to Amy Villarejo for being a generous reader and an eager interlocutor. Amy's insights are such a big part of this book—and, really, who I am as a scholar—that I will forever be grateful to her. Thanks also to Ron Becker; his gracious mentorship and careful notes inform many of these pages, as well. Thanks to my advisory committee at Northwestern—Nick Davis, Patrick Johnson, and Mimi White—for helping me identify the questions I wanted to wrestle with in the years after I graduated. Thank you to the Mellon Foundation for giving me a fellowship at Colby College; it provided me with the time and space I needed to start thinking about this project. Thanks also to my mentor while I was at Colby, Lisa Arellano, whose mix of wit, warmth, and wisdom saw me through more than a few dark moments in the period when I was first trying to imagine what this book might look like.

Thanks to my friends and colleagues at Denison—Suzanne Condray, Amanda Gunn, Alina Haliluc, Bill Kirkpatrick, Sangeet Kumar, Jeff Kurtz, Omedi Ochieng, and Laura Russell—as well as Lauren Araiza, Kristen Cole, Regina Martin, Anna Nekola, and Jo Tague. As I wrote (and continued to rewrite), their kind words and good energy helped me a great deal. Thanks to the students who enrolled in the Queer Studies Senior Seminar I taught in spring 2015. They read a draft of the introduction to this book for a class session, and I may have learned more from them that day than they learned from me. Also at Denison, thanks to Cheryl Johnson, Sally Scheiderer, and the Communication Department Fellows for their help in getting "the final product" in order for publication. Thanks to the Gerber/Hart Archives in Chicago and the Gay, Lesbian, Bisexual, and Transgender (GLBT) Historical Society and Archives in San Francisco for access to their collections. The materials I found there turned out to be the linchpin of this book.

And thank you to the Denison University Research Fund (DURF) for the grant that helped me finish that research.

Thanks to *Flow, In Media Res, MediaCommons*, and *Velvet Light Trap* for letting me make some rudimentary attempts to think through the issues that would only make sense to me when I wrote this book. Thanks to attendees and fellow panelists for their feedback when I presented this research at conferences, including meetings of Society for Cinema and Media Studies, Console-ing Passions, American Studies Association, International Communication Association, National Communication Association, and American Historical Association, as well as the conferences on Cultural Studies and "The Popular" at American University of Paris, TV in the Academy at University of Vermont, Queering the Media at Colby College, Interfaces of Play and Game at Università di Bologna, and A Hundred Years of Film Theory at Universität Leipzig. Thanks also to Diane Negra for inviting me to participate in the plenary at the Television Cities Conference at University College Dublin. It later proved to be a pivotal moment in my getting chapter 1 off the ground. An article that intersects with and then developed adjacent to chapter 4 appears in *Cinema Journal*. I thank the editors there, as well.

Thanks to the friends and colleagues who read chapter drafts: Ben Aslinger, Eric Freedman, Racquel Gates, Julia Himberg, Elana Levine, Elizabeth Nathanson, Michael Newman, Allison Perlman, Bryce Renninger, Avi Santo, Kyle Stevens, and Damon Young. The list of people who read early pages bleeds into the list of folks I want to thank for fielding the crazy text messages and e-mails I sent while writing (and, let's face it, also when I wasn't writing): Dean Allbritton, Henry Russell Bergstein, James Carlisle, Rob Curtis, Jimmy Draper, Ben Hladilek, Vicky Johnson, Ron Martirano, Kristine McMahon, Laura Montemarano, Kevin Ohi, Kevin Sanson, Ryan Warden, and Kristen Warner. Their encouragement has shaped these pages more than they know. And thanks to the friends I have made since moving to Ohio: Kurt Lavetti, Mary Anne Lewis, Meris Mandernach, Alison Sauers, Jordan Smith, Eric Teague, Mary and Erik Turocy, and Steven Weber. They have graciously listened to me talk about this book more often than they may have wanted. Among these friends, I owe particular thanks to Lisbeth Lipari for being a devoted mentor and a kindred spirit whose intellect challenges me and humbles me in equal amounts. And I am especially grateful to Jessica Bean for letting me be Romy to her Michele when I moved to Columbus. Jessica is a terrific dinner date and wonderful sounding board in addition to being my friend and partner in crime.

I would be remiss in not thanking my family members and loved ones because they are always my biggest cheerleaders. Thank you to my siblings, Jennifer Robertson and Rachel Griffin, because I have hit the lotto in this department: they are smart and kind and funny, and talked me off the proverbial ledge about the research and writing process more than a few times. Thank you to my parents, Donna and

Hollis Griffin, for encouraging me from the beginning and trying to impress upon me that I can do anything. And thank you to the grandparents, aunts, and uncles who have always helped me in my attempts to believe that. Yet my biggest thanks go to Alex Beekman. Alex has helped me understand the difference between what is internal and what is external and shown me that the road to contentment always travels through compassion. That we have begun walking that road together has filled me with more happiness and serenity than I have ever known. Writing this book transformed me as a scholar, and meeting Alex transformed me as a person. I owe him a debt of gratitude that I enjoy paying back very much.

But my final thanks are for my great-grandmother, Rose Steinmuller (1912–2009). To her family, she was known as "Nanny." Thank you to Nanny for getting on a boat in Europe and moving to New York City, where she had to live small but would only dream big. For her, those dreams made the hard times more bearable. Nanny lost herself and escaped her troubles, however intermittently, in soap operas and musicals. In Nanny's life I see a familiar conflict: the tension between one's investment in the good life as it is depicted in media forms and an understanding of how rarely those dreams ever come to fruition. Nanny's love for movies and television never delivered the kind of life she fantasized about, but they were no less compelling to her for that. This book could not possibly be for anybody else.

FEELING NORMAL

Introduction

I LIKE TO tell people that everything I know about being a gay man I learned by watching television. That claim is only partially true, however, as I probably learned just as much by renting movies and chatting with people online. Twenty years removed from my first struggles with sexuality, I understand now that I consumed so much gay and lesbian media in my youth because I wanted to put myself near bodies and places with parallels to my own narrative and history. In doing that, I was trying to situate myself in a world built around desire.[1] No matter how loving and supportive one's family might be, to experience same-sex desire while growing up in heteronormative culture is to doubt what you know about yourself. In this context, gay and lesbian cinema, television, and online media provide important though fraught resources. I, for one, looked to them because I wanted to "feel normal." A nebulous term for an affective state, "feeling normal" is an experience of freedom and belonging; it is both a flush of recognition and a fantasy of generality.[2] It is an experience of body and mind that you share with others, a sense of mutuality that can be difficult to come by without readily available scripts by which to model yourself.[3] While queer theory defines identity as being fluid and labile, the lived experience of that variability is often one of anxiety and doubt.[4]

If identity is a necessary fiction for politics and a convenient fiction of the marketplace, it is also a comforting fiction that helps people feel connected to others and make sense of the everyday. As an anchoring narrative, identity provides a sense of connection to both intimates and strangers. The stories about desire and identity available in gay and lesbian cinema, television, and online media are scripts that offer sexual minorities avenues through which they may understand their experiences. Such narratives are elaborate in that they affix people to certain practices and structures like communities and nation-states, as well as modes of consumption and habits of mind. At the same time, identity narratives are never elaborate enough: people get confused and feel hurt when the stories available to them in media culture are limited or confining.[5] People also experience insult and injury when those stories deviate from the ones that are validated by the social norms they encounter in the world around them. I consumed gay and lesbian media in search of those stories, and while I saw traces of my experiences in some of them, others were alienating and difficult for me. Through those stories, I hoped to place myself near a world I knew existed but often seemed far away from where I was. I wanted that closeness to help me "feel normal."

Years after I first rented gay movies, watched lesbian characters on television, and lurked in queer spaces online, I enrolled in graduate school to pursue a course of study that critiqued the very media forms and practices that had once provided me with so much solace. The appraisals of media culture and the gay and lesbian rights movement that I encountered there differed considerably from the more celebratory assessments of these topics I was used to reading in the popular press. In blogs, magazines, and newspapers, the visibility of gay and lesbian people in movies, television, and online media is often treated as less-than-complicated evidence of their inclusion in national culture. But in my classes, I learned modes of analysis that evaluated, often harshly, that very same visibility. More often than not, the assessments of gay and lesbian media I encountered in my courses were as convincing as they were sobering; I saw that the pleasures of such media were frequently limited, and that the celebrations of them that occurred in the popular press could be shortsighted.

The affective experience of gay and lesbian media is often one of normativity, so the experiences of agency and attachment most often found in cinema, television, and online media targeted to sexual minorities are predicated on many of the same power dynamics that they contest. Nevertheless, dismissing those feelings of freedom and belonging as being "merely normative" is to miscalculate their use-value to the people who consume them. I have also become wary of roundly dismissing the criticism of gay and lesbian media that takes place in the popular press, however parochial and obsequious it might be. The desire for social legibility is a compelling one, which most sexual minorities—most people, even—understand as being necessary if one is to have a livable life.[6] As such, this book takes seriously the desires presented in gay and lesbian movies, television programs, and online media—not to rescue them or condemn them, or even to argue that they are more progressive or regressive than they seem at first glance. Rather, the book considers gay and lesbian media evidence of the thorny terrain of politics in the twenty-first century, where ideas about sexual minorities are animated through narratives about individual happiness, and political claims get refracted through vague assertions related to personal transcendence. In gay and lesbian media, sexual politics present narrative problems that are solved by individual triumphs, which most frequently occur by amassing financial wealth or finding romantic love. This book identifies how such ideas about politics shape not just gay and lesbian media forms themselves but also the contexts of their production and distribution. My aim is to track the ideological labors that such movies, television programs, and online media perform in an effort to understand why so many people understand them as being progressive and liberatory, even when presented with persuasive arguments to the contrary.

Gay and lesbian media forms are sites of psychic investment and bodily experience for both the people who make them and the people who consume them. But feeling, emotion, and affect are so bound up in one another and so tightly linked to the texts and practices of media culture that they can be difficult to isolate and examine. While feeling is an individuated perception that one checks against previous experiences, emotion is a social phenomenon, a performance that becomes legible to others when it gets projected outward. In contrast, affect is prepersonal and unconscious; it is a not-yet-formed potentiality.[7] Although scholars take great pains to differentiate these categories, they are difficult to separate from one another in practice.[8] In gay and lesbian media culture, feeling, emotion, and affect slide together: an individual's experiences of body and mind are represented as being both involuntary and shared by many. Gay and lesbian movies, television programs, and online media emphasize that those experiences are worthy of respect because they are as natural as they are commonplace. *Feeling Normal* charts how feeling, emotion, and affect work together, marking the slippage between them as the ideological labor performed by gay and lesbian media: individual experiences get folded into the range of ideas associated with particular identity categories, experiences attributed to factors that people understand as being innate.[9] Gay and lesbian media blur feeling, emotion, and affect to present a range of ideas about desire and sociality. The pleasures of such texts are best understood as sensations generated by problematizing matters of sexuality and the public sphere.

Movies, television programs, and online media forms emphasize emotionally charged political issues that shape gay and lesbian lives: the joy of romantic partnership, the anger of being discriminated against, the fear of homophobic violence. Such framing renders the political as personal; structural issues are individuated and made intimate. Sara Ahmed calls the sensory dimensions of such issues "queer feelings"; they are the lived, felt experiences of bodies inhabiting the norms of heterosexist patriarchal culture.[10] Such a culture creates scripts about proper modes of being and wanting, which are compulsory but can be broken. Queer feelings involve the potential for bodies to inhabit norms differently—to desire differently, to love differently, or simply to feel different. Just because Western culture casts androcentric heterosexuality as obligatory does not mean that all who inhabit its norms embody them in the same ways. Having same-sex relations and desiring same-sex bodies show the incommensurability of hegemonic modes of being and wanting with many queer lives. Typically teleological in their emphasis on procreation, socially sanctioned types of desire leave little room for "feeling normal" about nonnormative sexuality. Even as gay and lesbian publics have made significant inroads in recent years in the vein of (certain, specific) political rights and (certain, specific) consumer subjectivities, the kinds of feelings engendered by gay and lesbian media are sometimes unsalvageably queer. If "good" feelings about marriage rights and employment protections circulate via many gay and lesbian media texts, those same texts are also often home to "good" feelings about unconventional sexual practices and subaltern cultural milieus. As such, the media forms and the feelings they validate among the people who consume them run afoul of many cultural norms about who or what those people should love, want, and be.

Yet in the contemporary moment, consumer capitalism valorizes individuality in ways that have corralled many of the identities and desires associated with queerness and placed them squarely in the cultural mainstream. This tendency toward centrism can be seen most plainly in the frequency with which ostensibly "queer media" becomes "LGBT [lesbian, gay, bisexual, transgender] media," or simply "gay and lesbian media." For all of their claims to inclusion, cinema, television, and online media that are created for sexual minorities frequently give short shrift to desire's multiplicities by privileging an identity-based definition of sexuality over and above a more fluid one rooted in acts. There are profound power dynamics embedded in such a distinction, where some ways of identifying and desiring are "more normal" than others. As such, gay and lesbian media are not frequently queer, per se, at all. To help keep those power dynamics in focus, this book makes an effort to delineate the consumers imagined by the media industries from the people who use and consume gay and lesbian cinema, television, and online media. *Feeling Normal* moves between the terms "gay and lesbian," "sexual minority," and "queer," but does not consider them to be equivalent. Rather, the movement between them marks the difficulties of parsing out the limited multiplicity created by media commerce from the more diverse people who look to media culture so that they might "feel normal" themselves.

The kinds of politics featured in the media forms examined in *Feeling Normal* typically culminate in markedly centrist rights claims, like demands for employment protections and marriage equality. Lisa Duggan calls this mode of politics "homonormative," a way of understanding ideological struggle "that does not contest dominant heteronormative assumptions and institutions, but upholds and sustains them, while promising the possibility of a demobilized gay constituency and a privatized, depoliticized gay culture anchored in domesticity and consumption."[11] This critique is a central preoccupation in scholarship on gay and lesbian media, and homonormativity is a defining element of each and every text examined in the pages ahead. But rather than reproduce this critique, as necessary and vital as it is, *Feeling Normal* attempts to unpack people's investments in it as a mode of politics. The book fleshes out the contours of how gay and lesbian media construct homonormativity in order to outline its logic and claims to universality. People cling to the notion that homonormativity can be emancipatory, even when they are confronted with compelling proof of its contradictions and limitations. The book connects the logics of homonormativity to developments in the media industries, focusing on the transition from analog to digital production and distribution. This transition has resulted in a proliferation of consumer categories in the media marketplace, shifts that have made gay and lesbian audiences eagerly courted demographics among cinema distributors, television networks, and mobile media companies at the turn of the twenty-first century.

While scholars debate the impact of digital technology on media culture, there is an understanding, though sometimes only tacit, that it marks a major shift in how cinema, television, and online media are produced, distributed, and consumed.[12] But *Feeling Normal* breaks with that consensus, arguing that the impact of digital technology on media made by and for sexual minorities at the start of the twenty-first century is evidence of a historical legacy dating back to the nineteenth century. The book historicizes digital media in the context of modernity, identifying in the relationship between sexual minorities and urbanization a parallel with how media forms are produced for and distributed to gay and lesbian audiences in the contemporary moment.[13] The first chapter casts modernity as a corporeal experience, underlining how the transformations that occurred at the end of the nineteenth century, particularly urbanization, changed how people lived and worked, placing bodies in new relations with one another. As it has occurred in the United States, modernity can be considered affective in two ways: (1) it is an experience of desire, where subjects' encounters with public cultures—bars, clubs, community centers—enable the enactment of identities built around nonnormative sexualities, and (2) it is an experience of Americanness in which subjects feel as though they belong to the nation-state as a result of their proximity to certain landmarks, like skyscrapers and bridges. The chapters that follow build on this understanding of commerce and desire as a mutually informing relationship wrought by proximate bodies. They cast sexual identity as an affective category in media culture that resonates through overlapping registers of politics, economy, and culture.

By using feeling, emotion, and affect as critical optics, *Feeling Normal* brings into focus the conflation of romantic longing, consumerist desire, and political personhood that characterizes the public sphere in the contemporary United States. It is an understanding of the political made material in gay and lesbian media, wherein citizenship becomes woven with consumption by way of sentiment. In this atmosphere, a lack of structural protections is surmountable with some fortitude and a little pluck, and each and every American is thought to be equally capable of achieving a "happily ever after." Media forms targeted to gay and lesbian people use this logic to rework what it means to be an American, making the desires of sexual minorities central to a sentimental experience of national culture. Many gay and lesbian people find great hope and comfort in this representational schema, even as many of them recognize the limitations of the terms by which those feelings of freedom and belonging can be realized.

Feeling Connected in/with Media Culture

I titled this book *Feeling Normal* because I want to raise the possibility that gay and lesbian people have unique experiences with gay and lesbian cinema, television, and online media that are both instinctive and cultural—as much of the body as they are of the mind. In her autobiographical essay "A Personal History of Lesbian Porn," Dorothy Allison describes being an eight-year-old and experiencing her first stirrings of lesbian desire in the cheap mass-market novels she found stuffed beneath the mattress of her mother's bed. After listing a series of Harlequin Romance and paperback detective novels that she read as a child and teenager, she insists that she knew the characters were not real in the way the women she knew were real. Yet even though these women did not resemble the women she encountered in her own life, Allison is adamant that the stories' lack of verisimilitude had little impact on her psychic and sexual investments in the characters and their stories:

> What the books did contribute was a word—the word *Lesbian*. When she finally appeared ... I knew her immediately. She wasn't true. ... She wasn't me. ... But she was true enough, and the lust echoed. When she pulled the frightened girl close after thirty pages, I got damp all down my legs. That's what it was, and I wasn't the only one even if none had turned up in the neighborhood yet. Details aside, the desire matched up. She wanted women; I wanted my girlfriends. The word was Lesbian. After that, I started looking for it.[14]

I find Allison's story illustrative insofar as she underlines the corporeality of gay and lesbian media for gay and lesbian people: the paperback novels she snuck out of her mother's room made her sweat and lubricate. The bodies and desires that Allison sought out in media forms during her youth are, in the contemporary moment, part of a vast commodity culture that courts people like her and people like me with promises that we too might "feel normal."

The texts examined in the pages ahead are as banal as the novels Allison found crammed beneath her mother's mattress, though not often as steamy. The cinema, television, and online media that comprise the archive for this book are imagined to create affective responses similar to but different than the ones Allison experienced when reading mass-market fiction. The experiences that sexual minorities have with media forms are meaningful to them but defy easy categorization: the affective dimensions of cinema, television, and online media rarely involve anything beyond emotional intelligibility and do not often operate in neat, linear ways. The phenomena detailed in this book are prosaic: feelings of validation, a sense of belonging. Even so, the movies, television programming, and mobile media applications examined in the pages ahead frame these conventional feelings as matters of great import. In gay and lesbian media, these mundane emotions get articulated as a mode of citizenship that is more imagined than tangible. As a signifier, it bears only a passing resemblance to its ostensible referent: the structural position of those protected under the aegis of the nation-state. But because it has such a strong affective resonance, many gay and lesbian people cleave to this idea of citizenship regardless, despite how often it provides little more than a poor analog.

Following Allison's lead, I share here a story of my own. Not nearly as erotic but just as seminal, my story is about how one of my own experiences with a fairly ordinary form of gay and lesbian media has been, because of its very conventionality, highly formative for me. Like Allison and her novels, I cannot help but question the nature of my investment in it:

My ninety-seven-year-old great-grandmother died as I was writing this book. Like so many other Jewish immigrants of her generation, Nanny retired to Florida but always called New York City "home." For decades, she commuted between her apartment in the Bronx and her job in the Hat Department at Saks Fifth Avenue in Midtown Manhattan. After living through a pogrom, the Great Depression, and two world wars, Nanny had an unmistakable romance about her. She used to take my grandmother on auditions for radio shows, had an insatiable appetite for melodramas and musicals, and dated men well into her eighties. She would also only wear high-heeled shoes, even when donning a bathrobe around the house. "Diva" does not even begin to describe her—Nanny was probably the grandest snowbird in the history of the Ft. Lauderdale-area retirement communities.

Because I am Nanny's eldest great-grandchild, my family asked me to write a eulogy in her memory, something short that could be delivered at her memorial service. I knew that I wanted to, needed to, write about *Angels in America*. With its intertwining stories about Judaism, American citizenship, and gay and lesbian life in New York City, *Angels in America* felt like the perfect way to highlight the hopes and dreams shared by a Jewish immigrant matriarch and her fagelah great-grandson. *Angels* renders American heritage prismatically, rearticulating Cold War controversies alongside Reaganite politics in a queer retelling of the past. Antisemitism and homophobia come into focus as deeply emotional elements of American history and public life. Multiple narratives unfold around New York City—sometimes in the AIDS unit of St. Vincent's Hospital in Greenwich Village or amid the greenery of Central Park. Many scenes take place in small apartments like the one Nanny commuted from in the Bronx through the 1960s, and like the ones I could barely afford when I lived in the gentrifying East Village forty years later.

The scene I wrote about for Nanny's memorial takes place at another memorial service, this one for a woman named Sarah Aronson. She is the grandmother of one of the main characters who, like me, is a gay man. At the memorial service in *Angels in America*, a rabbi shares Sarah's life story as part of his sermon to the congregation. Like Nanny, Sarah was an immigrant, a persecuted Jew who fled Europe and landed in the Bronx, planting roots and starting a family there. The rabbi talks about how hard it was for her, how she struggled, and how impossible things could seem for these people, in this place, at this point in time. But the rabbi also talked about how her hopes and dreams were carried on by her children, grandchildren, and great-grandchildren—like the gay main character and, of course, like me. In the version of *Angels in America* that aired on cable television, the character delivers these lines in a thick Yiddish accent. He says to the family: "She carried that Old World on her back. Across the ocean. In a boat. And she put it down near Grand Concourse Avenue in the Bronx." The rabbi tells them, "You can never make that crossing that she made. For such great voyages in this world do not anymore exist. But every day of your lives—those miles, that voyage, between that place and this one? You cross that every day. In you that journey is."

In the days after Nanny's death, I found this scene on YouTube and watched it again and again. As I did that, I cried onto my keyboard until I was nearly gasping for air. Narrated over grainy photos of immigrants and New York landmarks, and then against clearer shots of a glittering, more current urban landscape, the sequence connects me and Nanny to a history and mode of feeling that are bigger than either of us, yet part of both of us all at once. I see it as the intersection of Nanny's immigrant, early twentieth-century New York and my gay, more recent New York. The shots mark the convergence of similar yet not identical narratives whose discrepancies and blind spots are set aside in order to celebrate the American city's capacity to accommodate many different genres of dreams. In *Angels in America*, New York is a synecdoche for the United States; the scale of the city invokes the plenitude of the nation. The program suggests that the urban center enables agency for and attachment among minority people because it places them in proximity to towering skyscrapers and massive bridges, landmarks that link the spoils of consumer capitalism to the processes of American citizenship.[15] The version of US citizenship put forth in *Angels in America* emphasizes that minorities have a vexed relationship with the promises of national culture. Jewish characters are as self-hating as they are reviled. Gay characters struggle with access to health care as AIDS ravages their bodies. The disease kills even the most powerful, self-interested characters. All are marginalized by discourses on identity and desire that paint certain forms of being and wanting as "criminal intimacy."[16] The characters' experiences of the United States are as laden with frustration and disenchantment as they are filled with a yearning for freedom.[17] Truly, participation in national culture can be traumatic for members of minorities. Rendered via images of immigrant mobs, dying bodies, and colossal buildings, the New York depicted in *Angels in America* suggests that if the American Dream is widely available, it comes at a wildly uneven cost.

This representation of the urban is paradigmatic in that it underscores the extent to which modernity is an affective phenomenon in the United States: commerce puts bodies in new relations with one another, in the shadows of structures that place them amid capitalist democracy. In *Angels in America*, there are strong parallels between Nanny's coming to America and my own experiences as a gay man decades later. Both can be characterized by the possibility of inclusion and enfranchisement in an American national culture, even as we both have weathered suffering at the hands of that culture. The sense of belonging provided through this vision of American national culture is staked on notions of mutuality and equality. Yet such kinship is mitigated by the day-to-day difficulties of minority experience—as in those instances when Nanny was called "kike," and each time someone has called me "faggot." This vision of the American Dream is also informed and held in abeyance by broader structural concerns related to living and desiring differently—like when Nanny had trouble finding an apartment with a Jewish-sounding last name, and each time I have weathered homophobia in a workplace but was afraid to complain. Alas, minority people enjoy fewer assurances that the American Dream can be realized.

Nevertheless, the media forms that minorities produce and consume rarely, if ever, stop hoping that the American Dream will deliver on its promises. Crucially, many gay and lesbian people see such content as being meaningful for that very reason: movies, television programs, and online media targeted to them often promise that history and justice are on their side. If nothing else, such media assure consumers that they are not alone in their hopes and frustrations with a national culture that celebrates a good life that it does not provide in any uniform way.[18] I know that my great-grandmother believed the United States would always protect her family. Yet her optimism seems misguided considering she had run through her entire savings many times over by the time she died. It seems even more ill-advised in light of the fact that my family struggled to pay for her care, especially when her health declined. Part of me cries at *Angels in America* for those reasons too. Of course, the directors, producers, and marketing executives who created and circulated *Angels in America* hoped from the very start that gay and lesbian audiences would, like me, become invested in the sentimental vision of the United States put forth by the program.

Minorities making media for other minorities generate an affective politics that circulates across the cinema, television, and internet content examined in this book. As a cultural process, gay and lesbian media links producers and consumers in a circuit of mutual recognition, as if to say to one another: I know you, I hear you, I feel you. Lauren Berlant's *The Female Complaint: The Unfinished Business of Sentimentality in American Culture* was a major inspiration for this book, especially her framing of women's media culture as "a loosely organized, market-structured . . . sphere of people attached to each other by a *sense* that there is a common emotional world available to those individuals who have been marked by the historical burden of being harshly treated in a generic way."[19] Like the love plots that Berlant examines in women's middlebrow fiction and film melodramas, the narrative formulas of gay and lesbian media provide succor and sustenance to targeted consumers by imagining them as "intimate publics," audiences cultivated by "claim[s] to circulate texts and things that express . . . people's particular core interests and desires."[20]

Berlant characterizes the consumer appeals of minority media cultures as generating a sense of inclusion by their construction of "a subjective likeness that seems to emanate from their history and their ongoing attachments and actions."[21] Her analysis of how mass-produced media forms operate as sites of community and attachment for women features many parallels with how producers of contemporary gay and lesbian cinema, television, and online media imagine their target audiences. In both contexts, texts and promotional strategies suggest that "even before there was a market addressed to them, there existed a world of strangers who would be emotionally literate in each other's experience of power, intimacy, desire, and discontent."[22] Such media forms use personal modes of address to narrate stories about ostensibly impersonal public sphere issues, marking their target publics via rhetorics of mutuality and intimacy. Berlant characterizes such media as "juxtapolitical" in that stories unfold in the vicinity of a lived real and some notion of politics, but do so in order to "generat[e] *relief from the political*."[23] Identifying gay and lesbian media as "juxtapolitical" highlights how they operate "in *proximity* to the political, occasionally crossing over in political alliance, even more occasionally doing some political work, but most often not, acting as a critical chorus that sees the expression of emotional response and conceptual recalibration as achievement enough."[24] Such texts magnetize otherwise disparate individuals, inviting them to participate in a collectivity rooted in a shared experience of the world. Because that experience must always be constructed, it is inevitably more phantasmatic than it is factual.

Like Dorothy Allison's stack of novels and my viewership of *Angels in America*, people use media forms to understand their experiences. Berlant suggests that emotional modes of address cast "fantasies of vague belonging as an alleviation of what is hard to manage in the lived real, a market domain where a set of problems [is] . . . expressed and worked through incessantly."[25] Thus, media forms attempt to create affective bonds among the members of target audiences by emphasizing their commonalities and soothing their differences. These texts "solicit belonging via modes of sentimental realism that span fantasy and experience and claim a certain emotional generality."[26] In the instance of contemporary gay and lesbian cinema, television, and online media, producers and distributors anticipate some diversity in the range of audiences they court and ease some of the tensions between those publics via hazy though impassioned appeals to consumerist and sexual agency, erotic multiplicity, and a communal spirit of shared difference. Such claims to inclusion can only ever be imagined, and it is in the gap between signifier and signified that images of and stories about sexual minorities operate as catachresis in media culture. As metaphors, they are only partly relatable to the lived experiences of the people meant to consume them. The tensions that such representations create and the discursive limits they reach are primary concerns of the pages ahead, especially the ways that the weaving of sexuality, capitalism, and the nation-state in gay and lesbian media culture is staked on limitations of gender, race, and class. More often than not, texts pretend to transcend these shortcomings or just leave them aside altogether.[27]

By employing close reading as an interpretive method, I break with scholarship that considers affect nonrepresentational and unintentional.[28] On the one hand, I follow Eugenie Brinkema's insistence "that it is only because one must read for it that affect has any force at all."[29] On the other hand, I break with her by questioning the rationales and motivations of gay and lesbian media producers.[30] I see in gay and lesbian media a process of circulation that hinges on the shared investments of gay and lesbian producers and gay and lesbian audiences in particular practices, ideologies, and institutions. There is a palpable sense of intentionality in those investments, even though they are not wholly conscious or rational. As such, gay and lesbian media constitute a world making in which the aims of producers do not point directly to intended meanings as much as they suggest a media form's "feeling tone ... its general disposition or orientation toward its audience and the world."[31] I read for affect by looking to media forms as evidence of the terms by which media culture can understand sexual minorities as viable subjects, which can be located in the ways that texts situate sexual minorities in relation to the worlds that surround them. While my interest across the chapters is in gay and lesbian *subjects*, I heed Brinkema's warning about the *subjectivity* that can result from critics reading for affect. Here, the critic's experience of a text becomes overly generalized, as though others necessarily experience it that way too.[32] I mitigate the subjectivity of my readings via my archive, focusing on objects that are often considered to be without affect: low-budget movies, canceled sitcoms, and the pull-down menus of online databases. My gamble is that by reading for affect in objects that are widely thought to be *affectless,* the centrality of emotion and sensation to gay and lesbian media becomes evident.[33]

Focusing on feeling, emotion, and affect is also risky because imprecise definitions can veer toward universality, as though the essence of same-sex desire as an identity category can be located in a particular sensation or sensations. While that is a dangerous proposition for any analysis, it is particularly so in one that focuses on media made by and for minorities. Using Silvan Tomkins's work on cybernetics, Eve Kosofsky Sedgwick puts forth an understanding of affect that "gesture[s] toward the possibility of random, virtually infinite permutation" of emotions, even as it delimits those possibilities as being finite, as well as differentiated historically and politically.[34] Following this definition, *Feeling Normal* describes how media commerce makes affective experiences available to gay and lesbian people, but emphasizes that the range of those experiences is limited and contested. Sedgwick characterizes affect as a system that is multiple yet circumscribed, casting it as "attached to things, people, ideas, sensations, relations, activities, ambitions, and any number of things . . . [such that] one can be excited by anger, disgusted by shame, or surprised by joy."[35] *Feeling Normal* uses this understanding of affect to parse out how gay and lesbian media make political issues intimate in nature. It looks at texts and the conditions of their production and distribution to highlight how gay and lesbian media suggest a commonality of experience that no movie, television program, or online media form can ever achieve. Thus, the media forms examined in this book make political claims that are often facile and inelegant. Crucially, though, many people consider them no less vital for that.

Selling Emotion

Even with their profound shortcomings, the ways that gay and lesbian media allow consumers to "feel normal" do not disable all forms of political agency. Rather, they are evidence of a consumer citizenship that is manufactured over and over again in media culture.[36] This understanding of citizenship casts political life in terms of personal experiences and interpersonal connections, making identity a state of being that is achievable in the marketplace. The courtship of gay and lesbian consumers is only shortsightedly equated to the enfranchisement of all sexual minorities in the US body politic.[37] But that criticism is a familiar one in scholarship on media culture. I worry that it understates the intensity of the desire to "feel normal" and underestimates its use-value in the lives of sexual minorities. The processes of commerce always court minorities as citizens *and* consumers, enmeshing the economic, political, and cultural functions of media forms in ways that can prevent nuanced understandings of the relationships between them.[38] The tensions between media forms' different functions are precisely where feeling, emotion, and affect provide the most insight.

When the signifiers of sexual desire and identity are encoded as text and circulated via commerce, methods of production and distribution mark them as being worth something—economically, but also politically and socially. In her engagement with Marx in the essay "Scattered Speculations on Questions of Value," Gayatri Spivak defines value as a category that is coded in the economic sphere but is multiple and multivalent; value's different elements and charges are not one and the same but are "irreducibly complicitous" insofar as they can work both in concert and in tension with one another.[39] Commercial media forms are thus created and circulated by the logic of capital and, at the same time, have value functions that are related to and different from their economic functions. Moreover, those values are not static but are determined discursively, so they are always open to interpretation and critique. Spivak identifies the connections between different kinds of value even as she underlines their instability. This formulation of value offers a productive lens for examining how media commerce generates feelings of agency and kinship for gay and lesbian people because it gestures to capital's circulation of commodities that allow consumers to "feel normal." When considering the politics that attend these processes of use and exchange, media scholarship sometimes considers different kinds of value on static, binary terms, as in critiques where "The Media" is thought to propagate problematic ideological norms in the name of profit, which certain (wise, worldly) audiences may then resist.[40] This sort of hand-wringing about the relationship between politics and the marketplace precipitates a pointed tone of longing and disappointment in scholarship on media culture and sexual minorities.[41] As a critique, it often pits a profit-minded gay and lesbian consumer market against a potentially more transformative queer activism, pushing points of overlap out of focus and leaving little ground to parse out how the tensions between them play out in practice.[42] Spivak highlights the extent to which different forms of value cannot be isolated, and she underlines how such worth is always up for debate. The discontinuities of different forms of value are a vital topic in media scholarship, as are debates about whether or not the politics they foreground are progressive or regressive. I depart from these paradigms to follow Spivak's lead in identifying the numerous, vexing ways that redressing the conflation of different kinds of value can result in treating them as being isolated and/or fixed. When media scholarship determines value in those ways, it can prevent a capacious analysis of gay and lesbian media's value to the people who consume it.

The value of gay and lesbian media for people who consume it can be located in matters of feeling, emotion, and affect, or how such media allow them to "feel normal," in ways that are often simultaneously emancipatory and repressive. Amy Villarejo's scholarship on lesbian documentary cinema emphasizes the imbrication of different forms of value as well as the variability of the politics that attend them; she highlights how media forms encompass discontinuous systems that nonetheless circulate together. Villarejo builds on Spivak's analysis to generate "affective value" as a critical tool for media criticism, characterizing it as an abstraction that cuts across sign systems while preserving the continuities and discontinuities between them.[43] Through circuits of use and exchange, Villarejo sees lesbian documentary cinema making a particular experience available to audiences: one of identification and corporeality, in the psyche but also on the flesh. That is how Villarejo sees lesbian documentary generating economic value for the people who make and circulate it, and it is how she articulates its use-value for the people who consume it. Using affective value as a framework for analyzing sexuality and media culture ensures that "affect and desire are not banished from considerations of economy."[44] Villarejo uses affective value to consider how established categories of identity and conventional understandings of desire organize the identifications and sensations experienced by audiences of lesbian documentary cinema. In doing so, Villarejo also highlights how that process can disarticulate sexual desire from wholly related issues, like questions of race and class.[45]

What I find engaging and useful about Villarejo's engagement with Spivak is the way she uses affective value to link the people who make and distribute media with those who consume it. In my research on gay and lesbian cinema, television, and online media, I have been struck by how often the professionals who work for movie distributors, television networks, and mobile media companies that target sexual minorities understand their professional labor as serving important political and cultural functions. Many of these media workers also self-identify as consumers of the gay and lesbian content they help make and circulate, a scenario that Villarejo identifies in lesbian documentary as well. In order to parse out what is at stake there, she takes up what Spivak calls "the special case," the scenario wherein a worker consumes the results of her labor. "The special case" confounds capitalism's logic, complicating Marx's claims regarding the means of production being the genesis of power relations between classes because workers lack control over the conditions of their labor. Spivak disagrees, though only partially, stating that "one case of use-value can be that of the worker wishing to consume (the affect of the) work itself, that necessary possibility renders indeterminate the . . . predication of the subject as labor-power or super-adequation as calibrated and organized by the logic of capital."[46] The subject of Spivak's "special case" is rooted in affect, one whose work within capitalism's mode of production circulates her psychic, corporeal investments in the commodities she helps create and distribute. The worker's labor renders these investments as functions of capital—crucially, though, they are not wholly determined by the logic of capital. As such, Spivak sees this labor complicating "the mere philosophical justice of capital logic without shifting into utopian idealism."[47] Following Spivak, Villarejo highlights how media created by self-consciously political workers bears some relation to capital, but their labors also make ideas and sensations available to people via the processes of production and distribution.[48]

If a trenchant critique of gay and lesbian media is their tendency to conflate consumption (economic value) and citizenship (political value), I want to raise the possibility that this conflation requires a unique mode of criticism when cinema, television, and online media are produced by and for sexual minorities. In the labor performed in these milieus, affect becomes a commodity that is made and circulated for sale. The use-value of those emotions and sensations for the people who consume gay and lesbian media cannot be adequately assessed through critical paradigms that animate stark oppositions between different forms of value. If not for circuits of use and exchange, these media would not circulate at all. Villarejo's notion of "affective value" calls for careful analysis of gay and lesbian media workers making gay and lesbian media as being fundamentally different from the production and circulation practices characteristic of previous eras and other, more "mainstream" circuits of culture.[49] True, the gay and lesbian media examined in *Feeling Normal* often acquiesce to the requirements of capital and structures of power that perpetuate inequalities between different queer audiences. But those media are not completely determined by such requirements and structures. Gay and lesbian media professionals are often invested in the work they perform in niche-specific cinema, television, and online media because they understand that work as having important political functions for their lives and the lives of others like them. Those investments warrant more careful scrutiny than an evaluation in which they are deemed unproblematically "normative" as a result of being "commercial."

However complex and multiple value may be, the media industries are still motivated by the bottom line. Because Villarejo analyzes the politics of sexuality characteristic of a specialized, artisanal circuit of production, she is (rightfully) wary of applying affective value as a conceptual frame to the kinds of texts and practices that comprise the archive for this book. The people most valued in a paradigm that seeks to generate revenue by narrating stories about sexual minorities are often white, frequently middle- and upper-class, commonly male, and typically monogamously coupled. As such, parsing out the feelings of agency and kinship generated for such audiences in gay and lesbian media risks generating what Miranda Joseph calls "the romance of community," the processes by which capital aids queer public formation by exploiting power differentials along race, class, and gender lines.[50] In containing her argument to alternative public spheres, Villarejo stays within the bounds of activist media practice. Thus, her argument involves practitioners who are more likely to stay attuned to the politics of sexuality and the dynamics of power that shape them. Applying her paradigm to settings where profits are sought more lustfully, as in the objects examined in this book, requires careful attention to how affective value is a circumscribed category. It is hemmed in by the processes of commerce as well as by the mystifying natures of identification and desire. The feelings of personal empowerment and interpersonal connection made available in gay and lesbian media are not universally accessible and are often grossly normative. Even with such shortcomings, I cannot foreclose on the possibility that the feelings of freedom and belonging that inform the production and distribution of gay and lesbian media, specifically, can sometimes provoke new ways of being and wanting—or even just moments of self-reflexivity—among the people meant to consume them.

Furthermore, because Villarejo focuses on lesbian documentary cinema, the relations of capital are similar across different objects in her analysis. Using her argument about affective value in the context of more conventionally "commercial" media requires differentiating how revenue is generated in each circuit of production because the requirements of capital are constitutive elements of gay and lesbian media's affective value. The industry practices that are characteristic of digital production and distribution erode boundaries between the staid categories of "cinema," "television," and "the internet." Streaming platforms are often imagined as the primary distribution method for gay and lesbian movies, and television networks increasingly create online media content and become involved in the production of feature-length cinema. But content created for different delivery platforms still involves institutions, practices, and relations of capital that are at least somewhat disparate. For example, movie distributors do not sell advertising time, and mobile media companies do not profit from broadcasting rights. As such, there is no easy way of equating gay and lesbian cinema with gay and lesbian mobile media, or even comparing gay and lesbian content on network television with gay and lesbian content on cable television.

While there are profound parallels—affective, aesthetic—across the chapters in this book, the objects of analysis are disparate enough to thwart simple comparisons. Throughout, I resist the urge to evaluate certain movies, television programs, or mobile media applications more favorably or more harshly than others if only because it seems that subjective assessments are the enemy of rigorous analysis. After all, I learned everything I know about being a gay man by watching television. Truly, my own political and aesthetic judgments are as suspect as those made by anybody else.

Mapping the Chapters

This book considers gay and lesbian cinema, television, and online media created by and for sexual minorities as providing use-values for audiences rooted in feeling, emotion, and affect. It is a scenario that can be located in the context of digital production and distribution that simultaneously has historical parallels with the forms of agency and attachment made available to sexual minorities in the marketplace in the context of modernity. There are many similarities between looking for love at a bar and looking for love on a mobile media application. But gay and lesbian media also enact modes of feeling and belonging unique to their circuits of production, like when podcasts feature frank discussions about sexual practices for their finely conceived target audiences, or when characters on television sitcoms tell jokes about fashion trends among lesbians that are legible to queer and straight viewers alike. Commercial entities appealing to gay and lesbian consumers compete with one another in each circuit of production: cinema distributors vie for similar market demographics, and mobile media applications court overlapping categories of users. The processes of media commerce manufacture a range of affective experiences for target audiences in the process, using standard generic paradigms and exploiting multiple delivery technologies. The corporate rituals used to create and promote these media draw a flurry of attention in the popular press and media industry trade publications.

Feeling Normal reads gay and lesbian media content through its industry discourses to underscore that the affective experiences of cinema, television, and online media are shaped by a historical legacy dating back to the late nineteenth century as well as the political economy of twenty-first-century media culture. In chapter 1, I historicize digital media in the context of modernity, using the relationship between same-sex desire and urbanization as a way to describe how media forms are produced for and distributed to sexual minority audiences. In the chapters that follow, I trace the operation of sexual identity as a consumer category across different contexts, underlining how media forms articulate minority status as a market orientation that transcends the deprivation and subordination that characterize the experiences of structurally underprivileged minorities in US culture. In chapter 2, I contextualize gay and lesbian cinema amid the changes associated with digital distribution. In doing that, I trace a through line from the early 1990s to the present in order to identify how the activism of the New Queer Cinema movement has dovetailed with and been informed by ongoing transformations in cinema's methods of distribution and reception. The result is an aesthetic sensibility rooted in common cinematic techniques where characters overcome adversity related to their status as sexual minorities in ways that champion financial wealth at the expense of community membership.

In chapter 3, I analyze how the cable TV networks that target gay and lesbian viewers imagine themselves as doing political work. The chapter underlines the logic of activism that takes place by way of the commodity, demonstrating how particular modes of address are contoured by the political economy and technological makeup of cable television in the context of digital production and distribution. In chapter 4, I argue that prominent research methods in television scholarship can both prevent a nuanced understanding of how sexual minorities identify with television and leave unexamined the political implications of studying the medium. By rereading programs considered to be "failures" by trade publications and the popular press, I articulate a vision for "queerer" television scholarship that would operate in tension with the goals and preoccupations of industry critics and reviewers in the popular press. In chapter 5, I offer two ways of understanding geosocial networking applications designed to help sexual minorities make interpersonal connections on their smartphones. Where the first framework highlights feeling, emotion, and affect as they are made manifest in digital technologies, the second highlights how they are made material in the experiences of users. In this chapter, I build on scholarship related to technology and the body in order to parse out the mix of pleasure, pain, and amusement users experience when pursuing desire online.

The chapters point to trends in media commerce, highlighting the variety of feelings about sexual desire and identity that contemporary cinema, television, and online media make available to sexual minorities. The texts discussed in the pages ahead run afoul of many of the aesthetic, political, and economic value codings generated by industry professionals, reviewers, and academic critics. This book argues that such media are valuable for the people who consume them nonetheless, in ways that defy the terms of critique most often used to study the relationship between media, desire, and identity. Analyzing these texts, publics, and institutions in a systematic way is a crucial undertaking when trying to understand how ideas about sexual desire and identity are created, circulated, and consumed in twenty-first-century media culture.

Notes

1. David Halperin discusses the cultural forms that introduce gay men to gay male subculture. My project intersects with Halperin's a great deal, but is ultimately interested in a different set of questions. What is the pleasure of "feeling normal"? How does media culture accommodate those consumers? What are the historical precedents of such media forms? David Halperin, *How to Be Gay* (Cambridge, MA: Belknap, Harvard University Press, 2012).

2. I borrow this terminology from Lauren Berlant, who describes a similar process in women's media of midcentury America. Lauren Berlant, *The Female Complaint: The Unfinished Business of Sentimentality in American Culture* (Durham, NC: Duke University Press, 2008).

3. For more on how gay and lesbian media offer consumers "scripts" that they might use themselves, however loosely, see Alice Marwick, Mary L. Gray, and Mike Ananny, "'Dolphins Are Just Gay Sharks': *Glee* and the Queer Case of Transmedia as Text and Object," *Television and New Media*, February 26, 2013, doi: 10.1177/1527476413478493.

4. Michael Snediker discusses his experience being a depressed gay teen and then encountering queer theory as an undergraduate and graduate student. He stresses that the critique of normativity and the account of subject formation he encountered in that literature excited him intellectually, but did not dovetail well with his attempts to establish a sense of emotional well-being as a newly out gay man. See Michael Snediker, *Queer Optimism: Lyric Personhood and Other Felicitous Persuasions* (Minneapolis: University of Minnesota Press, 2008).

5. Lauren Berlant considers trauma the primary experience of citizenship in the contemporary United States; it is the means by which identity categories become intimate and personal. "The experience of social hierarchy is intensely individuating, yet it also makes people public and generic: it turns them into *kinds* of people who are both attached to and underdescribed by the identities that organize them." Emphasis in the original. Lauren Berlant, *The Queen of America Goes to Washington City: Essays on Sex and Citizenship* (Durham, NC: Duke University Press, 1997), 1.

6. I borrow this phrase from Judith Butler, who uses it to underline how one's self-understanding is achieved culturally, where even confining ideologies provide a sense of

belonging to a social world. See Judith Butler, "Doing Justice to Someone: Sex Reassignment and Allegories of Transsexuality," in *Undoing Gender* (New York: Routledge, 2004), 57–74.

7. For a brief outline of the differences between the concepts, see Eric Shouse, "Feeling Emotion Affect," *M/C: A Journal of Media and Culture* 8, no. 6 (December 2005).

8. On the relationship between affect and emotion, the literature is riven with tension. Baruch Spinoza defines affect as the ability to affect and be affected, which Gilles Deleuze and Felix Guattari frame as a corporeal experience beyond cognition. For Deleuze and Guattari, affect is an intensity of the flesh that has not yet taken shape as thought or representation, and thus differs from emotion. Nigel Thrift summarizes this position: "This roiling mass of nerve volleys prepare the body for action in such a way that intentions or decisions are made before the conscious self is even aware of them." It is this differentiation of affect from consciousness that is particularly divisive. For instance, Gayatri Spivak argues that the possibility of "a body without organs"—Deleuze and Guattari's metaphor for affect—is little more than "a metaphysical longing" for an experience of embodiment not burdened by the markers of race, sex, and gender. Spivak highlights how minorities shoulder that burden more than do those of dominant groups. Eve Sedgwick looks to cybernetics for a middle ground, where there is the possibility of affect as an essential experience of the body that is both innate and learned. In Sedgwick's framing, affect is as burdened by history as it is shaped by biology. Yet Ruth Leys remains skeptical of any critical move that hinges on "a commitment to the idea that there is a disjunction or gap between the subject's affective processes and his or her cognition or knowledge of the objects that caused them. The result is that the body not only 'senses' and performs a kind of 'thinking' below the threshold of conscious recognition and meaning but. . . . because of *the speed* with which the autonomic, affective processes are said to occur, it does all this before the mind has time to intervene." When critics differentiate affect from cognition, Leys charges that they "make disagreement about meaning, or ideological dispute, irrelevant to cultural analysis." The formulation of feeling, emotion, and affect in this book sits uncomfortably between Spivak, Sedgwick, and Leys. My goal in animating them together is to underscore how gay and lesbian media blur the distinctions between them as a matter of course. Baruch Spinoza, *Ethics* (New York: Penguin, 2005); Gilles Deleuze and Felix Guattari, *A Thousand Plateaus: Capitalism and Schizophrenia* (Minneapolis: University of Minnesota Press, 1987); Nigel Thrift, *Non-Representational Theory: Space, Politics, Affect* (New York: Routledge, 2007), 7; Gayatri Chakravorty Spivak, "Scattered Speculations on the Question of Value," *Diacritics* 15, no. 4, "Marx after Derrida" (Winter 1985): 73; Eve Sedgwick, *Touching Feeling: Affect, Performativity, Pedagogy* (Durham, NC: Duke University Press, 2003); Ruth Leys, "The Turn to Affect: A Critique," *Critical Inquiry* 37, no. 3 (Spring 2011): 450.

9. While many affect theorists make a hard, fast differentiation between affect and emotion, gay and lesbian media purposefully conflate them. As outlined, many theorists cast affect as a presubjective phenomenon and emotion as an ideological process. But the movies, television programs, and online media created for sexual minorities obscure those boundaries in order to position homosexuality as a viable, desirable way of being and wanting. One of the primary functions of gay and lesbian media is to highlight for consumers that same-sex desire is worthy of respect because it is both inherent and common.

10. Sara Ahmed uses the metaphor of sitting in a chair to describe normativity as comfortable in order to demonstrate that queerness involves contortion and discomfort. She sees in queerness the potential to rework such norms in order to better accommodate the bodies that inhabit them. See, in particular, Sara Ahmed, "Queer Feelings," in *The Cultural Politics of Emotion* (New York: Routledge, 2004), 144–167.

11. Lisa Duggan, *The Twilight of Equality? Neoliberalism, Cultural Politics, and the Attack on Democracy* (Boston: Beacon, 2003), 50.

12. This idea is a prominent one in media and cultural studies. See, in particular, Henry Jenkins, *Convergence Culture: Where Old and New Media Collide* (New York: New York University Press, 2006).

13. Several scholars make this connection between cities and digital technology. See, in particular, Jason Farman, *Mobile Interface Theory: Embodied Space and Locative Media* (New York: Routledge, 2011); Marita Sturken, "Mobilities of Time and Space: Technologies of the Modern and Postmodern," in *Technological Visions: The Hopes and Fears That Shape New Technologies*, ed. Marita Sturken, Douglas Thomas, and Sandra Ball-Rokeach (Philadelphia: Temple University Press, 2004), 71–91; and Adriana de Souza e Silva and Jordan Frith, eds., *Mobile Interfaces in Public Spaces: Locational Privacy, Control, and Urban Sociability* (New York: Routledge, 2012).

14. Dorothy Allison, *Skin: Talking about Sex, Class, and Literature* (Ithaca, NY: Firebrand Books, 1994), 187.

15. David Nye suggests that there is a fascination with bridges and skyscrapers in the United States because they bind ideas about national identity to developments in technology via narratives of progress and achievement. He sees in this process the reworking of Enlightenment ideals for an American context, charging that during the periods of Manifest Destiny and industrialization, notions of magnitude and mastery were recalibrated and incorporated into the mythos of the American Dream. See, in particular, David Nye, *American Technological Sublime* (Cambridge, MA: MIT Press, 1994), chap. 4.

16. Lauren Berlant and Michael Warner, "Sex in Public," *Critical Inquiry* 24, no. 2 (Winter 1998): 560.

17. Erica Rand parses out the silences and gaps in how the United States remembers its history by examining the mythologies surrounding Ellis Island. See Erica Rand, *The Ellis Island Snow Globe* (Durham, NC: Duke University Press, 2005).

18. Berlant, *Female Complaint*, ix.

19. Emphasis in the original. Ibid., 10.

20. Ibid., 5.

21. Ibid.

22. Ibid.

23. Emphasis in the original. Ibid., 10.

24. Emphasis in the original. Ibid., x.

25. Ibid.

26. Ibid.

27. Jasbir Puar uses the term homonationalism to refer to "a historical shift marked by the entrance of (some) homosexual bodies as worthy of protection by nation-states, a constitutive and fundamental reorientation of the relationship between the state, capitalism, and sexuality." See Jasbir Puar, "Rethinking Homonationalism," *International Journal of Middle East Studies* 45, no. 2 (May 2013): 336. Questions on the relationship between sexuality, liberation, and capital are also at the forefront of Judith [Jack] Halberstam's *In a Queer Time and Place: Transgender Bodies, Subcultural Lives* (New York: New York University Press, 2003).

28. See, in particular, Thrift, *Non-Representational Theory*; Brian Massumi, *Parables for the Virtual: Movement, Affect, Sensation* (Durham, NC: Duke University Press, 2002); and Steven Shaviro, *The Cinematic Body* (Minneapolis: University of Minnesota Press, 1993), and *Post Cinematic Affect* (London: Zero Books, 2010).

29. Eugenie Brinkema, *The Forms of the Affects* (Durham, NC: Duke University Press, 2014), 38.

30. Brinkema refers to the "intentional fallacy [that] suggests that each instance of cinematic affect is of or related to a spectator, that affect by definition represents or gives over something as some thing to an other." Ibid., 33.

31. Sianne Ngai, *Ugly Feelings* (Cambridge, MA: Harvard University Press, 2005), 28.

32. "Instead of positioning an exploration of affect as a mind/body problem, such writing makes affect a *my mind/my body* problem." Brinkema, *Forms of the Affects*, 33.

33. It is here that my project overlaps with Brinkema's considerably. She writes: "My gamble . . . has been that if I am persuasive that formal affectivity is operative in these texts in which affectivity would seem to be about anything other than form, then it should be even less controversial to read for the structure and forms of affects in other, less contested sites." Brinkema, *Forms of the Affects*, 179.

34. Sedgwick, *Touching Feeling*, 105.

35. Ibid., 19.

36. Sarah Banet-Weiser describes "consumer citizenship" through the cable television network Nickelodeon's targeting of children. It is a targeted appeal in which audience members are imagined as consumers and citizens simultaneously. In this way, commercial media "contribute to sets of meanings that form a contemporary notion of citizenship—meanings that invoke a sense of membership, community, and individual agency." Media forms of this sort "connect to a particular vision of political and cultural enfranchisement" that frames citizenship as an affective category rooted in "good feelings" about group membership and individual affirmation. Banet-Weiser underscores, however, that it is a form of citizenship with no referent. As a result, its connection to an actual citizenship, or the set of rights afforded to members protected by a nation-state, is hazy at best and misleading at worst. Sarah Banet-Weiser, *Kids Rule! Nickelodeon and Consumer-Citizenship* (Durham, NC: Duke University Press, 2007), 12.

37. In the instance of queer people and the public sphere, Eric Clarke states that "the justice conferred by public sphere inclusion involves value relations that at the very least tend to produce a heteronormative sanitation of queer life." Such a valuation of same-sex desire requires that "one act as if the material practices and organizations associated with the public sphere unproblematically embody the ideas of democratic publicness." While gays and lesbians often figure into contemporary political debates, the people most sanctioned to participate in these dialogues—and those whose interests they typically serve—are those who adhere to the "homogenized proxies" required of the public sphere. Michael Warner states that such "proxies," to use Clarke's term, conflate gay and lesbian visibility with queer political equality. He calls this "Rainbow Theory," a kind of "expressivist pluralism" that results in the representation of sexuality via "hyper-allegorized forms [that then get] interpreted as signs of inclusion and authenticity." He attributes the optimism of "Rainbow Theory" to its status as "a fantasized space where all embodied identities could be visibly represented as parallel forms of identity," one that does not and will never exist. Eric Clarke, *Virtuous Vice: Homoeroticism and the Public Sphere* (Durham, NC: Duke University Press, 2000), 6; Michael Warner, introduction to *Fear of a Queer Planet: Queer Politics and Social Theory* (Minneapolis: University of Minnesota Press, 1993), xix.

38. The overlapping registers of commercial media, or the ways in which they serve political functions alongside economic and social ones, is a prominent concern in scholarship on media and culture. See, in particular, George Lipsitz, *Time Passages: Collective Memory and American Popular Culture* (Minneapolis: University of Minnesota Press, 2001); and Herman Gray, *Cultural Moves: African Americans and the Politics of Representation* (Berkeley: University of California Press, 2005).

39. Spivak, "Scattered Speculations," 82.

40. Amy Villarejo calls this "the secret decoder ring" method of media analysis. Here, "a message is hidden in a given text, and it wends its way nefariously toward an unwitting receiver; the astute cultural critic knows better, decodes the hidden message, and exposes the lurking evil." Amy Villarejo, *Ethereal Queer: Television, Historicity, Desire* (Durham, NC: Duke University Press, 2014).

41. For her part, Katharine Sender criticizes this interpretive tendency, stating that "no pristine GLBT culture existed before, or outside of consumer culture, nor are gay people free of the need or desire to use products and services in socially meaningful ways." Her analysis examines the ways that gay and lesbian media professionals frame the political utility of such profit-minded labor. Katherine Sender, *Business, Not Politics: The Making of the Gay Market* (New York: Columbia University Press, 2005), 18.

42. Lisa Henderson uses the term "commercial repressive hypothesis" to connote "the idea that for queer culture, politics, and sexuality, the history of commerce is a history of repression." To highlight the very points of overlap and places of tension in which this book is most invested, Henderson offers the term "queer relay." She states: "While the critique of capital offers the language of market determination and appropriation, the subcategory of relay within commercial cultural production multiplies and redirects determination in favor of determinisms and other more reciprocal forms of influence. It imagines a historical braid of changing production conditions and the hunger of commercial systems for subcultural energy and artistry." What Henderson's notion of relay has in common with my interests in *Feeling Normal* is "a lively aversion to hardened categories in cultural analysis." By emphasizing the variability of value, I follow Henderson in underlining that the practices of media commerce involve more complicated relations between politics and economy than static binaries can ever bring into focus. Lisa Henderson, *Love and Money: Queers, Class, and Cultural Production* (New York: New York University Press, 2013), 102–103.

43. Amy Villarejo, *Lesbian Rule: Cultural Criticism and the Value of Desire* (Durham, NC: Duke University Press, 2003), 32–36.

44. Ibid., 35.

45. This critique is perhaps most salient in Villarejo's commentary on the documentary *Forbidden Love* (1992), a movie that examines lesbian themes in pulp fiction of the postwar era. Villarejo suggests that the documentary's labeling of these novels "lesbian" treats them as a coherent category when, in practice, they were not coherent at all. For Villarejo, the naming performs an isolation that "severs [the books'] connections to other forms of social abjection," particularly the circumstances of race and class that affected the characters and authors of the books in ways that were both informed and complicated by matters of sexuality. Villarejo worries about the ideological labors implicit in naming texts "gay and lesbian," seeing in it the potential for a rhetorical violence that separates what should be inseparable—mutually informing vectors of desire and identity. Ibid., 161.

46. Spivak, "Scattered Speculations," 80.

47. Ibid.

48. Villarejo, *Lesbian Rule*, 11.

49. Villarejo is careful to highlight that "alternative," self-consciously political cinema is both similar to and different from "Hollywood," or more conventionally commercial cinema. Ibid.

50. Miranda Joseph, *Against the Romance of Community* (Minneapolis: University of Minnesota Press, 2002).

1   Cities as Affective Convergences

CONVENTIONAL DEFINITIONS OF "convergence" understand the term as a "coming together" in which disparate things merge. The term has an adjacent meaning in the field of media studies, wherein it connotes the ongoing shift from analog to digital production and distribution; the dispersal of audiences across multiple delivery technologies; and the finer, more specific appeals made to consumers by increasingly conglomerated media companies.[1] This chapter considers these definitions in tandem, using the first definition of convergence to think through the second, charting a historical trajectory that connects the processes of urbanization to more recent developments in media commerce related to digital technology. Across both understandings of convergence, bodies are placed in new relations with one another via the circulation of capital. In the instance of urban centers, patterns of use and exchange orient people in space: crowds coalesce on city streets, communities concentrate in neighborhoods, and strangers bump into each other on sidewalks and public transit.[2] Urbanization is a corporeal experience that has enabled the development of public cultures among sexual minorities.[3] This chapter demonstrates that digital technologies converge audiences around media forms in similar ways. By doing so, it identifies a precedent for the courtship of sexual minorities as consumers that dates back to the advent of modernity.[4]

Using New York, Chicago, and San Francisco as case studies, this chapter demonstrates how the experiences available to sexual minorities in urban centers are similar to those offered to them by contemporary cinema, television, and online media. The processes by which sexual minorities form publics in urban centers feature a simultaneous *dispersal and concentration*, wherein publics can be found throughout cities, but cluster in particular locales.[5] Businesses that target sexual minority consumers, especially nightlife businesses like bars and clubs, use multiple attractions to court customers, like special events and theme nights that stretch across multiple levels and numerous dance floors. This *aggregation* of attractions is how businesses attempt to create variety, diversifying the kinds of experiences they make available to patrons and thus potentially diversifying the publics that form in them. Aggregation is one way that businesses compete with one another, a necessity given the fact that they target overlapping demographics. In fact, *marketplace competition* is so intense in urban centers that many businesses struggle to generate enough revenue to remain in operation. To do that, they often specialize in the kinds of experiences they provide to patrons. Because customers are more likely to frequent establishments where they think they will enjoy themselves, businesses differentiate themselves from their competitors by promising specific kinds of attractions, creating identities that can be thought of as *genres*. Cavernous dance clubs, intimate martini lounges, and campy dive bars provide different experiences to consumers.[6] But sexual minorities sometimes experience frustration with the opportunities for publicness available to them. As a result, online communities have developed in which people organize events where they crowd bars and clubs and usurp them, transforming the genres of publicness available to sexual minorities in urban centers.

These four patterns—dispersal and concentration, aggregation, marketplace competition, and genres—enable the formation of sexual minority publics by way of commerce, creating opportunities for sociality by bringing bodies together in city space.[7] Similar patterns can be seen in media industry contexts, where gay and lesbian audiences convene around cinema, television, and online media. In both cities and media forms, the bodies that come together through the practices of commerce form shifting, multiple, overlapping publics.[8] For all of the cultural mores that impel sexual minorities to come out of the closet, media criticism tends to imply private consumption, often framed in terms of individual spectatorship or group viewing.[9] In contrast, cities demonstrate how commerce enables an array of experiences for sexual minorities in public spaces, putting them in contact with others like themselves. Because same-sex desires—as well as the identities and communities they help form—are so often realized via people's circulation in public space, cities offer a framework for understanding the relationship between capital and affect found in all gay and lesbian media. Indeed, the public spaces of urban centers preexist the forms of sociality imagined in gay and lesbian cinema, television, and online media. Even as these ostensibly more "private" media have since proliferated, the publics that form in urban centers continue to operate via the patterns of commerce described here.

Moving between the terms "queer," "sexual minority," and "gay and lesbian" enables a differentiation of the diverse people who circulate in urban centers from the more limited ways the businesses that court them imagine target demographics. There is no single sexual minority public in any city, in any venue—just like there is no single subject position, nor is there one solitary, univocal audience. The convergence of sexual minorities in urban centers involves a tension between universals and particulars because the characteristics shared by individuals who form publics are not comprehensive. As a result, publics are structures in tension. Sexual minority publics feature heterogeneity in the form of gender, race, and class hierarchies. Thus, the sexual minority publics that converge in urban centers are embedded in systems of knowledge and power that are well established though always contested.[10] Like the media forms they predate, cities make sensory pleasures available to sexual minorities, but they are not equally accessible to all.

Cities and Their Ephemera

This chapter uses magazines that court queer readers in two ways: (1) as evidence of the patterns of commerce that develop in urban centers, and (2) as a bridge that links those urban centers to media forms created and circulated in the context of digital production and distribution.[11] The chapter focuses on locally published, advertiser-supported publications that inform readers of events and attractions in different locations and on particular nights of the week. In New York, Chicago, and San Francisco, such publications are distributed in businesses that serve sexual minorities and are piled in kiosks in gay and lesbian neighborhoods. Many of the attractions advertised and reported on in the magazines are commercial, as in the instance of bars, clubs, and restaurants. At the same time, many of those attractions are not commercial in the conventional sense, as in the instance of community centers, nonprofit organizations, LGBT (lesbian, gay, bisexual, transgender)-friendly churches, schools and universities, and so on. The magazines inform readers of the opportunities for entertainment, education, and community building available to them in cities, generating revenue by blurring advertising and editorial coverage of happy hours, neighborhood association meetings, charity benefits, and fetish parties. In each of the magazines, maps, event listings, and advertisements imagine the convergence of sexual minorities in public space. In essence, the magazines articulate urban centers as a collection of opportunities for personal agency and community belonging for their readers.

San Francisco's *Gloss*, New York's *HX* and *Next*, and Chicago's *Nightspots* and *Gay Chicago Magazine* do not simply describe urban centers as entities formed by other means, but participate in their production at the level of discourse. The magazines demonstrate how the convergence of sexual minorities in urban centers is affective in nature: advertisements and articles gesture to the joy of meeting friends at a community event, the laughter precipitated by nightlife entertainment, the wet heat of sticky bodies on a dance floor. The magazines announce guest DJs and television screening parties alongside discounted drinks, free food, dancing, giveaways, and similar entertainments. As a result, they underscore how the publics comprised of sexual minorities that form in urban centers are enabled and shaped by the circulation of bodies in public space. Cities foster a multiplicity of such convergences by virtue of their magnitude, both in terms of their spatial areas and population densities.[12] The magazines provide evidence of how that multiplicity is both fostered and hemmed in by the very nature of the metropolis.

Because cities enable contact between strangers, historians cast them as fostering the creation of identities and communities related to nonnormative sexual desires. John D'Emilio credits the expansion of industrialization and the spread of wage labor that occurred with the advent of modernity with freeing sexuality from the necessity of procreation. He argues that modernity—specifically, the growth of "free labor" and the processes of urbanization—created "conditions that allow[ed] some men and women to organize a personal life around their erotic/emotional attraction to their own sex."[13] Agrarian economies in the pre-industrial United States featured a mode of production in which people most often lived and worked with their biological families. In contrast, the modes of production that first emerged in the context of modernity involved people living and working outside of—and often away from—their kin. These changes allowed people to work in contexts other than household economies and create attachments to others in ways that differed from familial networks. Building upon that idea, D'Emilio argues that cities are central to gay and lesbian history in the United States because the urban migrations characteristic of modernity made it possible for one's "homosexual desire to coalesce into a personal identity."[14] Away from biological families, people sought out interpersonal connections in new ways, like participating in the communities that formed in their new urban environs. For people who experienced same-sex desire, the city precipitated a new set of relations between those desires, their notions of selfhood, and the means by which they forged relations with others. D'Emilio states that the Great Depression and World War II accelerated the pace and volume of these shifts, "severely disrupt[ing] traditional patterns of gender relations and sexuality and . . . creat[ing] a new erotic situation conducive to homosexual expression."[15] The legacy of these shifts can be seen in the locally published magazines that serve sexual minorities in urban centers.

Issues of gender, race, and class mitigate the applicability of urbanization as a historical trope for understanding sexual minorities and the publics they form. Jack Halberstam worries about the prevalence of cities as frames of reference in queer criticism, charging that there is a tendency among scholars to understand sexual desire and identity too simplistically via a set of city-centered, "metronormative" ideals.[16] While cities are unevenly experienced by sexual minorities—many live there, others visit, some never go at all—they provide many attractions, employment opportunities, and community-building resources to these populations. However tenuous, the connection between homosexuality and urban centers is so trenchant in American culture that it frequently functions as little more than a diffuse set of references. This operation of discourse is perhaps seen mostly plainly in the stereotype of the effete, worldly homosexual with high socioeconomic status and well-developed cultural tastes.[17] Such references construct a common sense that underscores the power relations implicit in all operations of discourse, where even considerable evidence to the contrary does not always lessen the veracity of their claims to truth.[18] Not every queer urbanite can afford season tickets to the opera, and many would not even want them. While the magazines themselves make broad assumptions and come to easy conclusions about the ways that publics form in urban centers, this chapter highlights the discursive limits of the feelings of agency and belonging they make available to sexual minorities.[19]

In their mixture of reportage and promotion, the magazines feature the slippage of consumption and citizenship that is the hallmark of all gay and lesbian media. In a sense, the magazines make going out for cocktails a civic matter, where particular modes of consumption are imagined to provide readers with a sense of personal agency and cultural membership. While the analysis in this chapter might have included any number of locales, I chose New York, San Francisco, and Chicago because I could access the locally published, advertiser-supported publications that circulate there. Even though such magazines are published and distributed across the United States, they are infrequently archived and not often available in online databases. Given away for free and thrown away in bulk, the magazines examined in this chapter are at once ephemeral and omnipresent. So even though they are a common feature of queer life in urban centers, they are less likely to be stored and analyzed than more self-consciously political press.[20] *Next, HX, Nightspots, Gay Chicago Magazine,* and *Gloss* have historical roots in publications that circulated information about same-sex leisure and entertainment in other eras.[21] Such magazines provided people who experience same-sex desire with information about the commercial attractions and community-building resources available to them in urban centers. Historically, these publications helped sexual minorities locate and patronize businesses where they could safely seek entertainment, education, and interpersonal connection.[22]

In the early 1990s, the marketplace for magazines that publish content of interest to sexual minorities transformed considerably. During that period, sex-related advertising was removed from the nationally circulating gay and lesbian publication the *Advocate* and circulated in the form of a stand-alone magazine, *Advocate Classifieds*.[23] This turn of events consolidated the marketplace for sex-related advertising in local magazines like *Next, HX, Nightspots, Gay Chicago Magazine,* and *Gloss*. It also swelled their circulation numbers and made them attractive to advertisers looking for ways to reach sexual minorities. So the local magazines published after this shift offer a substantive archive for examining how publics form in urban centers. This chapter uses a convenience sample of titles circulating between 2002 and 2010, which allows for an easier relation between them and the gay and lesbian media circulating around the same time. The magazines also provide long-term evidence of commerce forming queer publics. Their pages point to patterns in the relationship between capital and queer sociality, themes that have emerged over the course of many decades. Because the market for sex-related advertising is heavily gendered male, the magazines tend to showcase gay male cultural tastes and desires more prominently than those of other sexual minorities. Thus, the publications demonstrate the complicated roles that gender, race, and class play in the formation of sexual minority publics. At the same time, the publications are bound up in the processes of gentrification that occur in so many US cities, and they highlight the relationship between identity politics and those processes, as well.

Many of these locally published, advertiser-supported magazines are circulated by companies that also specialize in nightlife promotion, an arrangement that skews editorial coverage toward a focus on the commercial attractions available in the bars and clubs that buy advertising space in their pages. For instance, *HX* was initially owned and operated, in part, by an event promoter. And *HX*, *Next*, and *Gloss* all regularly host bar nights and cultivate "VIP" lists that they make available for sale to businesses interested in using them for promotional mailings. But while the magazines' editorial coverage is somewhat adjacent to more self-consciously "alternative" press, that differentiation is difficult to apply systematically. For instance, Chicago-based Windy City Media publishes several titles including the *Windy City Times*, which is focused on political issues and current events, as well as *Nightspots*, a publication focused on the city's queer nightlife. The magazines examined in this chapter resound with pictures of shirtless bartenders and near-nude dancers; they also feature listings for dance clubs and sex-related businesses, and include coupons for free drinks, reduced cover fees, and discounted erotic toys and pornography. Alongside their foregrounding of these decidedly consumerist pleasures, the magazines also do considerable charity work by hosting fund-raising events, sponsoring ad pages for public service announcements, and providing an avenue for elected officials and public health organizations to communicate information to sexual minorities.[24] As a result, these magazines demonstrate the convergence of sexual minorities in urban centers in all of its complexity, providing a historical basis and cultural logic for the kinds of appeals made to those audiences by cinema, television, and online media. A 2008 issue of San Francisco's *Gloss* includes a spread that promotes events for charities related to HIV/AIDS (figure 1.1). The spread's generally conservative content and tone is much different than a lot of *Gloss*'s content, which is often more sexual in nature.

By focusing on how magazines like *Gloss*, *HX*, *Next*, *Gay Chicago Magazine*, and *Nightspots* construct the urban center, the chapter illustrates how the convergence of sexual minorities involves strong parallels across disparate locations. The sections that follow are organized using patterns in how sexual minorities convene around commodities in New York, Chicago, and San Francisco.[25] While the process of public formation varies in each of the cities, the magazines illustrate how they operate in similar ways. It is tempting to see the parallels between the cities and the similarities of businesses as evidence of standardization. I have argued

Figure 1.1. An advertisement for events benefiting HIV/AIDS-related charities illustrates the civic functions that *Gloss* magazine serves for sexual minorities living in San Francisco.

elsewhere that this critique risks drawing too firm a connection between the promises of commercial spaces with the diverse, lived experiences of the people who convene in them.[26] Cities and the businesses that court sexual minorities in them demonstrate the mechanisms by which publics converge via commerce. They coalesce around markedly centrist, consumer-friendly attractions, as well as those that suggest more radical forms of being and wanting. The magazines provide evidence of these contradictions when they advertise (as is documented in the pages ahead) charity events for victims of natural disasters alongside fetish nights at sex clubs. What comes into focus in this analysis is an understanding of urban centers as sites where bodies circulate, forming publics that convene as a result of different patterns of commerce.

Dispersal and Concentration

The magazines publish maps to orient their readers in city space, demonstrating that businesses courting sexual minorities can be found throughout the locales,

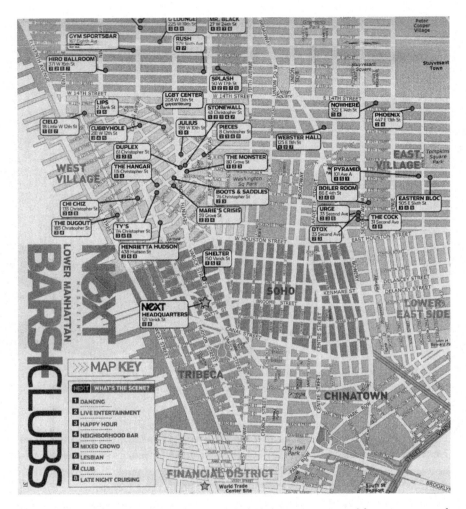

Figure 1.2. In most issues of *Next*, the centerfold is a two-page spread featuring a map of New York City.

and that they are also concentrated in particular zones and neighborhoods. For instance, *Next*'s regular weekly centerfold color codes the neighborhoods of Lower Manhattan, bullet pointing locations for the area's gay and lesbian bars and clubs (figure 1.2). While dispersed throughout the city, New York's gay and lesbian bars and clubs have several points of concentration: the historic Greenwich Village area downtown, the Chelsea neighborhood just north of there, and the area just west of Times Square in a neighborhood known as Hell's Kitchen. *Next*'s map identifies the multiple opportunities for education and entertainment that the city affords to sexual minorities, highlighting some of the most expensive, exclusive areas of the city in doing so. The map underlines a set of assumptions about where sexual minorities can be located, illuminating how businesses that court sexual minorities are bound to the processes of urban development that prevail in many US cities.

These patterns of dispersal and concentration are steeped in dynamics of power that remain largely unmentioned in the pages of *HX* and *Next*, enabling the formation of some publics even as they hinder the establishment of others. This dispersal and concentration is what Henri Lefebvre calls a society's "spatial practices," the process through which relations of production are situated in social space. Spatial practices are historical in nature and are cemented in symbolic objects like the maps found in *HX* and *Next*. They construct certain locales as being "desirable or undesirable; benevolent or malevolent; sanctioned or forbidden to particular groups."[27] While queer publics convene throughout New York City, they have a long history of concentrating in the Greenwich Village area. Although many scholars reject a narrative that marks the June 1969 riots at the Stonewall Inn as the beginning and epicenter of the US gay and lesbian rights movement, that narrative remains a common one that is reiterated in many discourses, including the pages of *HX* and *Next*.[28] For instance, the *Next* issue published during the week of June 22, 2007, was devoted to the city's annual Gay Pride celebration. Advertisements for the Stonewall Inn court customers with a pointed historical claim, gesturing to the bar's iconic status by referring to it as the place "Where Pride Began."

The dispersal of New York's gay and lesbian businesses throughout the city and their concentration in certain areas are firmly connected to the processes of gentrification. Samuel Delany outlines the impact of these developments on the ability of diverse publics to form in New York City. He charges that while cross-class contact flourished in the Times Square area's adult movie theaters in the 1960s through the 1980s, gentrification has largely exiled the queer, working class, and racial and ethnic minority publics who used to commingle there with relative ease. Beginning in the 1990s, city ordinances regulating sex-related commerce and renewed corporate interest in refashioning New York as a family friendly tourist destination marginalize some publics in the interest of generating profit from others. One result has been a sharp increase in rents and a large amount of new construction throughout the city, both of which have pushed many sex-related businesses out of operation. Because the Greenwich Village area is home to affluent residents as well as a place where sexual minorities from other parts of the city have historically converged, the neighborhood has seen tensions erupt between the interests of the wealthy people who own property there and the interests of those who visit to patronize the neighborhood's businesses.[29] In 2008, advertisements for the Stonewall Inn informed *Next* readers that the bar was renovated and placed under new management, making a veiled reference to the changing spatial practices of contemporary New York City in general, and Greenwich Village more specifically. These factors have helped make the Stonewall Inn a halting, uncertain business enterprise in the decades after the 1969 riots. The bar has closed, reopened, and changed hands multiple times since the early 1990s, providing evidence of the very transformations that Delany critiques. Urban development projects privilege demographics thought to have high disposable incomes, resulting in the segregation of sexual minorities along class and racial lines.[30] According to Delany, when such spatial practices are condoned and fostered by acts of governance, publics become "replaceable nodes" in networks more concerned with the generation of revenue than the welfare of citizens.[31]

At the same time, sexual minorities are also part of such gentrification because many of the businesses courting them as consumers thrive under the conditions that Delany describes. While sanctioned and unsanctioned publics are separated by dynamics of power, the local magazines blur those distinctions: kinky sex clubs are advertised alongside relatively conservative political benefits, leather bars are listed next to more pedestrian coffeehouses. For instance, the New York bar Posh is located in Hell's Kitchen, a midtown neighborhood near Columbus Circle and Times Square. The bar's central location is consistent with the fairly mundane attractions it advertises to consumers in *HX* and *Next*: cocktails and nosh, muscled waitstaff, and popular television. Posh's advertisements are similar to those published in magazines that circulate in all of the cities insofar as they foreground white gay men and their cultural tastes. The bar's location in a high-traffic area of New York demonstrates how gentrification enables the formation of particular publics even as it prevents others. Similarly, the bar Eastern Bloc is located a few blocks from subway and bus lines in the heart of the East Village. The sexual overtones in its advertisements are not at odds with the bar's central location in New York geography, especially because the ad features and the business caters to white gay men (figure 1.3). Enjoying more cultural power than do other sexual minorities, white gay men are most frequently depicted and courted as consumers in the advertisements of *HX* and *Next*. These representational trends demonstrate gentrification's uneven power dynamics.

The New York City neighborhoods most associated with white gay men are the focal points of the maps in both *HX* and *Next*, a tendency present in the magazines published in each of the cities. Off the maps entirely are Harlem and Queens, areas historically populated by racial and ethnic minorities, which require commutes to the gay and lesbian businesses that have long been concentrated in Lower Manhattan. In his history of gay male life in New York, George Chauncey notes how racial difference drastically altered the kinds of experiences available to sexual minorities in the city during the early twentieth century.[32]

Figure 1.3. Even though Eastern Bloc's advertisements refer to relatively taboo sexual practices, this ad highlights racialized dynamics of power in its feature of white gay men. Moreover, the venue itself is centrally located in New York City's trendy East Village.

White gay men tended to congregate in midtown and downtown Manhattan, while gay black men were more likely to meet one another uptown in Harlem. While this differential is still borne out in the pages of *HX* and *Next*, it is only partially revealing. The magazines also publish advertisements for Greenwich Village venues like the Dugout and Sneakers, which are situated close to the Port Authority Trans-Hudson (PATH) train and commuter rails between Manhattan and neighboring New Jersey. The proximity of these businesses to public transportation makes them particularly accessible to, and popular with, queer patrons from the large communities of racial and ethnic minorities in nearby Jersey City. However limited, such diversity is informed by the large number of businesses courting sexual minorities and the vast spatial area of the city. There are so many different businesses competing for patronage in urban centers that they often make direct appeals to finely conceived demographics. While the modes of publicness that New York City offers to sexual minorities may be more ethnically diverse than the pages of *HX* and *Next* suggest, they are decidedly more gender-specific. The key for *Next's* map differentiates the businesses that explicitly court women from the rest of Lower Manhattan's queer attractions. The tiny number of venues that cater to lesbians and other queer women underscores how the opportunities for publicness imagined by the magazines are predominantly male.[33]

The dispersal and concentration of queer publics in Chicago provide an even starker example of this gendered differential. Two of the neighborhoods on the city's North Side have long been associated with Chicago's sexual minorities: Lakeview with men and Andersonville with women.[34] In 1997, Mayor Richard Daley cited his commitment to the city's gay and lesbian communities and his gratitude to the area's businesses when he named Lakeview the first officially gay neighborhood in the United States. More than a symbolic gesture, Daley privileged the commerce along Halsted Street in material ways. Unlike Andersonville, Lakeview was included in the urban planning project "Neighborhoods Alive." Through this municipal investment program, Daley earmarked $3.2 million for a renovation project that placed twenty sculptures, each twenty-five feet high and ringed in the colors of Gay Pride, along a seven-block strip in the area. This act of governance resulted in the construction of structures that distinguish the strip from other sections of the city. As a symbolic act, "Neighborhoods Alive" marks Lakeview as an area where sexual minorities converge. It also has material consequences insofar as Lakeview businesses benefit from the campaign in ways that those operating in Andersonville, which more frequently cater to women, do not.[35]

The dynamics of power that concentrate and disperse publics in Chicago are visible throughout the city's advertiser-supported magazines. Businesses advertise in order to differentiate themselves with consumer appeals that point to the formation of distinct yet overlapping publics. For instance, a Halsted-area bar called the North End often courts gay men with advertisements depicting shirtless male athletes. Steamworks is a sex club located just a few blocks away from the North End, it also advertises in the city's locally published magazines, targeting gay men as sexual subjects in promotions that feature references to the business's saunas, locker rentals, and private fetish rooms. The multitude of such advertisements in *Nightspots* and *Gay Chicago Magazine* demonstrate how the publics convened by Chicago's businesses overlap considerably, underlining the gendered power dynamics that structure queer life in the city. Like the map in *Next's* centerfold, the maps in *Gay Chicago Magazine* and *Nightspots* leave out the regions where a large percentage of the city's racial and ethnic minority populations reside. As a result, the magazines portray the city's queer life, but concentrate on some of the priciest real estate in the city. Even so, the magazines' venue directories work differently. Because they are organized by neighborhood, the directories gesture to the dispersal of queer publics throughout Chicago. In *Nightspots*, the section "Where's My Bar At?" lists every gay and lesbian venue in the city. Here, the attractions of the city's North Side neighborhoods are featured alongside venues like Club Escape, Escapades, InnExile, and Jeffrey, located on the city's South Side, an area that has historically been home to the city's African American communities. Thus, Chicago's spatial area and the sheer magnitude of its population enable the formation of a range of queer publics that are simultaneously concentrated in particular zones and dispersed throughout the city. Those processes foster the convergence of publics, but simultaneously hook them into well-established power dynamics that mitigate their accessibility to all sexual minorities.

Like New York and Chicago, the convergence of sexual minorities in San Francisco is informed by the city's history. Nan Alamilla Boyd characterizes San Francisco's sexual diversity as an "overlap of cultures and communities," which she attributes to heavy port traffic and the sex-related businesses that flourished around it.[36] She argues that the sexual diversity often attributed to the city has historical roots dating back to the California gold rush of the nineteenth century. By the early 1900s, Boyd suggests that sexual minority publics were flourishing in the city because so many different communities "commingled in the intimate spaces of bars and baths, dances and house parties."[37] Boyd credits these developments with creating a cultural climate in San Francisco conducive to the formation of sexual minority publics throughout the city for most of the twentieth century and beyond.[38] San Francisco is itself a major attraction for sexual minorities. At the same time, the city's Castro neighborhood is often understood to be the center of the city's queer life. A combination of "white flight" to San Francisco's suburbs, the neighborhood's relatively low-cost real estate, and a handful of savvy entrepreneurs who converted existing businesses to gay and lesbian nightlife venues in the 1960s and 1970s helped make the Castro a major site for businesses courting sexual minorities during that period.[39] In the time since, the activism and notoriety of Castro Street business owner Harvey Milk in the 1970s, and frequent news coverage of the area during the height of the AIDS epidemic in the 1980s and 1990s, have underscored the neighborhood's status as a hub of queer San Francisco—as well as in the United States writ large.

Even though queer publics form throughout San Francisco, *Gloss* devotes more pages to the Castro than any other neighborhood. In doing so, the publication tacitly underlines it as the focal point of queer life in the city, devoting a great deal of attention to the gay men who frequent the Castro's businesses. For instance, the August 28, 2008, issue of *Gloss* features a promotion for a weekly event called "Boy Bar," sponsored by a gay adult website at a commercial space on Market Street. The advertisement depicts shirtless white male models with text reading "jocks, socks, c*cks," and "muscle music," and thus featuring strong similarities with the kinds of publicness available in New York and Chicago. Moreover, the promotion makes an explicit reference to San Francisco's geography, highlighting the event's location "in the Castro" as one of several attractions available to publics at Boy Bar. In *Gloss*'s July 11, 2008, issue, the "Frathouse" party at 440 Castro foregrounds a similar public with an advertisement depicting a young white male model alongside references to the venue's DJ and discounted drink specials. As in the instance of Boy Bar's advertisement, the promotion for Frathouse highlights the Castro as an attraction in and of itself, with prominently featured text reading "College Night in the Castro." In ways similar to those seen in these advertisements, *Gloss* privileges the Castro neighborhood as the epicenter of queer San Francisco in every issue.

This emphasis on the Castro performs acute elisions of gender, race, and class by foregrounding occasions for publicness associated with white gay men. Even so, queer San Francisco is more diverse than a passing glance at *Gloss* suggests. Although many pages of the magazine privilege the white gay male publics that convene in the Castro, *Gloss* also features promotions for attractions throughout the San Francisco Bay Area. The Castro has such a high cost of living that many of the city's racial and ethnic minority communities live elsewhere, either in other neighborhoods in San Francisco or, more frequently, across the bay in Oakland. The October 17, 2008, issue includes a promotion for the "Latin Explosion" party at a bar called Bench. Located in Oakland, Bench is geographically removed from San Francisco's more famous neighborhoods and largest concentrations of sexual minorities. Like New York's outer boroughs and Chicago's South Side, Oakland is home to many of the city's racial and ethnic minority communities, so pages devoted to attractions there demonstrate that San Francisco's queer publics converge throughout the city. *Gloss*'s focus on white gay men and the Castro animates class and racial dynamics that contour the formation of publics, but at the same time, the magazine also illustrates the dispersal of sexual minorities across the urban center.

The simultaneous dispersal and concentration of queer publics can be seen in each of the cities. The advertiser-supported magazines highlight how the concentration of those publics in particular areas reveals a great deal about the power dynamics that shape them, and the media forms created for sexual minorities operate in similar ways. Digital technology enables new modes of production and distribution, which in turn enable new sorts of representations that anticipate sexual minorities as audiences. But these practices are predicated on assumptions about those audiences, and they hinge on privileges associated with gender, race, and class that delimit the forms of diversity they are able to engender at all. This paradigm is most evident in cinema, where digital technology has resulted in a large number of distributors circulating movies to sexual minorities across different delivery platforms. Despite this multiplicity, the movies they distribute are striking in their similarities. They tend to animate narrative paradigms steeped in ideas about personal agency that actively curb attention to the different forms of diversity that characterize the very publics they convene.

Aggregation

In their advertisements, individual businesses construct a sense of multiplicity for consumers, suggesting that there are a multitude of attractions for them within the confines of a single venue, like live entertainment, drink specials, and video screens. This business strategy is a process of aggregation because it imagines a range of publics in a single venue, where each attraction is imagined to offer something different to customers.[40] It is a process that businesses use to exploit the mutability of space over time, and it opens the possibility that multiple (if also overlapping) publics can convene in a single venue. Advertisements for Hamburger Mary's demonstrate the process of aggregation when they promote events on different nights of the week: bingo hosted by a drag queen on Mondays, an event specifically for lesbian and bisexual women called "Lipstick Club" on Thursdays, and karaoke on Sundays and Wednesdays. Such advertisements create a sense of variety over time and appear frequently in the advertiser-supported magazines. They allow businesses to court a range of publics in trying to generate revenue. Although media content is not the only way that bars and clubs suggest variety, it is a common strategy used to aggregate multiple publics. For instance, advertisements for the San Francisco bar Midnight Sun highlight the venue's television viewing parties by constructing variety *within* a block of time. The venue's advertisements announce an assortment of programs screening at the bar, allotting an hour or half hour to each. In this way, the advertisement suggests that even in a single evening, the venue features an assortment of attractions. Advertisements for the Chicago bar Charlie's illustrate both dynamics; they announce different attractions on various nights of the week and schedule entertainment across different blocks of time within the same evening (figure 1.4).

Businesses also aggregate multiple publics by exploiting their spatial diversity, where different areas can be sectioned off to serve different groups of customers.

Figure 1.4. *Gay Chicago Magazine* informs readers of different events at a bar called Charlie's. Some of these events are scheduled on various nights of the week, while others are scheduled over the course of the same evening.

Advertisements for San Francisco's DNA Lounge invite patrons to listen to guest DJs mixing songs in one portion of the venue, and also promote the club's resident DJs who spin for the crowd in another area of the bar. Similarly, the city's Cat Club often advertises attractions in different spaces in the venue: "back room" DJs and "front room" DJs. The club aggregates different forms of entertainment in a single space, suggesting to customers that there are a bevy of attractions available there. By doing that, the advertisement suggests at least some variety in the publics that form there. Similarly, the Chicago bar Sidetrack uses its architecture to aggregate multiple publics. In an advertisement published in *Nightspots* in 2007, Sidetrack invites potential customers to participate in a beer tasting and product giveaway for a local microbrew on its roof deck. This design feature is one of several large alcoves that the venue has added over the course of several years. Sidetrack's website draws a timeline from the business's inception in 1982, "with no sign and beer cases as seating," to a 1984 addition that doubled its size; the 1988 construction of the "BackBar"; and additions of disparate bars and spaces coined with names like "CherryBar," "GlassBar," and "SideBar" in 1994, 1999, 2004, and 2009—with several renovations in between.[41] Advertisements for Hamburger Mary's in Chicago often highlight the venue's multiple spaces, branding its upstairs room "Mary's Attic"; its ads frequently point readers to different events upstairs and downstairs. Likewise, Krash, a bar that has operated in different venues around New York City, often collects a slew of spaces and attractions in its advertisements (figure 1.5). In the interest of invoking abundance, the venue's advertisement in *Next* features an aggregation of spaces: three floors, four rooms, and four bars. As such, it creates a sense of variety by way of space: suggesting to consumers (however tacitly) that each floor, room, and bar provides them with an opportunity to experience a different kind of attraction. A construction of marketing discourse, aggregation is another way in which public formation is fostered by commerce.

While the attractions that businesses provide are relatively similar, the aggregation of publics in single venues also enables some racial and gender diversity, as well as more recognizably civic attractions in the public spaces of urban centers. The Hideaway, a bar in suburban Chicago, announces a weekly party for women in the December 6, 2006, issue of *Nightspots*. Similarly, advertisements for the bar Big Chicks in *Gay Chicago Magazine* underline the venue's gender diversity, making a point to inform readers that everyone is welcome. Women are courted so infrequently by these businesses that their courtship by the Hideaway and Big Chicks is notable for the way it identifies women as one of several publics. These advertising practices indicate how aggregation is one way that commerce can create diversity. The Monster, a bar located in New York's West Village, makes an explicit appeal to Latino publics in the June 20, 2008, issue of *HX*. The business advertises itself with a promotion for a weekly "Sabor Latino" party, illustrating

Figure 1.5. Krash's advertisement in *Next* highlights different spaces at the same venue.

how aggregation enables specific appeals to racial and ethnic minorities. Similarly, the New York bar Escuelita announces a party for queer Puerto Ricans, scheduled so that it coincides with the city's annual Puerto Rican Day Parade (figure 1.6). Using the Puerto Rican flag alongside the word "Boricua," a slang term for Puerto Ricans living in the United States, Escuelita differentiates queer Puerto Ricans from the broader array of Latino consumers it courts. A 2005 *Gloss* advertisement for the EndUp in San Francisco invokes the anniversary of 9/11 to announce a benefit for the New Orleans Gay and Lesbian Community Center in the wake of Hurricane Katrina. In another advertisement, the EndUp targets San Francisco's Asian communities with a regular event called "Shangri-La." The venue announces that it will donate a portion of the evening's revenues to relief funds for people displaced by the 2008 earthquake that occurred in China's Sichuan Province. In these ways, aggregation convenes more recognizably civic-minded

Figure 1.6. Featuring vernacular and iconography that invoke Puerto Rico, the New York bar Escuelita advertises an event to a specific subset of its more diverse Latino customers.

publics alongside those that converge around more conventional attractions and entertainments.

The ways that businesses aggregate multiple publics parallel how that process takes place in media forms. In the travel content that circulates on gay and lesbian cable TV networks, programs feature a variety of different segments that showcase a range of different sexual minorities. Voice-over narration of these programs highlights this diversity as evidence of the multiple queer publics that can be found in any location around the world. The programs combine commodity pleasures with political commentary, imagining audiences comprised of diverse individuals. News content on the gay and lesbian cable networks also features aggregation, where a range of segments imagines a range of different viewers in the audience.[42] Aggregation can also be seen on mobile media applications that court gay and lesbian users. Mobile companies promote longer and more refined pull-down menus as better accommodating the diversity of sexual minorities who use mobile applications to make interpersonal connections. Like the aggregation that occurs in city businesses, the diversity created by aggregation in digital media is imagined, but it is a pattern of commerce that convenes multiple publics and fosters some diversity as a result.

Marketplace Competition

The dispersal/concentration and aggregation that form publics in urban centers are always in flux because the actors participating in any marketplace are competing with one another for similarly imagined demographics. In his theory of evolutionary economics, Joseph Schumpeter states that when entrepreneurs introduce an innovation to a marketplace it often causes existing businesses to lose their positions in that milieu.[43] So building a bigger bar, introducing more spectacular technology to a club, instituting special events on certain nights of the week, or adding multiple levels and rooms to an existing space provide evidence of the competition among businesses courting sexual minorities in the urban center. Up to this point, I have stressed that urban centers accommodate multiple, fluid sexual minority publics. At the same time, these publics overlap considerably because businesses target similar publics via comparable appeals. Thus, marketplace competition has a large impact on the public formation that occurs in urban centers. Within months of each other, two businesses closed in 2009: Rubyfruit in New York and Star Gaze in Chicago. In both cases, owners cited the difficulties of courting regular customers in a city where many businesses court similar demographics.[44] Moreover, the two businesses catered specifically to lesbians, demonstrating that competition is not a benign phenomenon. A focus on marketplace competition illustrates the extent to which the sexual minority publics that form by way of commerce overlap and precipitate deleterious effects on queer life in urban centers.

Various features of the magazines demonstrate how marketplace competition shapes the formation of queer publics in urban centers. For instance, in the magazines' calendar listings, the ways that different businesses court customers using similar appeals becomes particularly visible. The calendar listings in *Nightspots* note the drink specials, television viewing parties, CD giveaways, and special appearances occurring in businesses throughout the city over a seven-day period. In the August 19, 2008, issue, the magazine lists a series of attractions for queer Chicagoans to pick from on Thursday, August 20: a movie screening at Rumors, cocktails and videos at Sidetrack, cabaret at Mary's Attic and Spin, and simply "Cheap Booze" at Star Gaze. The calendar listings make material the process by which venues compete for customers by emphasizing that at any given point, there are time-specific pleasures available in a number of different businesses around the city. While a night on the town might involve stops at a few venues, *Nightspots* lists thirty-five different businesses hosting events on the very same night. Even the most spirited bargoers could not attend all of them at the same time.

The advertiser-supported magazines also participate in this marketplace competition themselves by featuring some businesses more frequently and/or more prominently than others. The magazines attempt to make their coverage serve an agenda-setting function, encouraging their readers to pick up each new issue. Each of the magazines spotlights a few key events and attractions occurring on particular nights of the week, which results in the privileging of a handful of businesses and events at the expense of those who do not make the cut. In the May 3, 2007, issue of *Gay Chicago Magazine*, the regularly featured "Calendar of Events" isolates a few events on each night of the week, drawing readers' attention to a handful of attractions: a CD giveaway at the bar Roscoe's on Thursday, May 3, and a benefit for the Women's Treatment Center at a downtown hotel that same night; or the Barbra Streisand party at Sidetrack against attractions at competing businesses on Monday, May 7. Listings and calendars help businesses push past the clutter of life in the urban center. After all, there is a slew of things for people to do, see, and enjoy in cities—bar nights and other events must echo above the din in order to generate profit. The magazines also attempt to make their coverage serve taste-making functions for consumers. *HX*'s editorial coverage is called "Homo Musts," where staff pick a list of events to highlight for their readership. In the February 1, 2008, issue, *HX* writers highlight a video and dance performance at Splash on Friday, January 25; a drink special at the bar Vlada the next night; and a special appearance by an adult video star and a benefit for an AIDS charity at different locations on Monday, January 28. On each of these nights, there are scores of other businesses courting consumers throughout the city. While *HX*'s features are often a matter of editorial choice, *Next* explicitly solicits submissions for its similar "Next Week" feature, providing promoters and managers with a regular e-mail address and a two-weeks-prior deadline.[45] Even so, the magazine emphasizes that inclusion in the weekly spotlight is "subject to editorial discretion." In the June 6, 2008, issue, *Next* promotes a bevy of events in the week leading up to the city's Gay Pride Celebration: an adult drawing class at a Chelsea gallery and a Shabbat dinner at the LGBT Community Center on Friday, June 6, as well as a party at the East Village bar Nowhere and a dance at the National Black Theatre in Harlem on June 8. In drawing attention to particular businesses and events, the magazines lure consumers away from other businesses and events, emphasizing how different interests compete for overlapping queer publics.

The marketplace competition that takes place between businesses courting sexual minorities in urban centers has many parallels with the competition between media companies that court sexual minority audiences. Cinema distributors and mobile media companies that target sexual minorities imagine overlapping target audiences and angle for broader market reach in the pages of trade publications. The industry practices that characterize network television result in strikingly similar programs courting parallel demographics. On cable TV, competition between networks targeting gay and lesbian audiences is so tight that it is difficult for networks to enter the marketplace at all. In each instance, the competition between different businesses points to broader issues related to political economy that differ considerably across media industries. But the competition seen among businesses in urban centers demonstrates the fine differentiations that various marketplace actors make when branding themselves, as well as the negative impact that competition can have on the processes of public formation.

Generic Appeals

In each of the cities, businesses court sexual minorities with similar ideas about identity, desire, and taste. They create niches for themselves to target consumers in highly specific ways. These differentiated appeals are generic insofar as they create expectations among targeted consumers. For instance, the sports-themed bar North End advertises its screenings of National Football League (NFL) and college football games to queer Chicagoans. A portrait of a turkey in a football helmet attracts target publics with some tongue-in-cheek double entendre, a reference to both Thanksgiving weekend's many televised sporting events and the slang term "chicken," used to describe young, athletic gay men. Thus, the business uses vernacular related to categories of identity, desire, and taste that circulate among gay men to signal to consumers what kinds of publics form there. Genre can be defined as a typology of identification and desire that creates affective expectations among consumers.[46] By cultivating distinct personas, businesses court returning customers and attract new ones.[47] Businesses construct different notions of genre on various nights of the week, inviting multiple kinds of publics to participate in the forms of entertainment and sociality they use to court consumers. Some bars cater to patrons interested in leather and BDSM (bondage, domination, sadism, and masochism) sex. Others target consumers interested in drag shows and other live entertainment. The use of generic categories is thus connected to the dispersal of attractions available to sexual minorities in urban centers, the aggregation characteristic of many gay and lesbian nightlife businesses, and the competition that pits those businesses against one another as they draw from a large though limited number of patrons. Genres feature both similarity and difference, as businesses use comparable attractions to court customers even as they attempt to distinguish themselves from others like them.

Bars and clubs that cater to sexual minorities in urban centers often construct their identities by specializing in certain genres of music: some play dance music, others play country and western, hip-hop, and the like. Screenplay is a company that provides music videos to businesses. Music and video screens are such common attractions in city businesses that court sexual minorities that many of them subscribe to this service. Via disc-based or direct-to-system download, Screenplay subscribers pay for access to a service called "VJ Pro," where they choose from different genres of music videos that loosely resemble radio formats: HitsVision, a Top 40 mix that promises subscribers "nothing but the hits from every source"; DanceVision, featuring "exclusive remixes, hard to find imports and popular mainstream hits and everything in between designed expressly for the fast paced dance environment"; UrbanVision, a rhythm and blues/hip-hop hybrid that purports "to be all inclusive"; RockVision, rock music featuring songs "from Classic . . . to Disco, New Wave to Old School"; CountryVision, "an upbeat mix of current hits and classic favorites"; and LatinVision, "designed specifically for the sophisticated Latin dance crowd that demands only the hottest and best in tropical, Caribbean, merengue dance and Latin pop."[48] Many gay bars subscribe to ClubVision, which features a mix of "techno, trance and euro-flavored . . . tracks."[49] For dance-themed bars, this subscription features "an extended autoplay feature and individual chapter stops for single track selection."[50] Via partnerships with record labels, Screenplay provides commercial venues with sound and screen media that allow them to differentiate their appeals to consumers from those of their competitors using similar attractions.

When using genre as a critical optic to examine the consumer appeals of businesses that court sexual minorities, the extent to which these appeals overlap becomes apparent. When I called Screenplay's customer service line to obtain samples, I learned that the staff's nickname for the ClubVision subscription is "the diva mix" because it is overwhelmingly popular with businesses that cater to gay men. This format features songs by artists like Beyoncé and Britney Spears, as well as other female singers who are popular among gay men for similar reasons. Remix-friendly songs, outsized media personas, and/or status as subcultural icons make artists like Robyn, Rihanna, and Nicki Minaj frequent fixtures on this service as well. Scholars often criticize the mainstreaming effect that industrialized cultural production can have on queer publics, a line of criticism that sees capital reducing subcultures to offshoots of a single monoculture. Admittedly, the development of mail-order video subscription services catering to nightlife businesses provides strong evidence supporting these claims.

Nevertheless, genre is a lived category that is shaped by both producers and consumers. The publics that converge in city businesses play an active role in how genres function in them, a phenomenon that the group Guerrilla Gay Bar illustrates well. A web-based effort among sexual minorities in cities around the United States, Guerilla Gay Bar co-opts public space by staging events at which ostensibly "straight" bars are descended on by hordes of bargoers in an effort to colonize venues and claim them for queerness. The organizations operating in different cities sometimes use different names: Guerrilla Gay Bar versus Guerilla Queer Bar, even "The Smoking Banana." The groups are only loosely affiliated; while some of the organizations direct website traffic to the organizations operating in other cities, many do not. And though all purport to meet monthly, some groups meet more regularly than others. The website for the Los Angeles–based iteration of the group lays out a tongue-in-cheek "manifesto" that demonstrates the sentiments that shape all of the groups. Their manifesto claims impatience with the city's queer bar culture, stating that "the gay scene in Los Angeles has ghettoized and sub-ghettoized itself so thoroughly that few of us are ever confronted with a person outside his or her own narrow demographic. Twinks mingle only with twinks, bears with bears, and many seem remarkably uncurious about life outside of West Hollywood."[51] The website suggests that the genres operating in gay and lesbian bars and clubs limit the possibilities for publicness in a city with countless opportunities available for consumption, congregation, and community. The organizers issue a call to action to queer people living in Los Angeles, urging them to work within the network of venues available to them in the urban center to expand the genres of queer publicness that operate there. They state: "We will take over the coolest bar we can find in greater Los Angeles for one night only, without any warning. Think of it as gay direct action. For one night a month, by our mere presence en masse, we recontextualize the bar you might not otherwise check out [turning it] into the . . . scene you've always wanted."[52] Using their irritation with the limitations of cities and the overlap of consumer appeals made to sexual minorities, the people who converge under the auspices of Guerilla Gay Bar attempt to expand the terms by which sexual minority publics form in urban centers.

All of the media forms created by and for sexual minorities feature some notion of genre insofar as they render same-sex desire typologically, making it an identity category that includes many different people but is organized around a recognizable set of experiences, feelings, and sensations.[53] When sexual minorities use mobile media apps to make interpersonal connections, they create profiles using pull-down menus that function like genres. These menus offer users legible terminology to articulate their needs and wants to others. Yet users often attempt to refine the categories of identity and desire provided to them in database designs, using text boxes to describe themselves more fully. At the same time, users often report that the apps result in as much miscommunication as they do interpersonal connection, demonstrating how genres are always fluid and open to contestation, featuring dynamics of power seen in the urban publics that predate them. But all gay and lesbian media draw on established genres in courting audiences. For instance, network television frequently uses the sitcom to court gay and lesbian audiences, using the genre's domestic setting to narrate issues associated with tensions between sexual minorities and their heterosexual family members. Similarly, several different gay and lesbian cable TV networks launched with nearly identical programming—news and travel—drawing on well-established genres to court viewers in cost-effective ways that have been prevalent among outlets courting similar audiences across different media platforms.

Connecting Convergences

The convergence of publics in urban centers provides a historical precedent for media marketed to sexual minorities in the cinema, television, and online media produced and distributed in the context of digital production and distribution. This chapter has laid out dispersal and concentration, aggregation, marketplace competition, and genres as patterns of commerce that emerge when an array of businesses court sexual minorities as consumers. The spatial area of urban centers disperses publics even as it concentrates them in particular zones. Thus, even as cities accommodate a range of sexual minority publics, they are home to power dynamics that foster the formation of some publics more easily and frequently than others. Individual businesses aggregate multiple publics by offering consumers a range of attractions, potentially accommodating diverse identities and desires in doing so. Nevertheless, businesses must compete with one another for similar demographics. They attempt to distinguish themselves from competitors by making generic appeals to consumers, identifying distinct demographics and targeting them with promises of particular experiences.

The chapters that follow describe the processes by which gay and lesbian audiences are courted via cinema, television, and online media. Contextualizing gay and lesbian media in the patterns of commerce that emerge in urban centers creates a new way of understanding the historical trajectory of media created by and for sexual minorities. Rather than locate "the first lesbian character on television" or "the first movie in which gay men kiss," modernity offers a more salient origin for recent developments in media culture. Yet the formation of sexual minority publics in urban centers is volatile. The magazines analyzed in this chapter are bound up in the shifting political economy and changing technological makeup of contemporary media culture more generally. During the time I was conducting this research, a soft advertising market pushed *HX* and *Gay Chicago Magazine* out of business entirely. To replace their advertisements in local magazines, city businesses are increasingly more likely to cultivate e-mail lists or use social media networks to court consumers. As such, the publications themselves are connected to the broad transformations occurring in media culture in the context of digital production and distribution. Similar changes can be seen in each of the case studies analyzed in the pages ahead, all of which have a profound impact on the publics that form around gay and lesbian media. Connecting the processes of urbanization to the changes attending digital production and distribution highlights how developments in gay and lesbian media culture are always in a state of flux. It also illustrates that the history of those developments is much longer than it appears at first glance.

Notes

1. Henry Jenkins offers a conceptualization of convergence that frames it as a cultural process that includes but is more comprehensive than just technological change. See Henry Jenkins, *Convergence Culture: Where Old and New Media Collide* (New York: New York University Press, 2006).

2. Georg Simmel's widely cited analysis of urban centers identifies how the particularities of city life shape the perceptions of individuals. More recently, Nigel Thrift has characterized cities as "roiling maelstroms of affect. Particular affects such as anger, fear, happiness and joy are continually on the boil, rising here, subsiding there, and these affects continually manifest themselves." Georg Simmel, "The Metropolis and Mental Life," in *The Blackwell City Reader*, ed. Gary Bridge and Sophie Watson (Oxford and Malden, MA: Wiley-Blackwell, 2002 [1903]); Nigel Thrift, "Intensities of Feeling: Towards a Spatial Politics of Affect," *Geografiska Annaler* 86, no. 1 (2004): 57.

3. John D'Emilio, "Capitalism and Gay Identity," in *The Lesbian and Gay Studies Reader*, ed. Henry Abelove, Michele Aine Barale, and David M. Halperin (New York: Routledge, 1993), 467–476.

4. Many scholars provide this genealogy for digital media more generally. For instance, Jason Farman places mobile computing in a historical context, arguing that such media "serve as contemporary examples of an ongoing relationship" between culturally situated bodies, technology, and the contexts in which those technologies are consumed. Jason Farman, *Mobile Interface Theory: Embodied Space and Locative Media* (New York: Routledge, 2011), 5.

5. These phenomena are spatial practices, which Henri Lefebvre defines as large-scale social operations that feature "production and reproduction, and the particular locations . . . characteristic of each social formation." He also characterizes them as the processes through which social formations achieve "continuity and cohesion." Henri Lefebvre, *The Production of Space*, trans. Donald Nicholson-Smith (Cambridge: Blackwell, 1991), 33.

6. This chapter uses queer nightlife in an oblique way, demonstrating how it indicates broad patterns of commerce that occur in cities in an effort to underline the parallels between urban centers and the marketplace for digital media. For a more thorough consideration of queer nightlife specifically, see Lucas Hilderbrand, "A Suitcase Full of Vaseline; or, Travels in the 1970s Gay World," *Journal of the History of Sexuality* 22, no. 3 (September 2013): 373–402.

7. Histories of same-sex desire often emphasize the ways that different permutations of commerce and space enable queer sociality. One example is George Chauncey's work on gay men and prewar New York: "Gay men had to take precautions, but, like other marginalized peoples, they were able to construct spheres of relative cultural autonomy in the interstices of a city governed by hostile powers. . . . The 'gay world' actually consisted of multiple social worlds, or social networks, many of them overlapping but some quite distinct and segregated from others along lines of race, ethnicity, class, gay cultural style, and/or sexual practices." As they are in Chauncey's work, the tensions in and limitations of queer sociality in the urban center are central issues in this chapter. George Chauncey, *Gay New York: Gender, Urban Culture, and the Making of the Gay Male World, 1890–1940* (New York: Basic Books, 1994), 2–3.

8. Michael Warner defines a public as "a concrete audience, a crowd witnessing itself in visible space . . . A public also has a sense of totality, bounded by the event or by the shared physical space . . . [It] comes into being only in relation to texts and their circulation." The term names the phenomenon wherein bodies coalesce around texts. Michael Warner, *Publics and Counterpublics* (Cambridge, MA: Zone Books, 2002), 65–66.

9. See Judith Mayne's distinction between "spectatorship" and "viewership." Anna McCarthy's work on television outside the home is another study that seeks to problematize private media consumption. Judith Mayne, *Cinema and Spectatorship* (New York: Routledge, 1993); Anna McCarthy, *Ambient Television: Visual Culture and Public Space* (Durham, NC: Duke University Press, 2001).

10. I refer here to the relationship Warner sees between publics and counterpublics, which features the give-and-take of Gramscian hegemony. Both publics and counterpublics are "publics" insofar as they both "offer . . . members direct and active membership through language [and] place strangers on a shared footing." But members of counterpublics are marked socially by their participation in a discourse organized by a power differential, wherein the counterpublic "maintains . . . an awareness of its subordinate status" to a broader public. Warner, *Publics and Counterpublics*, 108, 119.

11. My use of the magazines is best described as "intermedial" insofar as they offer the analysis a connection between the affective publics that form in urban centers and the affective publics that form around media texts. Lars Elleström puts forth this notion of intermediality-as-bridge in "The Modalities of Media: A Model for Understanding Intermedial Relations," in *Media Borders, Multimodality, and Intermediality*, ed. Lars Elleström (New York: Palgrave MacMillan, 2010), 11–50.

12. The relationship between urban spaces and sexual minorities is a major area of study in sociology and geography; see David Bell and Gill Valentine, eds., *Mapping Desire: Geographies of Sexualities* (New York: Routledge, 1995). In particular, Jon Binnie's essay discusses how the practices of commerce facilitate sites for queer sociality; see John Binnie, "Trading Places: Consumption, Sexuality, and the Production of Queer Space," in ibid.

13. "Free labor" is the term D'Emilio uses to describe the dialectic of worker autonomy and exploitation that drives capitalism. His argument is that modernity involved new forms of worker autonomy that, in turn, enabled new forms of sexual autonomy. D'Emilio, "Capitalism and Gay Identity," 468, 470.

14. Ibid.

15. Ibid., 471.

16. A more in-depth discussion of metronormativity can be found in chapter 2. See also Judith [Jack] Halberstam, *In a Queer Time in Place: Transgender Bodies, Subcultural Lives* (New York: New York University Press, 2005).

17. For a more in-depth analysis of how this stereotype of wealthy sexual minorities functions in media culture, see chapter 4.

18. See Kara Keeling's application of Antonio Gramsci's notion of "common sense" to Gilles Deleuze's idea of "the cinematic" in Kara Keeling, *The Witch's Flight: The Cinematic, the Black Femme, and the Image of Common Sense* (Durham, NC: Duke University Press, 2007).

19. Here again, this critique is Jack Halberstam's main undertaking in Halberstam, *In a Queer Time and Place*. For a comparable interpretation of these issues, see Scott Herring, *Another Country: Queer Anti-Urbanism* (New York: New York University Press, 2010).

20. There are numerous studies of gay and lesbian newspapers that describe the important roles these publications have played and continue to play in the politics of sexuality in the US. See Rodger Streitmatter, *Unspeakable: The Rise of the Gay and Lesbian Press in America* (Boston: Faber and Faber, 1995). Yet the objects examined in this chapter have something of a vexed relation to those publications and that scholarship. For instance, historian Michael Bronski dismisses locally published, advertiser-supported magazines as little more than "bar rags," dismissing their worth as objects of analysis because of their more visibly commercial functions. Thus, the epistemological value of the publications examined in this chapter is not always readily apparent. Michael Bronski, *Culture Clash: The Making of Gay Sensibility* (Boston: South End, 1984), 151.

21. Martin Meeker, *Contacts Desired: Gay and Lesbian Communications and Community, 1940s–1970s* (Chicago: University of Chicago Press, 2003). See chapter 5, in particular, where Meeker talks about *Lavender Baedecker* and the regional publications detailing places where consumers could be openly gay in the mid-century United States.

22. For specific discussions of local gay press, see Marc Stein's discussion of the Philadelphia-area publication *DRUM* in his book, *City of Sisterly and Brotherly Loves: Lesbian and Gay Philadelphia, 1945–1972* (Philadelphia: Temple University Press, 2004). Martin Meeker examines how handmade publications and advertising circulars aimed at gay and lesbian readers evolved from an underground DIY movement to an enterprise indicative of a broad, extensive social network that developed over several decades. Meeker, *Contacts Desired*.

23. Katherine Sender discusses the cultural logic that animated this process in greater detail in "Gay Readers, Consumers, and a Dominant Gay Habitus: 25 Years of the *Advocate* Magazine," *Journal of Communication* 51, no. 1 (March 2001): 73–99.

24. The magazine issues published in the weeks leading up to Gay Pride festivals often feature open letters from city politicians, and health organizations like Chicago's Howard Brown Health Center and New York's Callen-Lorde Community Health Center frequently publish notices and promotions for their services in the free publications.

25. For historical analysis of same-sex desire in a wider array of locations, see *Creating a Place for Ourselves: Lesbian, Gay, and Bisexual Community Histories*, ed. Brett Beemyn (New York: Routledge, 1997).

26. Hollis Griffin, "Your Favorite Stars, Live on Our Screens: Media Culture, Queer Publics, and Commercial Space," *Velvet Light Trap* 62, no. 2 (Fall 2008): 15–28.

27. Lefebvre, *Production of Space*, 228.

28. See Chauncey, *Gay New York*, as well as Scott Bravmann, *Queer Fictions of the Past: History, Culture, and Difference* (New York: Cambridge University Press, 1997).

29. These tensions are discussed at length in Lauren Berlant and Michael Warner, "Sex in Public," *Critical Inquiry* 24, no. 2 (Winter 1998): 547–566.

30. For more information on the racial politics that attend gentrification, see Christina Hanhardt, *Safe Space: Gay Neighborhood History and the Politics of Violence* (Durham, NC: Duke University Press, 2013).

31. Samuel Delany, *Times Square Red, Times Square Blue* (New York: New York University Press, 2001), 161.

32. See, in particular, chapter 9 in Chauncey's *Gay New York*, where he discusses the development of gay male social networks among the city's African American publics in the Harlem neighborhood. Allen Drexel also discusses the history of gay male communities on Chicago's South Side, emphasizing that they developed apart from the white communities in the city's loop area in "Before Paris Burned: Race, Class, and Male Homosexuality on the Chicago South Side, 1935–1960," in Beemyn, *Creating a Place for Ourselves*. Roey Thorpe underscores the role that race and class played in the different fates of various lesbian bars in mid-twentieth-century Detroit in "The Changing Face of Lesbian Bars in Detroit, 1938–1965," in ibid.

33. Tamar Rothenberg details how this phenomenon shapes the formation of lesbian commercial spaces in "'And She Told Two Friends': Lesbians Creating Urban Social Space," in *Mapping Desire: Geographies of Sexualities*, ed. David Bell and Gill Valentine (New York: Routledge, 1995), 165–180.

34. I witnessed this phenomenon firsthand as a resident of the city between 2005 and 2010. It is a "local knowledge" that is widely reproduced in most guidebooks to the city. See, for instance, *Frommer's Chicago 2010* (New York: Frommer's, 2009).

35. For more detail on queer life in Chicago, see Timothy Stewart-Winter, *Queer Clout: Chicago and the Rise of Gay Politics* (Chicago: University of Chicago Press, 2016).

36. Nan Alamilla Boyd, *Wide-Open Town: A History of Queer San Francisco to 1965* (Berkeley: University of California Press, 2003), 4.

37. Ibid., 5.

38. Ibid., 4.

39. Randy Shilts, *The Mayor of Castro Street: The Life and Times of Harvey Milk* (New York: St. Martin's Griffin, 1988), 85, 118.

40. This phenomenon can be understood as a "concatenation of texts through time," Warner, *Publics and Counterpublics*, 90.

41. Descriptions of these spaces can be found on the bar's website: http://sidetrackchicago .com/about.html.

42. Gregory Woods highlights how this construction of diversity has long been a goal of television news content directed to sexual minorities. Gregory Woods, "'Something for Everyone': Lesbian and Gay 'Magazine' Programming on British Television, 1980–2000," in *Queer TV: Theories, Histories, Politics* (New York: Routledge, 2009), 108–120.

43. See Joseph A. Schumpeter, *Business Cycles: A Theoretical, Historical, and Statistical Analysis of the Capitalist Process* (New York: McGraw-Hill, 1964 [1939]). Yuichi Shionoya explains this in some depth in *Schumpeter and the Idea of Social Science*, English ed. (New York: Cambridge University Press, 1997), esp. chaps. 7 and 9.

44. The circumstances of Star Gaze's closure are discussed on a local Chicago gay website: ChicagoPride.com, "Lesbian Themed Bar Star Gaze Closing," December 31, 2009, http://www .chicagopride.com/news/article.cfm/articleid/9114016. Gregory Beyer covered efforts to keep Rubyfruit open for business in "Bailout for a Local Bar," *New York Times*, October 12, 2008, city section.

45. Personal e-mail correspondence with *HX*'s former associate publisher Gary Lacinski, January 3, 2010.

46. Jason Mittell applies Michel Foucault's notion of the discursive formation to genre, shifting attention away from television programs to the myriad ways in which different institutions and players use programs in the cultural practice of television: promotion, criticism, fandom, and so on. He casts genre as a "cultural category," whereby television networks, content distributors, and audiences create different meanings in a text as it circulates in culture. I borrow this term here to situate the vernaculars of queer nightlife as genres, cultural categories that venue owners, bar managers, and consuming publics define as they make use of commercial spaces. Jason Mittell, *Television and Genre: From Cop Shows to Cartoons in American Culture* (New York: Routledge, 2004).

47. Thomas Schatz considers genre a kind of contract between media organizations and audiences that creates expectations among consumers about the kinds of entertainment they will consume. Genres thus generate return customers as institutions look to notions of genre to court potential publics. Moreover, audiences themselves consider genre as a way of understanding which pleasures certain forms of entertainment will provide. Thomas Schatz, *Hollywood Genres: Formulas, Filmmaking, and the Studio System* (New York: McGraw-Hill, 1981).

48. "Programs" Screenplay VJ Pro Series, July 25, 2013, www.vj-pro.net/Home/Programs.

49. Ibid.

50. Ibid.

51. "Guerilla Gay Bar, Los Angeles Manifesto," *Guerilla Gay Bar*, November 13, 2007, www.guerillagaybar.com.

52. Ibid.

53. For a longer discussion of how gay and lesbian media render identity generically, see chapter 5.

2 The Aesthetics of Banality after New Queer Cinema

CLICKING THROUGH THE offerings of online streaming services brings users to many different kinds of gay and lesbian movies. On Netflix, algorithms divide hundreds of titles into different categories: Gay and Lesbian Movies, Gay and Lesbian Dramas, Gay and Lesbian Comedies, Romantic Gay and Lesbian Movies, Gay and Lesbian Documentaries. Even within these groupings, though, vastly different movies appear alongside one another: a contemporary, studio-distributed melodrama might appear alongside a low-budget, independent documentary from the same period, as well as an art house movie from decades prior. Online platforms like Netflix, Amazon, and Hulu—common modes of cinematic distribution and reception—ease movement between different sorts of gay and lesbian cinema, offering consumers vastly disparate spectatorial experiences. This chapter uses gay and lesbian movies released between the early 1990s and the second decade of the twenty-first century to think through the fantasies of identity they provide for the people meant to consume them. As is detailed in the pages ahead, the different kinds of gay and lesbian movies released in the 1990s have profoundly shaped the gay and lesbian cinema released in the time since. The chapter begins with a personal story about my experiences watching a pair of movies from this period to illustrate how different yet related kinds of gay and lesbian cinema emerged after. In weighing the two movies' similarities against their differences, the chapter highlights how tensions between distinct categories of gay and lesbian cinema are connected to ongoing transformations in how all movies are made, sold, and consumed.

It might go without saying that cinema is always ideological, but many gay and lesbian movies work to curtail any commentary they might make on the politics of sexuality. The second section of this chapter focuses on this sort of gay and lesbian cinema, movies in which an anodyne politics is made manifest in a routine system of telling stories. Where prevailing methods of understanding these movies dismiss their purview on questions of identity and desire as being apolitical, this chapter suggests that this apolitical viewpoint *is* their politics. Using close readings of the movies in tandem with attention to their press discourses, the chapter demonstrates how this cinema underscores the terrain of the political in neoliberal governmentality, a context in which stories about sexual minorities provide little more than fantasies of normativity. Even so, dismissing the movies as being apolitical misses a chance to understand why people find their world-views so seductive. Using Lauren Berlant's national sentimentality trilogy, the chapter highlights how these gay and lesbian movies construct sexual identity as an affective modality, where a character's proximity to certain places codes them as agentic members of an American body politic.

Through a highly routinized representational system invoking the plenitude of urban centers, these movies forge a relation between spectators and a broader national culture. This representational system casts identity as an individual achievement in the contemporary United States, one that involves only a vague relationship to the circumstances and histories of sexual minorities. Berlant highlights changes in the sign system used to represent minority identities and feelings of national belonging that occurred at the end of the twentieth century. She argues that minority media forms like gay and lesbian cinema create a sense of attachment among disparate individuals through narratives in which characters struggle with feelings of deprivation. Like the movies discussed in this chapter, such media forms do not often understand those feelings as being the result of structural conditions. Instead, such media rework fantasies about people overcoming subordination through force of will, achieving happiness by amassing wealth and finding love. When they narrate sexual identity in this way, gay and lesbian movies perpetuate other hierarchies, most notably those of race and class, even as the stories suggest that they are doing the opposite.[1] As ordinary as they are illuminating, the spectator positions opened by such movies provide gay and lesbian people with "a way of experiencing one's own story as part of something social, even if one's singular relation to the belonging is extremely limited, episodic, ambivalent, rejecting."[2]

Many gay and lesbian movies feature the conventional aesthetics of classical Hollywood's invisible style, telling stories about sexual minorities through mundane narratives and formal systems. The movies examined in this chapter present a contradictory politics, where a minority character's personal agency offers a route to membership in national culture. That only occurs through a disavowal of his or her minority status and a softening of the histories and particularities of minority experiences in the US. Understanding these movies as being "political" is to appreciate that politics often operate in silly, convoluted ways. The workings of hegemony in the texts of media culture are more emotional than they are rational. Such normative fantasies are compelling because they provide people with feelings of freedom and belonging, offering them visions of the good life without forcing them to reimagine what that looks like.

Conflicting Legacies

Two movies underscore the changes in gay and lesbian cinema that occurred in the 1990s and demonstrate their impact on films released in the time since: *The*

Living End (1992) and *Jeffrey* (1995). Their differing styles and disparate politics helped create a consumer marketplace for gay and lesbian cinema, influencing the kinds of stories told about sexual minorities in movies that circulate in the twenty-first century. When I first watched *The Living End*, I thought it was sexy but unsettling. The main character is diagnosed with HIV in the opening scenes, but the movie never pities him. In fact, the story is largely unconcerned with how his diagnosis might make other characters feel. Instead, it details his affair with a male hustler named Luke. Although the main character, Jon, identifies as gay, Luke's identity and desires are more fluid: he flirts with women and has sex with men. Luke is HIV-positive as well. *The Living End* is exciting but confusing. On some level, it is a road movie in which the characters drive from Los Angeles to San Francisco. In such movies, the metaphor of the open road underlines the psychic "journeys" of characters, where the setting is an indeterminate space in which anything might happen.[3] Conclusions of these movies often involve examining how much, or how little, the characters have changed from the beginning to the end.

In *The Living End*, the open road is so indeterminate that it is sometimes hard to know which plot points relate to the narrative as a whole.[4] Unidentified characters wander in and out of the frame. Even though the camera lingers on them, they do not have anything to do with the story. A scene that takes place in the parking lot of a convenience store depicts a conversation between the two main characters. As they talk, a third character drifts into the frame, blurts out a nonsensical sentence or two, and then ambles offscreen. The movie also involves entire sequences that command the viewer's attention but then do not relate to the plot in any straightforward way. In one such scene, an argument between two unidentified characters ends in a shooting. It closes with the camera lingering on a house pet (bizarrely, comedically) licking blood off a corpse's arm. *The Living End*'s mise-en-scène does not enable a discernible journey as much as it sets the stage for random, seemingly disconnected events.

While such elements are unrelated to the story, they are integral to establishing the movie's disconcerting tone. A lot of what happens in *The Living End* is simply difficult to pin down, an uncertainty that is most palpable in the movie's treatment of HIV and AIDS. Sometimes the characters seem distraught about having contracted the disease. At the end of the sequence in which Jon receives his diagnosis, he is so upset that he vomits in a bathroom stall. In another scene, Luke's despondence about his HIV status leads him to cut open his hand so he can look at his infected blood. Yet, at other moments, the characters seem to embrace the disease as an opportunity for self-interested nihilism. In one scene, Jon says to the audience via voice-over: "Live fast, die young, leave a beautiful corpse." Referring to a quote made famous in the film noir *Knock on Any Door* (1949), the line paints the characters' HIV status as being tragic yet also romantic. In *The Living End*, it is difficult to know how the main character feels about anything at all. Jon speaks in a monotone that suggests feelings of jadedness, but his voice never really signifies resignation or defeat. The movie's road metaphor enables my favorite part of *The Living End*: a sex scene set in a shower at a motel off a freeway. Even twenty years after seeing it for the first time, it can make my heart race. In this scene, the two characters talk candidly about having sex without condoms. Such dialogue offers a marked contrast to the safe sex rhetoric that circulated so heavily during the 1990s. Nevertheless, I never understand this scene as suggesting either character's acquiescence to illness or death. Rather, I see it as demonstrating how they live deliberately, giving in to their desires even as—or maybe just because—doing so defies prevailing cultural norms.[5] *The Living End* is enticing and unnerving, it is shot with camera angles that leave this spectator feeling off-kilter in ways that are simultaneously scary and erotic; they force me to consider the characters and their story closely. The movie does not conclude as much as it ends; the characters never resolve anything and I always leave it wondering how the story might continue.

Jeffrey also features a gay man navigating sexuality in relation to AIDS, but unlike the characters in *The Living End*, Jeffrey is HIV-negative and is terrified of contracting the virus. He also dreads the possibility of experiencing grief should he fall in love with someone who dies of AIDS. When Jeffrey meets and falls in love with a man who is HIV-positive, the disease becomes the movie's main narrative problem: will the main character let go of his fears and allow himself to experience love? One of the pleasures of watching this movie is that the spectator never doubts that Jeffrey will find Mr. Right. Even though the protagonist's fears of sickness and sadness animate every scene, *Jeffrey* is comedic and corny. Jeffrey repeatedly breaks the fourth wall to make humorous asides to the camera. Numerous montages depict his life as a comedy of manners. Consistently, his sexual encounters go awry and his dates end in awkwardness. The plot segues to dream sequences in which characters break into elaborate song and dance numbers as the protagonist fantasizes about a dating life that culminates with him falling in love. One scene features a telephone conversation between Jeffrey in New York and his parents in the Midwest. His mother attempts to convey her support for him by asking pointed questions about his sex life: Is he a top or a bottom? Has he considered having phone sex? Does he groom his body hair? Played for laughs, the scene ends with Jeffrey hanging up in mock horror.

Jeffrey is hokey and hopeful; the protagonist's anxiety about AIDS is played for gentle comedy and the movie never loses its optimistic tone. The movie examines issues related to sexuality and desire, but its emphasis is always on how the main character might be happy. Transitions and camera angles never draw the viewer's attention away from the character's desires and problems, and every scene moves the plot forward to its inevitable conclusion. *Jeffrey*'s plot unfolds in the public spaces of New York: parks, bars, and gyms. In an early scene, the character walks around the city as he talks to the audience about his fears and desires. As the scene progresses, the frame becomes increasingly more crowded as random passersby become part of the narrative action. Even strangers on the street tell Jeffrey to give in to his feelings for the HIV-positive man. The movie's secondary plot involves a supporting character coping with the sickness and death of his partner. That too gets mobilized in the service of the main character achieving happiness. The penultimate scene takes place in Central Park, at the start of New York City's Gay Pride parade. When Jeffrey encounters his suitor there, the two have a tense conversation in which the paramour calls Jeffrey a coward for being so scared of getting hurt that he is willing to sacrifice his own happiness for a sense of security. It is in the sheer obviousness of this moment that *Jeffrey* renders the protagonist's happiness a political problem. The movie concludes with the main character embracing the relationship with some innuendo and a kiss. I enjoy *Jeffrey* not *in spite* of knowing what will happen next, but *because* I know what will happen next. In *Jeffrey*, the confusions of desire give way to the stability of identity. I find *Jeffrey*'s ending to be tremendously comforting, no matter how many times I see it.

Even though *The Living End* and *Jeffrey* feature some plot parallels, they involve vastly different styles and politics. Understanding the movies' intersections alongside their disparities is central to understanding the hundreds of gay and lesbian movies released between the period of their release in the 1990s and those created and circulated in the twenty-first century. *The Living End* is associated with the New Queer Cinema of the early 1990s, movies whose creators told stories about sexuality by toying with the conventions and categories associated with classical Hollywood cinema.[6] *The Living End*'s nonlinear narrative and formal play highlight its frank representation of sexuality, providing evidence of the innovations that critics recognize and appreciate in New Queer Cinema.[7] The movie's plot and style are borne from a particular set of historical events that transformed both cinema culture and gay and lesbian life during the early 1990s: the AIDS crisis, conservative cultural politics, consumer-friendly video technology, and urban blight. B. Ruby Rich states that the combination of these factors precipitated a movement "in search of new languages and mediums that could accommodate new materials, subjects, and modes of production."[8] She characterizes New Queer Cinema as "as an evolution in thinking [that] reinterpreted the link between the personal and the political envisioned by feminism, restaged the defiant activism pioneered at Stonewall, and recoded aesthetics to link the independent feature movement with the avant-garde."[9]

By self-consciously defying cinematic norms, New Queer Cinema actively champions a progressive sexual politics in the face of AIDS and social conservatism. The affordability of video technology allowed filmmakers to experiment with style, and the low rents available to people in economically depressed cities enabled collaboration between artists and activists, all of which help New Queer Cinema tell unique stories about sexual minorities in innovative ways.[10] New Queer Cinema's popularity at independent cinema festivals in the early 1990s alerted commercial interests to the revenue potential of gay and lesbian movies. Soon, gay and lesbian moviegoers like me could watch movies like *The Living End* after distributors released them more widely. New Queer Cinema's circulation on video provided movie culture's increasingly dispersed audiences with a connection to the worlds that the stories narrate and the places in which the movies themselves took shape. Rich identifies some legacies of New Queer Cinema in more recent gay and lesbian movies. In international cinemas, art gallery screenings, and some big-budget Hollywood releases, she hears echoes of the movement's commitments and innovations.

At the same time, Rich identifies a second, vastly different legacy of New Queer Cinema. She calls these movies "happy-ending popcorn movies . . . cheese-cake gay male romances and chocolate-box lesbian confections."[11] Following the popular and critical success of New Queer Cinema in the early and mid-1990s, the specialty divisions of several major Hollywood studios used the market demographic created by movies like *The Living End* to create another kind of cinema about sexual minorities. These movies featured a more classical Hollywood style and received limited releases in the gay and lesbian neighborhoods of urban centers before being released more widely on video. Many of these movies were like *Jeffrey*—not just comforting in content but also classical in style.[12] Rich characterizes movies like *Jeffrey* as being made by people "without commitment to community, claim[ing] a market where New Queer Cinema pioneers had worked for a broader good."[13] Of the pleasures found in such gay and lesbian movies, Rich states: "I [am] troubled by a pronounced audience tendency: the desire for something predictable and familiar up there on screen."[14]

Rich worries that one of the legacies wrought by New Queer Cinema is a cinema culture where the proliferation of mundane stories about sexual minorities results in audiences with "narrow limits of tolerance . . . when confronted with uncomfortable ideas, stories, and representations."[15] Rich's comments mark an important differentiation and offer a vital critique. There is a big difference between the spectatorial experience of *The Living End* and that of *Jeffrey*. Yet understanding *Jeffrey* as being *non*political misses a chance to examine the conflicting registers of "politics" in the cinema cultures of sexual minorities. Rich has elaborated well how the movies associated with New Queer Cinema put forth distinct, radical ideas about sexuality. Their unconventional styles defy the expectations that spectators bring to cinema, forcing them to confront the movies' ideas about sexuality. The critical vocabulary for identifying the politics at work in movies like *Jeffrey* is less well established. *The Living End* and *Jeffrey* feature different takes on sexuality because their modes of production differ: the movies originated in different places, were created by different means, and are imagined for different (if also distinctly overlapping) audiences.

As of this writing, *The Living End* and *Jeffrey* are two of hundreds of gay and lesbian movies that stream online via platforms like Netflix, Amazon, and Hulu. The abundance of gay and lesbian movies in twenty-first-century cinema culture has much to do with the production and distribution of New Queer Cinema like *The Living End*. And these movies enabled the circulation of movies like *Jeffrey* to gay and lesbian audiences in ways that would not have been possible otherwise. Like many gay and lesbian movies of the 1990s constructed in Hollywood's classical style, *Jeffrey* was circulated by one of the divisions at a major Hollywood studio. Like those who were drawn to New Queer Cinema, the gay and lesbian audiences of more conventional, mainstream fare often experienced those movies outside of theaters. Since the 1980s, the medium "film" has been something of a misnomer insofar as movies do not often involve "film" per se. Changes in the technology and economy of cinema culture have made moviegoing an at-home activity for audiences far more frequently than it is a public one in theaters. As a result, cinema's storage media and viewing platforms do not often involve "film" at all. Rather, over time, moviegoing has shuffled across an array of delivery technologies: cassette tapes, digital video discs (DVDs), downloads, and streaming online. These changes have transformed the ways that people make, circulate, and consume movies. More specific to gay and lesbian cinema, the corporate consolidation and technological diffusion that occurred after the 1990s resulted in a change in the kinds of companies that most frequently circulate movies created by and for sexual minorities.[16]

Rather than specialty divisions of Hollywood studios, small independent firms are now the predominant distributors of gay and lesbian movies, and these companies frequently specialize in cinema imagined for gay and lesbian audiences. The movies released by these companies are not often released in theaters and their consumption is imagined as an individual experience rather than a collective one. The changes precipitated by digital technology have increased the number of companies that create and circulate gay and lesbian cinema, and have influenced the kinds of stories about sexual minorities told in movies.[17] Feature-length cinema circulated by companies like TLA Releasing, Wolfe Video, Picture This!, Ariztical Entertainment, Water Bearer Films, and Strand Releasing does not have the market reach or cultural influence of the handful of gay and lesbian movies that continue to be released by larger media companies.[18] In fact, the movies' small budgets and low production values frequently mark them as "bad objects."[19] They overwhelmingly feature classical cinematic style, which animates a distinct representational paradigm rooted in widely circulating beliefs about sexual minorities. Coverage of these companies in the trade press highlights how the distributors simultaneously embrace and disavow the forms and sensibilities of New Queer Cinema. Such rhetorical moves gesture to the peculiar politics of movies about sexual minorities that feature conventional aesthetics. In interviews with trade publications, professionals who work in gay and lesbian cinema distribution identify the late twentieth century as a period of struggle for gay and lesbian people. They suggest that more recent improvements in the lives of sexual minorities have become so widespread that the cultural problems addressed by New Queer Cinema are largely in the past.

In connecting gay and lesbian cinema to the advancements they see in gay and lesbian rights, employees at the small distributors suggest that these changed political circumstances have precipitated different desires among gay and lesbian moviegoers. They characterize the companies they work for as serving this politicized—yet not "too" politicized—target audience. In differentiating more recent gay and lesbian movies from New Queer Cinema, the workers suggest that gay and lesbian cinema has evolved as a cultural form and moved away from its roots "after years of oh-so-serious art house-friendly stories."[20] As Rich points out, historicizing gay and lesbian cinema in this manner disarticulates the movies from their predecessors, which had more activist ambitions and, in many ways, made the movies possible in the first place. But the trade articles construct this as a populist evolution, casting particular viewing experiences as both a consumerist desire and a political right. In one article, a distribution worker casts his companies' releases as being about "gay people enjoying a funny, sexy film. We deserve that as much as anybody else. . . . Gay people have a place in pop culture and it doesn't always have to be serious."[21] The articles characterize gay and lesbian cinema's shift toward a more moderate politics as evidence of the progress New Queer Cinema helped achieve.

In trade publications, employees at the small distribution companies characterize the pleasure of these gay and lesbian movies as conventionality: stories that look and feel familiar, which put viewers in some relation to people like themselves.[22] One distribution worker argues that gay and lesbian moviegoers have a "desire to see their lives and dreams reflected onscreen. . . . Gays and lesbians grow up transposing themselves into the heads and hearts of straight characters in romantic movies, so it's not much of a leap to say that we deserve and will flock to gay versions of those kinds of films."[23] So industry workers see the movies as being political, but only in the sense that the stories place gay and lesbian audiences in proximity to a world where sexual identity is achievable and comforting. One professional uses a similar characterization to describe her own preferences as well as her company's vision: "Every distributor has a sensibility. . . . Our [movies] are generally less edgy. My personal favorite is one with a 'feel good' aspect to it."[24] The distribution workers imagine the politics of their movies on prosaic terms, where characters achieve happiness but the stories never unsettle or challenge viewers in the manner of New Queer Cinema.

It is tempting to rank the wishy-washy political aspirations of the small distribution houses below the more activist intentions that Rich identifies in the creators of New Queer Cinema. As powerful as that urge may be, I resist it here in favor of elaborating on the aspirations of the companies and the gay and lesbian movies they circulate. The people who work for the companies do, in fact, understand their labor and the movies they work on as being "political." But those politics do not operate on the same plane as those associated with and championed in New Queer Cinema.[25] For instance, in one article, a distribution worker states: "It's not about money. It's about good, solid films with a good message that have nowhere to go and deserve to be seen."[26] More frequently, distribution professionals connect their labors of love to the logics of the marketplace. One worker characterizes her company as "an agent for social change. We need to be profitable but we want to give back to the community."[27] The interviewee casts her company as having some impact on the lives of gay and lesbian moviegoers, describing that impact in guarded yet sentimental ways.

No less self-consciously political than New Queer Cinema, the movies circulated by the small distributors are decidedly more middle-of-the-road in their politics. In parsing out the movies' politics this way, the professionals who work for these companies actively distance the gay and lesbian movies that their companies circulate from the cinema that came before them and, in many ways, enabled them. New Queer Cinema is more easily identifiable as being "political." Even so, the professionals who work at the small distribution companies understand themselves and their employers as serving gay and lesbian audiences on distinctly political terms. But those terms are never the kind that would seek contestation or transformation. Such aspirations operate in a different register, which can be identified in the aesthetics of movies that circulate in this more centrist cinema. In looking at how a disparate group of gay and lesbian movies employ classical Hollywood style, their distinct though contradictory politics come into sharper focus. As Lucas Hilderbrand points out in his work on videocassette tapes and Caetlin Benson-Allott argues in her research on viewing platforms, cinema aesthetics and spectatorial experiences are profoundly informed by the medium through which movies circulate and the method by which people consume them.[28] The economic and technological transformations that have altered both medium and platform in cinema culture more generally have resulted in the proliferation of a specific kind of gay and lesbian movie.

Continuity Editing and Conventionality

Gay and lesbian cinema circulated by small distributors features aesthetics that rarely differ at all insofar as they are the aesthetics seen in most movies. They animate a set of stories that can be boiled down to the following narrative arc: a protagonist confronts a problem related to his or her same-sex desires and, by doing so, achieves happiness. The variations between the stories are delimited by the ordinariness of their style. The result is an overwhelmingly common regime for representing sexual identity in gay and lesbian cinema. In classical Hollywood cinema, all shots, cuts, camera movements, and editing patterns communicate information to spectators relatively seamlessly. Referred to as "invisible style" or "continuity editing," it is an aesthetic that strings together shots in order to clarify protagonists' goals and organize plot points by way of cause and effect.[29] Such an aesthetic never draws attention to the process of its construction. Continuity editing relies on prevalent cultural beliefs in making associations between characters, plots, and mise-en-scène. For instance, *Leave It on the Floor* (2011) begins with a medium shot of a black teenage boy looking at his computer and then cuts to a medium close-up of the computer screen, which reveals that the character is looking at gay pornography. Action then cuts to shots of a woman entering the room, which then cut to two-shots of the pair in dialogue in front of the computer. These shots then cut to longer shots of the two characters framed separately, though the shots are spliced together so the spectator understands that they are still in dialogue. Shots then alternate between the two characters as the backgrounds of the frames change: the mise-en-scène shifts from bedroom furniture to kitchen appliances to a front porch and driveway. In this sequence, Brad, the teenage gay black male protagonist, fights with his mother when she catches him looking at gay pornography on the internet. The two characters argue as Brad packs a bag and attempts to leave their house, fighting with his mother as he makes his way from his bedroom to the front door and, finally, outside. Continuity editing directs the spectator's attention by smoothing any disjoint between shots and cuts, connecting narrative spaces into a linear story.

A sequence in *Gypsy 83* (2001) further demonstrates how continuity editing takes place in gay and lesbian cinema. In one scene, close-ups alternate between the movie's protagonists, Clive and Gypsy, as they are in dialogue while sitting in a car. Narration then cuts to an extreme long shot of the New York City skyline. This shot is followed by more close-ups of the pair, which then cut to two-shots of the characters. From that point, narration cuts back and forth between two-shots of the characters, extreme long shots of the skyline, and long shots of the entrance to a commuter tunnel. This sequence is followed by another sequence where the two-shots are obscured by the reflections of lights as the characters look up and out of the frame. From these sequences, the spectator understands that the characters have driven into Manhattan and are looking up at the buildings from the street. Like *The Living End*, *Gypsy 83* is a road movie. The characters drive from Sandusky, Ohio, to New York in order to go to a singing contest at a bar in Greenwich Village. The protagonists are misfits at home in Ohio, where Clive weathers a great deal of homophobia from his high school classmates. The movie frames

New York as the place where he might ultimately experience happiness. Unlike *The Living End*, Clive's journey and transformation are one and the same, and his behaviors are infinitely predictable over the course of the movie.

Continuity editing also underscores character development and the cause-and-effect relationship of plot elements. For instance, in the movie *Latter Days* (2003), one scene crosscuts between shots of a male character dancing and drinking at a bar and shots of a second character receiving aversion therapy and electroshock treatment in a hospital. The story is set in an apartment complex where neighbors meet and fall in love: Christian is a gay "party boy," while Aaron is a closeted Mormon missionary. In *Latter Days*, Christian realizes how much he loves Aaron, and while Aaron also loves Christian, Aaron's feelings are thwarted by his homophobic upbringing. Over the course of the narrative, the characters come together and then part ways. But like the ending in *Jeffrey*, the ending in *Latter Days* is never in doubt. The crosscut sequence animates the heavy-handed binary that *Latter Days* establishes throughout the plot: shots of a blissful Christian underscore shots of a miserable Aaron. By way of continuity editing, *Latter Days* creates a cause-and-effect relationship between different narrative threads.

Looking at Hollywood cinema over several decades, David Bordwell argues that Hollywood's "invisible style" is increasingly one of augmentation, where the continuity editing of classical Hollywood cinema prevails but its pace has quickened over time. Calling this style "intensified continuity," Bordwell details how it "tries to rivet the viewer to the screen . . . even ordinary scenes are heightened to compel attention and sharpen emotional resonance."[30] Intensified continuity is a style that he locates in specific conventions, including rapid editing and close framings in dialogue scenes. Since the height of New Queer Cinema in the early 1990s and after the consolidation of a consumer market by gay and lesbian movies released by Hollywood studios, continuity editing is the primary style by which gay and lesbian cinema distributed by the small independent companies tells stories about sexuality. Consistent with the intensification that Bordwell notes in cinema of recent decades, the use of rapid editing and close framing of dialogue are the conventions by which many gay and lesbian movies frame the personal experiences of characters as political issues. In examining these two aesthetic conventions across a snowball sample of gay and lesbian movies, the ideological underpinnings of the relationship they forge between the personal and the political come into view as the site of this cinema's politics.

Editing speed is most noticeable in the preponderance of establishing shots in gay and lesbian movies, which are then followed by a cycle of shots that repeatedly orient the spectator in the story's narrative space. In this way, a conspicuous pattern occurs across many gay and lesbian movies. It begins with several extreme long shots of buildings at a distance (figure 2.1), which cut to a long shot or two of a single building's exterior (figure 2.2.), and then to shots of characters (figure 2.3).

Figure 2.1. Extreme long shots of city skylines invoke the grandeur of the urban center, combining ideas about US citizenship, financial wealth, and the history of sexual minorities.

Figure 2.2. Long shots of building exteriors construct a sense of urbanness, functioning as a connection between cities and the lives of characters.

Figure 2.3. The sequences of extreme long shots and long shots conclude with tighter shots of narrative action. In *Dorian Blues*, they situate the characters and their story on the streets of New York City.

The pattern establishes and reestablishes narrative space by cycling through a series of increasingly tighter shots. Movies frame the narrative space first, and then frame the characters. In extreme long shots and long shots, gay and lesbian cinema often features shots of skylines and building exteriors that construct a city-like mise-en-scène before focusing on the experiences of the characters. This editing pattern distills the operation of a distinct representational paradigm across different kinds of stories. For instance, in *Dorian Blues* (2004), a white gay male protagonist, Dorian, leaves home to go away to school. The movie cuts from scenes that take place in Dorian's childhood home by way of a fade to black. A fade-in brings the narrative to New York City with an extreme long shot of the Empire State Building followed by a series of quick cuts and other shots of New York landmarks. A shot of the New York Public Library then cuts to shots of the Metropolitan Museum of Art and Central Park. Frames become tighter over the sequence, as narration eventually cuts to a dialogue scene. In *The Skinny* (2012), a group of gay black college friends reunite for a long weekend. Extreme long shots of a city skyline cut to long shots of buildings that then cut to increasingly closer shots of the characters in dialogue. The movie situates and resituates the plot in different areas around New York: Harlem, Midtown, and Central Park.

An editing pattern that constructs a sense of urbanness can also be seen in *And Then Came Lola* (2009), where extreme long shots of the Bay Area and then long shots of buildings situate and resituate the narrative in the streets of San Francisco.

In this movie, a lesbian woman rushes through the city in an attempt to run a time-sensitive errand for her girlfriend. The plot involves the many obstacles that stand in her way: a curmudgeonly police officer, a talkative ex-girlfriend. A campy homage to the German thriller *Run Lola Run* (1998), *And Then Came Lola* reestablishes the narrative in San Francisco over and over again. *Molly's Girl* (2012) probably demonstrates the editing pattern best because it works the same way yet does not set the story in a specific location in any obvious way. Many scenes begin with extreme long shots of a skyline and then cut to long shots of individual buildings, which then cut to tighter shots of characters in dialogue. The main character, Mercedes, is a lesbian woman who works as a lobbyist for same-sex marriage rights. The plot revolves around a one-night stand she has with the daughter of a conservative senator. Filmed on location in Iowa, *Molly's Girl* features this editing pattern throughout the movie. The movie places the plot in an urban-*like* environment, but is ambiguous about where the story takes place precisely. Moreover, extratextual information suggests that the narrative's location is, in fact, Iowa because that state was the site of an extended struggle between political parties over its marriage laws.[31] Even so, Iowa rarely signifies as being "urban" per se, although editing patterns in *Molly's Girl* construct the movie's setting with those associations nonetheless.

This editing pattern establishes narrative spaces by casting urban settings as places conducive to characters overcoming their struggles related to sexuality. In *Gypsy 83*, the characters flee the close-minded Midwest in search of happiness in New York City. In *Dorian Blues*, the main character comes to terms with the difficult relationship he has with his homophobic father. In *The Skinny*, the characters realize their affection for one another and find suitable romantic partners in the process. The main character in *And Then Comes Lola* manages to complete the errand that her girlfriend needs her to accomplish and solidifies their relationship. In *Molly's Girl*, the main character shames the conservative senator about his politics and makes headway in her quest to legalize same-sex marriage.

The stories differ, but the editing patterns work the same way: extreme long shots of skylines cut to long shots of buildings that then cut to tighter shots of characters in a way that suggests city-like environs as the mise-en-scène of a character's happiness. The spaces constructed in these movies often lack precise details, fabricating a sense of urbanness that does not rely too heavily on the specificities of any single locale.[32] In doing so, the movies draw on trenchant associations that people make with cities, a uniformity of style that offers profound evidence of what Jack Halberstam calls "metronormativity": the notion that urban centers uniformly "allo[w] for the full expression of the sexual self in relation to a community of other gays/lesbians/queers."[33] The feelings and fantasies that perpetuate metronormativity can be found in the historically contingent meanings associated with urban signifiers in American culture.[34] Narration of sexuality with this editing pattern links the movies to a shifting range of ideas about sexuality, capitalism, and citizenship.

The ubiquity of gay and lesbian rights rhetoric rooted in terminology associated with national citizenship—in which mentions of "equality" and "civil rights" abound—imbues gay and lesbian cinema's urban-like editing pattern with feelings of agency and belonging. Establishing shots that repeatedly situate action in city-like spaces connect the movies to the sign system that Lauren Berlant calls "the National Symbolic," a collection of the United States' "traditional icons, its metaphors, its heroes, its rituals and narratives [that] provide an alphabet for collective consciousness or national subjectivity."[35] I see the urban signifiers that are so prevalent in gay and lesbian cinema as part of this system insofar as they link ideas about US citizenship to the processes of capitalism, where skylines and buildings perpetuate ideas and feelings of progress and transcendence.[36] Berlant notes that this sign system became markedly more sentimental in the later decades of the twentieth century, arguing that the increase of conservatism in the United States during the 1980s was a response to the gains made by minority rights movements in the 1960s and 1970s. As a result of conservatism's ascendance, political life in the United States has become a discursive space wherein "a citizen is defined as a person traumatized by some aspect of life in the United States."[37] Berlant emphasizes this understanding of citizenship as being "intensely individuating" in that citizens become "*kinds* of people who are both attached to and underdescribed by the identities that organize them."[38] Berlant characterizes this experience as one of "partial legibility" and "misrecognition" that people work within and work against; identity discourses enable feelings of validation that then chafe if they threaten to overdetermine the experiences of disparate individuals.[39] She sees this as the "desired effect of conservative cultural politics, whose aim is to dilute the oppositional discourses of the historically stereotyped citizens—people of color, women, gays, and lesbians." The result is an understanding of citizenship as being intimate: "something scarce and sacred, private and proper."[40]

In their similarities with Berlant's notion of the "National Symbolic," the gay and lesbian movies examined in this chapter display this understanding of sentimentalized citizenship, where the urbanness constructed in continuity editing connotes the freedom and agency of characters. In doing so, the movies articulate sexual identity as a mode of belonging to the nation-state. At the same time, they work to evacuate the signs of the subordination and disempowerment that so often characterize minority experiences. If the narrative settings suggest that the movies place characters in proximity to the gay and lesbian communities long located in and associated with cities, the movies frequently dissociate characters from those milieus. In fact, in gay and lesbian movies, minority subcultures are often narrative problems, obstacles that characters must overcome in order to achieve happiness. In *Latter Days*, the "party boy" disavows barhopping and cruising for sex so that he may realize his ultimate goal: romance. In *The Skinny*, one of the characters gets drugged at a bar and then raped; the movie's continuity editing places the characters in an urban milieu only to underscore the dangers they find there. Continuity editing in *Dorian Blues* places the protagonist in the bars, clubs, and cafes of New York City. But Dorian only encounters bad dates and failed friendships there. The movie casts gay and lesbian communities as impeding the only thing that will make Dorian happy: embracing his individuality. In *Leave It on the Floor*, Brad becomes friendly with other queer people in Los Angeles' drag scene. But the ball scene ultimately makes him unhappy because it features temptations that threaten his relationship with his boyfriend. The movie creates a binary opposition that pits the cattiness and jealousy that characterize casual sex in the ball scene with the happiness and stability provided by his monogamous relationship. In *Gypsy 83*, the denouement involves a scene in which Clive gets so humiliated that he ultimately moves back to the Midwest. A group of gay men he meets at a bar make fun of him for pretending to be better enmeshed in New York life than he actually is. The city and its gay and lesbian subcultures stand in the way of the only thing that will make Clive happy: embracing his identity no matter what others think or say about him.

Cities are highly politicized signs in post-9/11 America, which many gay and lesbian movies use to narrate characters who must transcend the complications that result from their involvements with the minority subcultures found in them. The establishing shots in gay and lesbian cinema's continuity editing perpetuate fantasies of independence and happiness, but the associations between those establishing shots and actual cities are more fantasies of capital than they are fantasies of subculture. Where B. Ruby Rich identifies blighted, economically depressed cities as a vibrant point of origin for New Queer Cinema, more recent gay and lesbian movies imagine city spaces that have been "made safe" by gentrification.[41] City iconography in more recent gay and lesbian cinema individuates protagonists, casting their stories about identity as fantasies of mobility in which characters transcend the deprivations associated with being an underprivileged minority. The pattern of continuity editing so prevalent in gay and lesbian cinema demonstrates how the movies operate like most minority media forms insofar as they "solici[t] belonging via modes of sentimental realism that span fantasy and experience and claim a certain emotional generality . . . even though the stories that circulate demonstrate diverse historical locations of . . . the audience."[42]

While city signifiers are elastic insofar as they accommodate different kinds of gay and lesbian people in the stories they narrate, the feelings they attempt to construct are highly static. For instance, establishing shots early in *East Side Story* (2006) place the spectator at a remove from Los Angeles' downtown skyline. In one shot, a glittering urban landscape shines in the background while a homeless man pushes a shopping cart in the foreground. This shot cuts to an extended tracking shot of storefronts with Spanish-language signs. In voice-over, a radio announcer with a thick accent situates the plot in the city's heavily Latino East Side. *East Side Story* points to the elasticity of the gay and lesbian cinema's continuity editing. The movie sets an interracial gay romance amid the politics of gentrification in Los Angeles, underlining the class and ethnic significations embedded in city iconography. The main character, Diego Campos, waits tables at his family's restaurant but dreams of opening his own business. When a white gay couple moves into Diego's neighborhood, tensions flare as he forges a bond with one of the partners but weathers elitist scorn and racist invective from the other. Over the course of the movie, Diego feels stifled by his class status, which the story yokes to his Mexican heritage: the plot features several fights with the homophobic relatives he works with at the family restaurant. The plot of *East Side Story* suggests that Diego might overcome his problems by way of professional success. At the same time, the character is at odds with the bourgeois lifestyle of the gay men he meets through his neighbors. In the scenes where he interacts with the emerging gay and lesbian community in his gentrifying neighborhood, Diego experiences a barrage of class disparagements and ethnocentric insults.

While the signifiers of gay and lesbian cinema's urban representation are variable, the ideas they signify are not. Sequences that cut from long shots of Los Angeles to tracking shots of storefronts with Spanish-language signage recur throughout *East Side Story* (figure 2.4). They orient and then reorient the spectator in the movie's class-stratified, ethnically diverse city. The story eases the racial and ethnic tensions embedded in these aesthetics with narrative developments similar to those seen in all gay and lesbian movies. One of the neighbors is progressive and open-minded, and Diego develops romantic feelings for him. As *East Side Story* progresses, Diego also evolves as a chef, which makes him more confident in his ability to run a restaurant on his own. Shot sequences in *East Side Story* situate the story in the ethnic and class politics of Los Angeles, but the narrative involves the main character transcending the minority communities located there. The narrative problems get resolved when Diego becomes a business owner and falls in love with one of his white neighbors. Thus, the frictions attending the gentrification of city neighborhoods populated by ethnic minorities get smoothed over by the conventional aesthetics of gay and lesbian cinema. These conventions set aside the notion that minority communities might create a welcoming environment for the character.

The variability of city signifiers suggest that this editing pattern can accommodate racial and ethnic diversity in its representation of sexual minorities, but the ideas about freedom and belonging that the city imagery are meant to signify

Figure 2.4. The Spanish-language signage that appears throughout *East Side Story* demonstrates the diversity enabled by urban signifiers.

ultimately close down that diversity. *East Side Story* can only imagine the character's happiness by way of professional ambition and individual transcendence. Variations in continuity editing enable some variety in the kinds of stories gay and lesbian movies tell about sexual minorities. For instance, in *East Side Story*, the variations mark an experience of urban America with some ethnic specificity. Yet those variations never threaten the ultimate goal: the freedom and self-actualization of the protagonist. In *East Side Story*, the underpinnings of gay and lesbian cinema's editing style become apparent, and the movie resolves its main narrative problem by reinvesting in the very ideologies its plot started to question. The continuity editing animates a paradigm wherein the experience of a newly empowered gay character is one of personal agency and capital accumulation. In rendering sexuality with these conventions, gay and lesbian movies never call attention to themselves as a "homogenizing threat to people's sovereignty and singularity."[43] In fact, they do quite the opposite. The stories work to make the vexed connections they forge between identity, community, and capital "a true expression of something both deep and simple in the human."[44]

In *Julie Johnson* (2002), continuity editing plays with the meanings attributed to urban signifiers, but ultimately features a representational logic similar to the one seen in *East Side Story*. The movie opens with an extreme long shot of New York City's skyscrapers. But the camera quickly pans across the Hudson River, where a series of shots frame the grittier, more industrial New Jersey skyline. *Julie Johnson* narrates the life of a working-class wife and mother who falls in

Figure 2.5. A city skyline looms in the background of many shots in *Julie Johnson*, connecting plot elements to what Lauren Berlant calls the "National Symbolic."

love with her best friend. While the protagonist dreams of going to college and becoming a scientist, her husband ridicules her, even forbids her from finishing high school. Over the course of the story, Julie realizes these dreams by leaving her husband and beginning a romantic relationship with her friend Claire. The story differentiates the gendered division of labor in the household of Julie's marriage from the egalitarian home she shares with Claire. The pair raises Julie's children together and splits the housework, an arrangement that enables the protagonist to realize her dreams of going back to school. Julie and Claire first confess their feelings for each other while watching Julie's children play in a neighborhood park, wedding the emotions of same-sex attraction to the world of women's work. The city skyline looms in the background of these shots, connecting the couple's romance to the fantasies of freedom attached to urban signs in the "National Symbolic" (figure 2.5).

Much of the narrative action in *Julie Johnson* takes place in domestic space, where the couple's romance fits into the rhythms of family life that unfold in Julie's living room and kitchen. Consistent with cultural narratives that relegate female characters to domestic realms, the movie frames the home as a space that enables lesbian desire and attachment, where plain decor and tight quarters are the site of lesbian possibility.[45] Yet proximity to the city is crucial in *Julie Johnson* insofar as it provides the primary tension. Although the protagonist wants to circulate in the gay and lesbian communities found in New York City, her girlfriend finds them intimidating and prefers their working-class neighborhood in New Jersey. In one scene, Julie refuses to give up her studies, but offers to stop spending so much time with her new friends in New York if it will make Claire happy. But Claire refuses. The scene precipitates their breaking up, and the editing cuts back and forth from medium shots of the couple in a car to long shots of New York's commuter tunnels and exteriors of the city's buildings.

If plot elements in *Julie Johnson* seem to reject the city as a site of agency and happiness, their logic does not. While the extreme long shots and long shots of urban iconography have a causal relationship to the couple's demise in *Julie Johnson*, the plot variation still works within the representational paradigm seen in other movies. The romance between Julie and Claire ends when it clashes with Julie's happiness. As with Diego in *East Side Story*, the main character in *Julie Johnson* ultimately does not need the succor of the gay and lesbian communities found in urban centers. After all, the protagonist was willing to stop spending so much time there. But she would not give up her professional ambition, predicating the movie's representation of sexual identity on the achievements that individuals might realize as a result of capital. Even though the plot varies, the logic is consistent. As Berlant says of such conventionalized stories, "moments of potential collapse that threaten the contract . . . with the viewer . . . are usually *part* of the convention and not a transgression of it."[46] In that sense, slight variations in plot across gay and lesbian movies still maintain fidelity to a system that imagines minority status as a challenge that individuals overcome through class ascendance.

Continuity editing yokes sexuality to notions of membership in national culture by way of agency and will, which are most often achieved by amassing wealth. Like *Julie Johnson*, the continuity editing in *Shelter* (2007) involves some variation in how it uses urban signifiers, but the narrative's emphasis on the protagonist's class status ultimately offers the same logic. The extreme long shots and long shots interspersed in the movie's narration depict an urban space comprised of rusty buildings and peeling industrial spaces. A story about a white gay man living in Southern California, *Shelter* employs a visual aesthetic rooted in the decaying remnants of Southern California's heavy industry. Against this backdrop, the main character, Zach, shares a cramped home with his family and works as a short-order cook. The plot revolves around his difficult relationship with his underemployed sister and his fondness for her son, as well as his dream of enrolling in art school. In *Shelter*, Zach also begins a secret romance with his wealthy friend's brother. A recurring sequence features Zach skateboarding past industrial buildings where, in extreme long shot, his body is dwarfed by the rot and rust of abandoned factories. The mise-en-scène in these sequences emphasizes the difficulty of the character's circumstances: he wants to go to school but cannot afford tuition, and he wants to move out of his shared home but cannot pay rent. By the end of *Shelter*, Zach comes out of the closet and is public about his relationship with his boyfriend. Not only does the relationship provide him with the money he needs to enroll in art school but it also allows him to adopt his nephew from his sister.

Figure 2.6. One of the final images in *Shelter* sets the newly wealthy protagonist against the drab industrial backdrop of his youth.

The closing sequence underscores the discursive limits of continuity editing that features urban signs. When Zach and his boyfriend, Shaun, confront Zach's sister about his nephew, the shot is framed so that the couple is situated in the foreground. They stand in stark relief from the background, where rotting smoke-stacks and decomposing electrical towers loom behind them (figure 2.6). Thus, the movie begins by examining the class politics of cities, where the processes of late capitalism have corroded entire swaths of urban America. Like *East Side Story* and *Julie Johnson*, it even animates a story of love and possibility there. Yet the story hinges on the logic of the other gay and lesbian movies, a conventionality that Berlant characterizes as involving "more movement within a space than toward being or wanting to be beyond it."[47] The continuity editing of *East Side Story*, *Julie Johnson*, and *Shelter* seems to question the justice of uneven capital accumulation. But by the conclusions of the narratives, the movies circle back and reinvest in the same dynamics they initially critiqued. In these movies, characters achieve happiness by conceding to the same beliefs and practices that disempowered them from the beginning.

In the relationship they forge between sexuality, citizenship, and capitalism in their continuity editing, gay and lesbian movies "sublimate singularity on behalf of maintaining proximity to a vague prospect of social belonging."[48] In doing so, they make sexual identity an individual achievement that transcends the lack of structural privilege endured by many minorities. The movies' continuity editing creates such fantasies through particular, historically specific associations.

Like the employees who separate the small distributors' movies from the New Queer Cinema that preceded them, the narratives of more recent gay and lesbian movies distance themselves from the political sphere by casting minority status as a blockage that individual protagonists must move beyond in order to be happy. The political ambivalence of gay and lesbian movies comes to the fore rather clearly when continuity editing places characters in proximity to the spaces associated with subcultural milieus and ethnic diversity only to then tell stories that disconnect characters from those contexts and the struggles connected to them.

The ambivalence of this cinema is underscored further in terms of how shots organize screen space. Spectators process information in shots by depth cues, delineating planes within the image: foreground, middle ground, background. Frames construct depth through shallow-space composition, where the closest and most distant planes are close to one another, or through deep-space composition, where the planes are farther apart. In the movies examined in this chapter, many shots feature deep-space composition, where characters are in the foreground and buildings are in the background. For example, in one sequence in *Latter Days*, Aaron sees Christian from across the courtyard in their apartment complex, and the city looms behind him. Aaron is in the foreground, Christian is in the middle ground, and the Los Angeles skyline is in the background. In *Molly's Girl*, Mercedes talks on the telephone with her girlfriend while standing on the roof of her office building. Narration cuts between shots of the character from different angles, framing her in the foreground with various buildings in the background. *Leave It on the Floor* also includes a rooftop scene in which two characters discuss their burgeoning relationship; shots alternate so that the pair are in the foreground and various buildings are in the background. *The Skinny* also includes a scene where two characters have an argument on a roof deck. They are in focus in medium shots and medium close-ups in the foreground, while the city skyline is a smudge of lights in the background behind them.

The depth of field in these shots highlights the discursive limits of the relation that the movies construct between the personal and the political. In their use of selective focus, where some planes stay in focus as others blur, the movies direct the spectator's attention to the most important information in the frame. When backgrounds blur, a shot's composition focuses the spectator's attention on characters in the foreground (figure 2.7). These aesthetic conventions appear in all movies; they are tools used to direct the spectator's attention toward certain formal elements. But in the movies examined in this chapter, I see the blurring of background planes involving a blurring of their referents as well. The inclusion of such shots in continuity editing underlines the extent to which the movies imagine a relation between the personal and the political: they frame characters against iconography rich in significations of power and agency, casting a character's happiness as a political achievement. In focusing narration on the emotional lives of

Figure 2.7. Selective focus blurs background planes, separating characters from the milieus from which they come. This formal element underlines the political limitations of gay and lesbian cinema's urban signifiers.

characters, the movies do not represent the city to stage "the personal as political" as much as they use such imagery to stage "the political as personal."[49] Characters overcome their struggles and find happiness, but the stories only register as being political insofar as they narrate a person experiencing contentment by exercising his or her agency. I see this element of the movies' invisible style underlining their narration of sexuality as an individual experience, where one's proximity to urbanness fosters national subjectivity by way of independence. Crucially, such feelings of freedom and belonging are more individual than they are communal. In that way, the politics of these movies can only ever be personal: their classical style subordinates any structural critique they might make about their narration of a character's emotional journey. Thus, gay and lesbian movies rarely reconceive a paradigm that casts minority status as an individual experience realized in the marketplace. Spectators are connected to a "National Symbolic" by characters who find happiness in city space, but they only do that by transcending socioeconomic forces that are more powerful than they are—with little to no help from anybody else.

Mundane Transcendence

It is tempting to point to the gay and lesbian cinema circulated by the small distributors as conclusive proof of everything that is wrong with commercial media, specifically, and consumer capitalism, more generally. However compelling, such a critique leaves aside the extent to which gay and lesbian people find sustenance in the stories told in these movies. It is also a critique that overlooks the degree to which many people understand this cinema as fostering cultural change. In talking about the relationship between queerness and socioeconomic class, Lisa Henderson casts "survival as the first condition of thriving," where merely getting by is a necessary first step in one's ability to live or think differently.[50] Henderson parses out the difference between redistribution and recognition, identifying how the enfranchisement of certain sexual minorities—frequently white, professional gays and lesbians—rarely restructures the schema in which rights are bestowed on people. As she points out, "class ascendancy is . . . the route to enfranchisement for nondominant subjects, be they gay, female, persons of color, or all three."[51] Even so, in a critique I admire, Henderson highlights how wholly dismissing such class-based fantasies of transcendence as being problematic or less desirable than a more visibly progressive politics of solidarity "disables other forms of reading, other insights, and, ultimately, other forms of living."[52]

In equating happiness with agency achieved through accumulation, the gay and lesbian movies discussed in this chapter exhibit a prevalent, maybe even timeless sensibility in American culture. But the movies' disavowal of minority deprivation also suggests more historically specific cultural logics associated with neoliberalism, where one's ability to amass wealth is thought to be the best way to supersede any experience of disempowerment. Given the acceleration of class dis-parities in the twenty-first-century United States, and considering how often gay and lesbian people suffer as a result of those inequalities, it is easy to see why such fantasies of self-actualization might be appealing. When I talk with students, I am struck by how frequently they cleave to the logic of these movies in their under-standing of identity as an individual experience rather than a communal one. Even more frequently, they cast minority deprivation as being epiphenomenal and not structural; they see it as a temporary state that is best surmounted through perseverance and ingenuity. Like the movies examined here, my students do not often question institutions that perpetuate inequality as much as they hope they can make a place for themselves inside structures that predate them. Students tell me they find respite in movies like the ones described here because such cinema helps them manage anxieties in their own lives, where finding employment after graduation is a perennial, recurring concern. Seeing characters succeed in that vein gives them faith that they might do the same. They do not frequently imagine that they can change anything even though many of them want to.

Because New Queer Cinema is a mode of cultural production more easily read as being political, it is also more easily interpreted as having the ability to affect its audience. Nick Davis describes movies like those of New Queer Cinema as "a sudden effulgence of sexual protoplasm," characterizing his interest in them as being "less in 'identifying' with these images than in surmising through them that if *these* unexpected relations were possible, surely countless others were too."[53] My gambit in this chapter has been reading for affect in cheaply made, quickly released movies in order to identify sensation as being inextricable from every cultural form created by and for sexual minorities. Unlike those in the movies discussed by Davis, the sensations associated with the movies examined in this chapter are ordinary and small: feelings of validation, shimmers of optimism. Against the startling sensations precipitated by movies associated with New Queer Cinema—movies whose formal arrangements evoke descriptions like Davis's, suggesting floods, bursts, and seeping energies—the movies discussed here seem blank, as devoid of feeling as they are of innovation. Alas, movies do not always challenge or confound. Perhaps more regularly they do neither. Of movies like those associated with New Queer Cinema, Davis writes: "Movies, like lovers, have always been more interesting as windows than as mirrors."[54] Yet the movies discussed in this chapter aspire to be mirrors more than windows, inviting spectatorial identification through claims to universality that have profound limitations. If the movies of New Queer Cinema are "lovers," the movies discussed in this chapter are perhaps better described as romantic entanglements that persist because they are an improvement over sleeping alone.

Gay and lesbian movies with happy endings like the ones that prevail in the cinema discussed in this chapter point to a historically specific relationship between sexuality, capitalism, and the American nation-state. In casting minority identities as problems that people must overcome more often than identifying them as locations that people might embrace, the movies paint identity as an affective experience that transcends the struggles and deficits that characterize minority experiences in the United States. The movies understand such worries as problems that require independence more than they necessitate collectivity because structural subordination is always conquerable if characters try hard enough. In my repeated viewings of the gay and lesbian movies discussed in this chapter via Netflix, Amazon, and Hulu, I became aware of the continuity editing's reliance on shots of buildings and skylines to narrate sexual identity. The stories insist on a timelessness of physical structures, an emphasis on buildings and bridges that generates a curious tension with the movies themselves insofar as they are most often consumed in ephemeral ways, as digital downloads or streaming online. Even as cinema's circulation becomes more abstracted from a physical object, gay and lesbian movies seem to insist on sexuality as an embodied problem that involves the persistence of place and how a character feels while inhabiting it. That these movies are so banal highlights the pervasiveness of the political vision they put forward.

Notes

1. This concern is a primary one for Lauren Berlant in her discussion of the intimate publics created by minority media forms. She writes that "embedded in the often sweetly motivated and solidaristic activity of the intimate public . . . is a white universalist paternalism." Lauren Berlant, *The Female Complaint* (Durham, NC: Duke University Press, 2008), 6.

2. Ibid., x.

3. See Steve Cohan and Ina Rae Hark, eds., introduction to *The Road Movie Book* (New York: Routledge, 2002), 2–4.

4. In his analysis of *The Living End*, Damon Young writes: "Jon and Luke's road trip allows them to . . . circulate without destination . . . the diagnosis of HIV . . . situates this journey, truly, in a queer time and place." Damon Young, "*The Living End*, or Love without a Future," in *Queer Love in Film and Television: Critical Essays*, ed. Pamela Demory and Christopher Pullen (New York: Palgrave MacMillan, 2013), 16.

5. For more analysis of the sexual politics at work in Araki's movies, see Kylo-Patrick Hart, *Images for a Generation Doomed: The Films and Career of Gregg Araki* (Lanham, MD: Lexington Books, 2010).

6. Writing in part about this cinema, Nick Davis suggests that "these films deterritorialize sex, gender, and desire to extravagant degrees from their gay and straight coordinates." In Davis's words, this category of cinema is often discursively constructed as "'weird,' 'ambiguous,' or 'confusing,'" whereas the movies examined in this chapter are anything but. The movies I examine feature a territorialized politics that reifies identity categories and perpetuates existing vocabularies for organizing desire and identity through narratives and aesthetic sensibilities °that champion ideological and cinematic norms. For more on territorialized versus deterritorialized politics, see chapter 5 herein. See also Nick Davis, *The Desiring-Image: Gilles Deleuze and Contemporary Queer Cinema* (New York: Oxford University Press, 2013), 30, 8.

7. Narrative form in *The Living End* is consistent with art cinema narration, where protagonists lack clear goals, style is made readily apparent, plot elements are disconnected, and the narrative ends ambiguously. See David Bordwell, *Narration in the Fiction Film* (Madison: University of Wisconsin Press, 1985), 205–233.

8. B. Ruby Rich, *New Queer Cinema: The Director's Cut* (Durham, NC: Duke University Press, 2013), xv.

9. Ibid.

10. Other examples of movies associated with New Queer Cinema include *Looking for Langston* (1989), *Paris Is Burning* (1990), *Poison* (1991), *Swoon* (1992), *Go Fish* (1994), and *The Watermelon Woman* (1996).

11. Rich, *New Queer Cinema*, xxii.

12. Other examples of studio produced and distributed gay and lesbian movies from this period include *Bound* (1996), *Kiss Me, Guido* (1997), *In and Out* (1997), and *Trick* (1999).

13. Rich, *New Queer Cinema*, xxiv.

14. Ibid., xxii.

15. Ibid.

16. There is a great deal of literature on the various financial and technological changes shaping cinema culture in the twenty-first century. See, in particular, Chuck Tryon, *On-Demand Culture: Digital Delivery and the Future of Movies* (New Brunswick, NJ: Rutgers University Press, 2013); and Jennifer Holt and Kevin Sanson, *Connected Viewing: Selling, Streaming, and Sharing Media in the Digital Age* (New York: Routledge, 2013).

17. For more background on the development of gay and lesbian media distribution in this context, see Candace Moore, "Distribution Is Queen: LGBTQ Media on Demand," *Cinema Journal* 53, no. 1 (Fall 2013): 137–144.

18. As Chuck Tryon points out, "theatrical distribution and other classical 'gatekeeping' mechanisms . . . shap[e] the reception and marketing of movies." Chuck Tryon, *Reinventing Cinema: Movies in the Age of Media Convergence* (New Brunswick, NJ: Rutgers University Press, 2009), 96.

19. The gay and lesbian movies circulated by the small independent distributors have another predecessor in direct-to-video cinema, a category that can be characterized by the movies' vexed relations to standard notions of value as coded in cinema culture and scholarship. See Jeffrey Sconce, ed., *Sleaze Artists: Cinema at the Margins of Taste, Style, and Politics* (Durham, NC: Duke University Press, 2007); Joan Hawkins, *Cutting Edge: Art Horror and the Horrific Avant-garde* (Minneapolis: University of Minnesota Press, 2000); and Linda Ruth Williams, *The Erotic Thriller in Contemporary Cinema* (Edinburgh: Edinburgh University Press, 2005). For a discussion of the relationship between direct-to-video movies and gay and lesbian cinema specifically, see Glyn Davis, "A Taste for *Leeches!* DVDs, Audience Configurations, and Generic Hybridity," in *Film and Television after DVD*, ed. James Bennett and Tony Brown (New York: Routledge, 2008), 45–62.

20. This chapter draws on eighty-three published articles. Todd Longwell, "Gays Just Wanna Have Fun," *Hollywood Reporter* 389, no. 44 (July 5, 2005): 18–19, Film & Television Literature Index with Full Text, EBSCOhost Research Databases, https://www.ebscohost.com/title-lists.

21. Ibid.

22. In her interviews with gay and lesbian workers in the advertising industry, Katherine Sender identifies a double bind in which the job requirements and career pressures of minority professionals often result in them having to both draw on and disavow their subcultural knowledge and minority status. This phenomenon can be seen throughout the press discourses on gay and lesbian cinema. Katherine Sender, *Business Not Politics: The Making of the Gay Market* (New York: Columbia University Press, 2004), 64–94.

23. Quoted in Todd Longwell, "Gays Just Wanna Have Fun."

24. Quoted in Erik Haagensen, "We're Here, We're Queer, We're on DVD," *Back Stage West* 12, no. 35 (August 25, 2005): 10–12, Film & Television Literature Index with Full Text, EBSCOhost.

25. These political commitments are akin to ones that Sender identifies in gay and lesbian advertising workers. Because industry constraints prevent more transformative goals, Sender's interviewees conceive of their roles in the creation of gay and lesbian media as more "progressive" than "radical," identifying themselves as "educators." Sender, *Business Not Politics*, 90.

26. Quoted in Stuart Levine, "Wolfe Keeps Market at Bay," *Daily Variety* 282, no. 65 (March 26, 2004): A10–A12, Film & Television Literature Index with Full Text, EBSCOhost.

27. Ibid.

28. Lucas Hilderbrand, *Inherent Vice: Bootleg Histories of Videotape and Copyright* (Durham, NC: Duke University Press, 2009); and Caetlin Benson-Allott, *Killer Tapes and Shattered Screens: Video Spectatorship from VHS to File-Sharing* (Berkeley: University of California Press, 2013).

29. David Bordwell, Janet Staiger, and Kristin Thompson, *The Classical Hollywood Cinema* (New York: Columbia University Press, 1985).

30. David Bordwell, "Intensified Continuity: Visual Style in Contemporary American Film," *Film Quarterly* 55, no. 3 (2002): 24.

31. Livia Cole, "Iowa's Filmmaking Future: What's the Impact on Local Economies?" *Iowa Source*, http://www.iowasource.com/movies/2010_11_iowafilm.html.

32. John David Rhodes argues that scholarship on cities and cinema frequently "assume[s] a rather abstract, diffuse character; often 'the city' might be only an imagined city—a fabrication of set design and cinematography." I am mindful of this critical tendency, but the movies analyzed here only rarely problematize the specifics of any single location. The movies themselves bracket most of the differences between various locales, requiring a critical optic that addresses the political implications of the very tendency that Rhodes criticizes. Thanks to Dan Bashara for pointing me to this research. John David Rhodes, *Stupendous, Miserable City: Pasolini's Rome* (Minneapolis: University of Minnesota Press, 2007), xv.

33. Judith [Jack] Halberstam, *In a Queer Time and Place: Transgender Bodies, Subcultural Lives* (New York: New York University Press, 2005), 36.

34. For another analysis of developments in cinematic representations of cities, see Pamela Robertson Wojcik, *The Apartment Plot: Urban Living in American Film and Popular Culture, 1945–1975* (Durham, NC: Duke University Press, 2010).

35. Lauren Berlant, *Anatomy of a National Fantasy: Hawthorne, Utopia, and Everyday Life* (Chicago: University of Chicago Press, 1991), 20.

36. In her discussion of cinematic representations of skyscrapers, Merrill Schleier writes: "Skyscrapers in cinema are often invested with ideological significance, economically based philosophies, and gender positions." The long shots and extreme long shots in gay and lesbian movies work by this logic as well. Merrill Schleier, *Skyscraper Cinema: Architecture and Gender in American Film* (Minneapolis: University of Minnesota Press, 2009), vii.

37. Lauren Berlant, *The Queen of America Goes to Washington City: Essays on Sex and Citizenship* (Durham, NC: Duke University Press, 1997), 1.

38. Emphasis in the original. Ibid.

39. Ibid., 1–2.

40. Ibid., 3.

41. B. Ruby Rich's analysis of gentrification and its effects on queer cinema are most pointed in her discussion of New York. Of the period during New Queer Cinema's heyday, she writes: "The artists whose live-work lofts made SoHo and TriBeCa safe for financiers and chain stores had not yet been bought out, fled, or been evicted . . . New York City wasn't yet the post-Giuliani, Bloomberg-forever, Disneyland-Vegas tourist attraction of today, trademarked and policed to protect the visitors and the tourism industry." The historical narrative Rich writes for New York City between the early 1990s and the second decade of the twenty-first century is analogous to the representations of cities in New Queer Cinema and those seen in the gay and lesbian movies circulated by the small independent distributors in the decades after. Rich, *New Queer Cinema*, xviii.

42. Lauren Berlant, *The Female Complaint: The Unfinished Business of Sentimentality in American Culture* (Durham, NC: Duke University Press, 2008), 5.

43. Ibid., 3.

44. Ibid.

45. Lee Wallace calls for a special consideration of spaces that foster the representation of lesbian sexuality, articulating a series of "lesbian chronotopes" that can be considered privileged sites in the narration of same-sex attraction and romance between women. She identifies the prison, the schoolhouse, and the bar as sites for understanding how lesbian desire is challenged by different circumstances of visibility than gay male desire. She adds the apartment to this list—and it seems to me, that while *Julie Johnson* does not evolve in an apartment per se, its narration of lesbian desire is particularly attuned to the spatial forces at work in delimiting the female characters' romantic and sexual possibilities. Thanks to Pamela Wojcik for directing

me to this research. Lee Wallace, *The Sexual Life of Apartments: Lesbianism, Sex, and Cinema* (New York: Routledge, 2009).

46. Emphasis in the original. Berlant, *The Female Complaint*, 4.

47. Ibid., 12.

48. Ibid., 11.

49. For a variant on the idea "the political is personal," see Lauren Berlant, *The Queen of America Goes to Washington City*, 178.

50. Lisa Henderson, *Love and Money: Queers, Class, and Cultural Production* (New York: New York University Press, 2013), 13.

51. Here, Henderson refers to Beverly Skeggs's work on class friction among sexual minorities. Beverly Skeggs, "The Appearance of Class: Challenges in Gay Space," in *Cultural Studies and the Working Class: Subject to Change*, ed. Sally Munt (London: Cassell, 2000), 129–151. Quoted in Henderson, *Love and Money*, 100.

52. Henderson, *Love and Money*, 13.

53. Davis, *Desiring-Image*, 28.

54. Ibid.

3 Cable TV, Commodity Activism, and Corporate Synergy (or Lack Thereof)

In the summer of 2007, the gay and lesbian cable television network Logo hosted a debate between candidates vying for the Democratic nomination in the 2008 election for the US presidency. In an interview about the program with the Associated Press, a Logo executive states: "Simply seeing the candidates step on a stage to speak to a national gay television audience may be as moving as anything they say."[1] Another Logo executive uses the debate to differentiate the network from its competitors, telling a trade reporter that the event will "solidify the position [Logo has] been building . . . as a really legitimate place to tell stories by and for our audience."[2] A televised debate in which contenders for the US presidency address issues of import to sexual minority audiences illustrates a mode of address peculiar to identity-based cable TV, one best described as commodity activism. In this entanglement of consumption and citizenship, political energies circulate as items for sale. With a rationale rooted in the marketplace, commodity activism creates an equivalence in which the branding opportunities that the debate opens up for the network are coterminous with any civic function it might serve. According to this line of thinking, gay and lesbian cable TV's staging of political dialogue is important simply because it exists, and any impact the debate might have on the lives of viewers is left unexamined.[3]

There is a temptation to use this anecdote in order to restage familiar debates, where a critique of identity-based television might lobby for representational justice and/or lament the impact of media commerce on progressive politics. This chapter resists these urges in order to examine how the cable TV networks that court sexual minorities imagine themselves to be doing political work. Whereas most studies of gay and lesbian cable tend to limit their purview to the most prominent and frequently studied gay and lesbian cable network, this chapter demonstrates that Logo cannot be isolated from the competition of the media marketplace, where Here TV and Q Television Network court similar demographics with nearly identical programming. The first section articulates commodity activism as an audience appeal specific to cable TV that courts minority audiences, one that is simultaneously commodified and progressive and thus exploitative and liberatory, as well.[4] Without making apologies for gay and lesbian cable TV's political limitations, the chapter examines the medium's programming and online content to illustrate how the networks Logo, Here, and Q construct consumption as a mode of citizenship.[5] Here, ideas about ideological struggle get packaged as individual troubles that are then rendered conquerable through assorted commodity purchases.

The shifting political economy and changing technological makeup of cable TV are often cast as having linear relations to marketplace viability and an inverse relationship with progressive politics, a consensus that this chapter questions. The chapter demonstrates that cable TV industry practices have had less straightforward effects on the programming and online content that the gay and lesbian networks produce and distribute. Even though the three networks examined in this chapter feature different modes of financing—one is a basic cable channel, one is a pay cable channel, and one is an on-demand service—each launched with original news content and travel programming. The chapter charts the evolution of these genres across the networks over a ten-year period, 2004 to 2014. It teases out the effects that different funding models and corporate structures have had on programming and online content, underscoring their role in shaping the kinds of commodity activism seen on gay and lesbian cable TV.

The second section focuses specifically on news content, detailing how it frames public sphere issues on intimate terms for its audiences. It also demonstrates how news content provides evidence of the corporate synergy that media conglomerates attempt to create across their different holdings, an industry practice that has had different results for each of the networks. The third section focuses on travel programs, analyzing how their representations of sexual minorities around the world attempt to manage the tensions that attend cultural difference. It also demonstrates the impact of different funding models on the programs' modes of address. News content and travel programming are the genres where the networks have most clearly attempted to exploit the multiple modes of interactivity made possible by digital technology. The circulation of programs and other content across multiple delivery platforms further enmeshes citizenship with acts of consumption, like when news content about the financial issues unique to same-sex couples is punctuated by click-through links to the bank that created it, or when travel programs gesture to the history of persecution of sexual minorities around the world and then facilitate access to plane tickets and hotel accommodations to those locations shortly thereafter. Attempts to encourage viewer interactivity across multiple delivery technologies have precipitated disparate results across the different networks, as well.

News content and travel programming offer explicit examples of gay and lesbian cable's commodity activism: the networks construct politicized modes of address that are routed through the medium's imperative to generate revenue. It is a sensibility in which consumer experiences create a path toward political collectivity in limited, often counterintuitive ways. Even as the chapter emphasizes the discursive limits of political claims made in the name of commerce, it explains how and why people find them meaningful. The chapter closes with some thoughts about how scholarship might intervene in the cable TV marketplace on behalf of sexual minority audiences.

Cable TV Spectatorship as Commodity Activism

The gay and lesbian cable networks have many parallels with those created for women and African American audiences and are thus a dense site for mapping the peculiar connections that cable TV forges with identity politics. The production of identity-bound cable TV is often framed as having "twin missions: . . . to be both socially responsible and profitable, serving both public interests and private (corporate) needs."[6] Beretta Smith-Shomade registers her skepticism of the emancipatory powers attributed to identity-bound cable TV by industry publications and the popular press, wondering how well "the audience, democracy, and narrowcasting actually mesh."[7] Similarly, Lisa Parks worries about press discourses framing the multiplatform content of cable TV as a progressive improvement over more traditional television programming. She argues: "Despite . . . efforts to claim the computer as a platform for social transformation, the dominant social, economic, and cultural discourses continue to position computer technologies as domains of . . . activity, authority, and control."[8] Capital is also cast as a corrosive influence in the realm of sexual minorities and cable television. In his analysis of Logo, Ben Aslinger argues: "Efforts to offer more complex and egalitarian representations of queerness are ultimately circumscribed by the requirements of capital."[9] Looking at gay and lesbian cable networks in the United States and Canada, Anthony Freitas charges that their "representation of a unitary lesbian and gay market niche erases much of the variation within and between these communities. . . . [T]hese channels . . . mirror other commercial television by taking a status quo and 'centrist' perspective on social and political issues."[10] Eve Ng sees this political centrism increasing at Logo over time. She casts the network-wide recalibration toward "gaystreaming" in 2008 and 2009 as the result of programming efforts "designed to draw in a larger general audience, particularly heterosexual women . . . [which] marginalizes some LGBT [lesbian, gay, bisexual, transgender] subjects even as others are integrated into the mainstream."[11] In conducting interviews with Logo employees and looking at internal documents that circulated among network staff, Ng emphasizes that this strategy evacuates the evolution in programming strategy of any negative connotations.[12] All of this research emphasizes that marketplace developments in cable TV's identity-bound appeals get framed in press discourses and corporate communications as evidence of an inevitable march toward progress and justice for sexual minorities. At the same time, the studies accuse these appeals of rarely, if ever, precipitating social change. While these critiques are apt and compelling, I worry that they seek a justice that television can never provide.[13]

Where scholarship on cable TV identifies a limited, sometimes even hollow politics in the medium's courtship of minorities, I see an ability to generate ever more consumer categories. Alas, these are not mutually exclusive endeavors. Understanding the political claims made by gay and lesbian cable TV requires analyzing how it constructs an activist sensibility not *in spite* of its consumerist thrust, but *because* of it. Across the networks, audience appeals imagine the very act of watching television to be a mode of civic engagement rooted in the pleasures of consumption. Sarah Banet-Weiser and Roopali Mukherjee use the term "commodity activism" to define such political acts: "As is characteristic of the commodity form—produced through labor for purposes of trade and profit within markets and fetishized in culture—commodity activism, as we encounter it today, offers critical insights into both the promise and the perils of consumer-based modes of resistance as they take shape within the dynamics of neoliberal power."[14] The spectator positions engendered by gay and lesbian cable TV are rooted in feelings of social mobility and thus consistent with the ethos of neoliberalism.[15] They are constructed in an effort to empower audiences, so that viewers might make particular kinds of life choices. This mode of spectatorship yokes political transformation to capital accumulation, suggesting that agency and thus happiness are best achieved through a viewer's shrewd functioning in the marketplace. Commodity activism trumpets "self-reliance, entrepreneurial individualism, and economic responsibility," so facilitating the use and exchange of consumer products is its governing rationale.[16] News content and travel programming in particular are imagined to inspire viewers, providing them with opportunities to participate in consumer culture in meaningful ways.

Following Banet-Weiser and Mukherjee's lead, my aim is neither to condone nor condemn commodity activism's vision of politics. Even as I find it tempting to dismiss commodity activism as being relatively meaningless, maybe even dangerously complacent, I worry that such determinations ultimately prevent a nuanced understanding of how media commerce, progressive politics, and sexual identity become intertwined in this circuit of culture. Gay and lesbian cable TV engages politics for the sake of profit, a process that recognizes minorities but does not redistribute resources.[17] Gay and lesbian cable TV constructs a mode of address rooted in the specificities of sexual minorities' experiences, but does so in the interest of circulating capital upward.[18] The commodity activism enacted by Logo, Q, and Here features "the conflation of selfhood with neoliberal modes of governmentality, the economic logics of post-Fordism, hyperconsumerism, and promotionalism, and marries this conflation to social activism."[19] It is a mode of address that is enabled, delimited, and contoured by the shifting political economy and transforming technological makeup of cable TV.

News Content and Disparate Conglomerations

In its first decade, gay and lesbian cable TV's commodity activism is especially evident in news programming, and the tensions and limits that structure it in this content are informed by the business practices the networks employ in order to finance their programming. All cable TV networks promise audiences up-to-the-minute news reporting, an abbreviated news cycle intensified further by the medium's convergence with the internet. Throughout on-air broadcasts, reporters and anchors urge audiences to obtain information via different delivery technologies because revenue potential increases when viewers make multiple contacts with content.[20] Creating such programming is costly, and start-up businesses often struggle to amass the resources and capital required for such endeavors. The ways that the different gay and lesbian networks navigate this scenario differ considerably, contrasts that underline the difficulty of courting sexual minorities in the cable marketplace at all.

Because Logo is owned by international media conglomerate Viacom, the network was able to forge relationships with the company's other subsidiaries to create original news content and avoid many of the attendant production costs. Between 2004 and 2009, Logo's partnership with CBS News resulted in the creation of on-air programming in which story selection, the structure of segments, and the performances of on-air talent presented a range of ideas about sexuality via an advertiser-supported business model consistent with the network's status as a basic cable offering. Using on-location reporting and footage culled from local CBS affiliates, Logo's news programming was initially called *CBS News on Logo* (2004–2007) and then, in an effort to connect news programming to the network's web acquisitions, *365Gay News on Logo* (2007–2009). Working in conjunction with CBS News, in-house Logo reporters produced three- to five-minute segments and half-hour-long specials for the network and its websites. Segments aired during commercial breaks throughout on-air broadcasts and specials aired and then repeated throughout the network's schedule. The network's website streamed segments and featured longer-form reportage.

The news programs that aired on Logo during the first week of February 2008 are representative of the network's news content as a whole. Like newspapers and magazines before them, the programs tailored coverage for a target audience comprised of sexual minorities.[21] In one segment, news anchor Jason Bellini interviewed then presidential candidate Hillary Clinton about her positions on issues related to LGBT rights, and another showcased a new release from lesbian singer k.d. lang. But another news program that aired during this period, the news special *Money Matters*, demonstrates most plainly how Logo addresses its audience in this content. Chicly dressed in a blazer, dress shirt open at the neck, and blue jeans, Bellini opens the finance-themed special by informing viewers that Logo created the two-part special so that "the worldwide resources of CBS News" can be used to bring financial advice to the network's viewers. Bellini's performance is consistent with the sincerity associated with TV news anchors, but his relaxed dress and intermittently playful demeanor are somewhat atypical for the sober tone that is perhaps most common on television news.[22] For instance, when introducing a segment covering the financial aspects of ending a gay marriage, Bellini breaks into a sly grin and, in tongue-in-cheek fashion, says to the camera: "Breaking up is hard to do."

With a mixture of candor and gay-inflected hipness, the anchor introduces each segment and is the organizing presence in the news special. One segment features an interview with a white, professional gay man struggling to manage his student debt, and another segment features a black lesbian couple merging their finances in order to launch a business together. In between these segments are two shorter segments: one in which a middle-aged, white gay male couple adopt a baby, and another that discusses the financial fallout of the dissolution of a lesbian marriage. Bellini's voice-over narration casts the program's enumeration of financial problems experienced by the upper- and upper-middle-class interviewees as typical of those experienced by viewers in the audience. Demonstrating what Mimi White has identified as television's therapeutic rhetorical mode, the *Money Matters* news special offers solutions for the people on-screen and advice for people in the audience, constructing a mode of address steeped in ideas about financial empowerment and assertive decisions.[23]

One of the special's final segments is a report on automobile sales, which demonstrates the corporate synergy at work in Logo's news content. Bellini introduces the segment by telling the gay and lesbian audience that buying a car is "one of the biggest purchases" they will ever make. Narration then cuts to reporter Teri Okita, who reports on *Consumer Reports* car rankings and the popularity of hybrid vehicles among car buyers. Bellini introduces Okita as being based in Los Angeles because the report was originally produced for broadcast on the local CBS affiliate there. The synergy created by integrating content from different divisions of a conglomerate in a single broadcast is a common occurrence in television news, but it is unique to Logo in the context of gay and lesbian cable. In November 2007, Logo announced that in addition to specials and brief interstitial segments, *CBS News on Logo* would be a weekly half-hour-long program airing several times a week and streaming on a website.[24] In mid-2008, Bellini left the network and was replaced by Ross Palombo, a staffing change that was attended by a rebranding of the network's news programming overall. The second iteration of Logo's news programming, *365Gay News on Logo*, was similar in style and function to its predecessor. The broadcast was renamed to shift the network's news content to a new website following the network's purchase of Toronto-based internet domain 365gay.com. And while Palombo's performance and sartorial presence were more earnest and conventionally polished than Bellini's, the new anchor signified in similar ways: young, urbane, and white. In press releases, the network cast the program change as allowing it to better serve its audience as members of the body politic: "LGBT Americans will be a key voting bloc in the 2008 election, and we hope [Logo's news programming] will be a dynamic new platform for keeping our community informed and involved."[25] Like its predecessor, *365Gay News on Logo*'s half-hour newscasts include a combination of on-location reporting, stock footage, and coverage culled from its partnership with CBS. Also like its predecessor, all segments foreground an audience-specific engagement with political issues that is consistent with commodity activism, exploiting resources available to producers as a result of Logo's corporate ownership.

News content on gay and lesbian cable engages audiences on intimate terms, a process that can be seen in *365Gay News on Logo*'s coverage of Barack Obama's first presidential inauguration. The January 23, 2009, episode begins with Palombo in voice-over; he tells the audience that Barack Obama frequently addressed gay and lesbian issues when campaigning, but did not mention them during his inaugural address. Narration then cuts to a segment that describes a controversy related to a gay bishop's invitation to participate in the inauguration. The segment begins with footage of the bishop speaking at the event, then cuts to footage of spectators crowding national monuments, and then to a shot of the president taking the oath of office. In voice-over, the host reports that the inauguration organizers also included antigay evangelist Rick Warren in the festivities, telling viewers that the invitation was met with criticism from media outlets and the president's gay and lesbian supporters. Palombo speculates that the bishop only participated in the inauguration so that the organizing committee could appease critics who disagreed with the evangelist's invitation. The host then frames this appeasement as being mitigated by the speech's exclusion from the event's television broadcast, suggesting that the omission was met with still more disapproval.

Palombo's voice-over relates this information in a causal way and the footage is used in an evidential manner. The result is a linear narrative that engages viewers' emotions by casting the events at the inauguration as evidence of homophobia. Although bias in television news is a frequent criticism of current events reportage from both ends of the political spectrum, Michael Schudson casts such reportage as, by definition, an interpretive act. Subjective interpretations "allow the reporter to write about what he hears and sees, and what is unheard, unseen, or intentionally omitted as well."[26] Schudson's claim underscores how Palombo's—or, perhaps more accurately, Logo's—interpretation of the inauguration events are common narrative techniques deployed in news reporting of all kinds, dating back to the late nineteenth and early twentieth centuries. On Logo, they are used to frame national news stories for a target audience comprised of sexual minorities, engaging viewers as consumer citizens by making public sphere issues personal for them.

It is through this emotional interpretation of events that Logo constructs a mode of address consistent with commodity activism. As the segment about the inauguration controversy progresses, Palombo's voice-over continues, though images on-screen change from footage taken at the inauguration to stills of newspaper headlines and then highlighted pull quotes from articles. These images are offered as evidence of the outrage precipitated by the events that unfolded at the inauguration. Palombo describes other news outlets' coverage of these events as images of mastheads from different newspapers and magazines collect in the frame. The editing is such that the time between cuts decreases as the segment continues; the pace suggests that people's anger became more intense over time. The segment continues with Palombo reading an apology issued by the inauguration committee, which is accompanied on-screen with text laid over a long shot of the Lincoln Memorial. The segment concludes with brief interviews of gay and lesbian inauguration attendees, all of whom express their disappointment with the Inauguration Committee and the president.

The clip's growing sense of anger coupled with concluding shots of enraged interviewees is evidence of a mode of address that attempts to involve viewers in the events unfolding on-screen. But outrage is not the only emotion constructed in Logo's news content. In another segment, reporter Chagmion Antoine interviews Charlotte Smallwood, an elderly black woman who the program identifies as a longtime political activist. A voice-over accompanies decades-old stock footage of black civil rights demonstrations, feminist protests, and LGBT rights rallies, which Antoine associates with Smallwood's multiple political identities and investments. Antoine charges that Smallwood's numerous identifications are representative of gay and lesbian African American voters, who the reporter claims are heartened by the election of a black president yet apprehensive about his dedication to winning rights for sexual minorities. Antoine's voice-over narration suggests a generational conflict in that it casts Smallwood as being disappointed with young gay and lesbian voters' lack of familiarity with the struggles of mid-century black and feminist activists.

The segment leaves unspoken the different tensions that have attended political struggles over the course of US history—the vital disagreements over sex, gender, race, and class that shaped twentieth-century rights movements, and how generational disparities complicate simple conclusions about ideological change over time. Yet Antoine refers again and again to Smallwood's self-reliance and stoicism, and the shots of the interviewee that are interspersed among the other footage always depict the elderly woman by herself: either in medium close-up as she walks down the street or via long shot as she prays in a church. The segment represents the political through the personal, constructing Smallwood's independence as facilitating multiple political affinities. This mode of address is a common one in feature reporting; it identifies a locus of politicization at the level of the individual, thereby alleviating ideological tensions latent in examinations of contentious issues. Antoine finishes the segment by relaying Smallwood's advice for younger generations: "Be yourself." Thus, Logo's news content engages in some political dialogue about the lives of sexual minorities but manages the tensions that attend it by advocating for individual agency rather than political collectivity. It is a mode of address that works within Logo's business model, which must remain sensitive to advertiser concerns.

Logo's business model was a frequent talking point in press discourses leading up to the network's launch. Executives heralded Logo's corporate parenthood and program financing as ensuring its viability in the marketplace. In interviews during early to mid-2004, Logo staff promised reporters that the network would "attract blue-chip advertisers hungry for an audience segment that overindexes on disposable income,"[27] and that Logo benefits from advertisers "drooling for TV's largely untapped homosexual audience—an estimated 15 million gay adults in the United States, with disposable income projected at $485 billion [per] year."[28] This triumphant rhetoric can also be seen in industry press in the months leading up to Logo's launch: "Madison Avenue can only see deep green when it comes to gay consumers with disposable incomes and the means to drop several thou on a BMW."[29] Press coverage suggested that Logo's courtship of gay and lesbian audiences was resolving a deficit in the marketplace, speculating that corporations and brands like Miller Lite and Subaru view the network as an attractive advertising outlet because they "have been frustrated by limited options" for courting gay and lesbian consumers.[30] Logo couched its corporate goals in similar terms. In a July 2004 press release, Logo characterizes its launch as "the first time there is an outlet dedicated to this important, loyal audience with disposable income."[31] In a 2005 interview, Logo's then head of sales calls gay cable television audiences "a completely underserved market.... Advertisers ... will see their specific competitors on our air and ... come to us."[32] Throughout Logo's corporate communications and coverage in the press, the channel's advertiser-supported business model was articulated as a good indication that the network could be profitable.

Like the network's news content, press discourses on Logo's launch also feature a careful avoidance of controversy.[33] In one interview, an executive characterizes Logo as a "full-service, mainstream network," stressing that "we don't think it's indecent. We're not using profanity, we're not using sex. This is going to be mainstream programming that you see everywhere else."[34] Executives repeatedly highlight the network's ability to recirculate preexisting content, simultaneously underlining the benefits of Logo's corporate ownership and stressing the moderate politics of its programming.[35] In one interview, a sales executive dismisses the notion that advertisers will be scared of conservative backlash by advertising on a gay and lesbian cable TV network: "Once they really understand . . . the breadth of the audience and the breadth of the programming, they [will] understand there is a great business opportunity."[36] Executives frame Logo's repackaging of Viacom content as a boon to advertisers, characterizing it as being "pretested for audience acceptability."[37] Logo executives attempted to blunt anxieties about the kind of programming it would circulate by characterizing the network as "not an edgy, boundary-breaking venture," emphasizing its advertiser-friendly political vision.[38]

In contrast, Q was an independently financed and distributed pay cable channel launched by a group of investors, and trade reporters were skeptical that the network could compete with Logo for advertisers or audiences. In interviews, Q executives defended the network's business model. When one interviewer labeled Q gay and lesbian cable's "underdog," an executive countered: "I think there's room [for different gay and lesbian cable networks]. We're different types of channels, just like you have ABC, NBC and CBS."[39] Like Logo, Q's launch featured mostly news programming. Unlike Logo, Q had to build a news division from scratch, without the benefit of other holdings in a conglomerate. In November 2004, the network announced *On Q Live* (2004–2006), a two-and-a-half-hour news program airing two times daily with gay and lesbian-themed news, entertainment, and political coverage in a talk format with three different hosts. The program was conceived as "a truly interactive show" in that viewers would be invited "to join in discussions with the hosts using their Web cameras."[40] In June 2005, Q promoted *On Q Live*'s plans to broadcast from different Gay Pride festivals around the world. Anchors Jack E. Jett, Chrisanne Eastwood, and Scott Withers were to bring "live coverage of events as they happen around the nation and the world . . . explor[ing] the unique aspects of the LGBT community, interview celebrities, [and] delve into [each] location's queer arts and celebrate the rich history of [each] city."[41] In 2005, Q announced plans for a morning news show akin to those seen on the major networks, called *Good Morning Gay America* (2005–2006). Press releases promised viewers and cable systems operators an on-air staff of two in-studio anchors and twenty-five reporters who would cover a wide range of topics: news, entertainment, business, and sports.[42] And with *QTN Worldcast* (2005–2006), the network announced plans for a nightly program with many similarities to Logo's regular newscasts. Promising "live, in-depth interviews with newsmakers, discussing everything from politics, current events, technology, and business, to how the topics relate to the GLBT community," press releases described *QTN Worldcast* like Logo described its half-hour newscasts, a form of commodity activism that would be an integral aspect of the network brand.[43]

Where press discourses framed Logo's news programming as being cost-effective, Q's were cast as overly ambitious. Trade reporters and gay and lesbian print press underscored how Q lacked the libraries of stock footage, video feeds, and a ready stable of topical beat reporters associated with Logo's corporate ownership. These reports suggested that Q's lack of cost-saving conglomerate infrastructure contributed to its disappearance from the marketplace. Press coverage indicates that Q struggled to meet its financial obligations as early as the fall of 2005, and began laying off staff in early 2006.[44] Most of Q's senior executives left the company in March of that year, and another group of investors attempted to stage a financial turnaround, ultimately announcing the network's closure a few months later.[45]

In interviews, Here TV's CEO, Paul Colichmann, actively differentiated his network from Q, telling reporters: "If you assigned [Q's] business plan to any niche, it wouldn't work," suggesting that Q's plans for its many news programs were impractical.[46] In comparison, he casts Here's model as being simultaneously less ambitious but more financially sound, claiming that Q was "promising the sun, moon and stars. . . . [Here] could afford one star, but we would actually deliver on one star."[47] Here's news shows cover a range of political and cultural issues, but without the benefit of Logo's production resources, the network initially only offered them in podcast, a relatively inexpensive way of creating and circulating content. Between 2005 and 2009, Here offered gay and lesbian audiences a range of different talk format podcasts that covered issues related to gay and lesbian life and culture. Cheaply produced and hybrid in form, podcasts allow television networks to diversify their programming and aggregate a range of publics.[48] On *Here with Josh and Sara*, hosts Joshua Rosenzweig and Sara Logue talk about current events and interview guests familiar to the network's target audiences: gay director John Cameron Mitchell, lesbian cartoonist Alison Bechdel, and transgender activist and author Kate Bornstein. Promotional materials position the podcast as bringing "intelligent and entertaining conversation while serving as a new voice of the developing community at large,"[49] aligning the program with other elements of the network's branding efforts that paint a corporate mission rooted in commodity activism. In their discussions of current events, Rosenzweig and Logue interview a variety of guests: members of the AIDS Community Research Initiative, publisher of the fetish publication *A Bear's Life*, lesbian tennis player Martina Navratilova, and the president of the National Lesbian and Gay Journalists Association. Episodes traverse a range of topics in an informal though markedly political tone. For example, the program's August 2005 launch began with an episode in which Rosenzweig talks about his support for openly gay political candidates in New York City elections, and the hosts shared their knowledge and feelings about antigay legislation pending in California at that time.

Here's marketing discourses frame the hosts' dialogue as a source of insider knowledge, casting audiences as participants in timely discussions.[50] Press releases characterize Rosenzweig as offering audiences "extensive knowledge of pop culture, entertainment and gay media as well as New York nightlife" in addition to "a unique perspective and singular interviewing style" as a result of having "worn many hats in the entertainment industry both behind and in front of the camera."[51] In contrast, the network positions Sara Logue as "bring[ing] to the table a female perspective," emphasizing her involvement in "organizations doing big things for the LGBT community," which allows her to offer "out-of-the-box insights on many of today's important issues."[52] On Here's podcasts, hosts invited viewer feedback via e-mail or telephone, read selected correspondence on the air, and played some of these voice mail messages during the programs. While *Here with Josh and Sara* featured a relaxed yet refined narrational tone, the other podcasts were hosted by stand-up comedians and tended to be more ribald by comparison. Specifically, *Bent* and *Girls on Girls* featured risqué chat and an augmented sense of spontaneous exchange with their animated dialogue and frequent explosions of laughter.

In Here's podcasts, political dialogue is folded into conversation, inviting listeners as participants through topics and vernacular familiar to the target audience. With fewer regulatory concerns, the talk that takes place on Here's podcasts is more frank and explicit than talk that takes place in more traditional television broadcasts. For instance, the hosts of *Bent*, J. C. Chavez and Paul Case, often talked about Chavez's experiences as a Latino man. In many episodes, Case asks Chavez pointed questions about waxing or "manscaping," and jokes that because he has a crush on MSNBC anchor Rachel Maddow, he secretly wants to be a lesbian. But the hosts also discussed the incidents surrounding Pastor Rick Warren's involvement in the presidential inauguration, a discussion in which Chavez actually defended President Obama's invitation to the evangelist, characterizing it as a savvy political tactic. Another episode featured Chase welcoming then Alaska governor Sarah Palin's involvement in national politics, suggesting that her status as a working mother gives her a unique perspective on current events. In almost the same breath, he issued a catty insult to Cindy McCain, the wife of 2008 presidential candidate John McCain. Referring to her coiffed appearance and careful public persona, Case called her "a tranny robot"—a remark that precipitates robust laughter from his cohost. Fostering interactivity is a feature of all political coverage on cable. Jeffrey Jones identifies such politicized entertainment as part of a broader industry trend, a move toward making cable TV's news programming more engaging for viewers.[53]

Because of the network's business model, Here's podcasts could be "edgy" in ways that Logo's news content could not. In contrast to both Logo and Q, Here was initially distributed to television audiences as an on-demand feature and, at the time of its launch, its content was available for download over the internet. Viewers paid a fee for a changing list of programming, though the podcasts were all free to audiences. The podcasts' edgy sensibility can be seen in *Girls on Girls*, which was hosted by comedians Anne Neczypor and Jackie Monahan and featured discussion about topics like the etiquette of one-night stands between women, the proper use of sex toys, and cultural norms regarding female masturbation. Throughout its episodes, Monahan comfortably recounted personal experiences, though Neczypor cracked jokes more than she divulged any private information. Episodes dealt with conventional political and cultural issues of interest to target audiences like homophobia on the internet, ex-gay therapy, and the history of lesbian butch/femme couples, but always engaged those topics informally and humorously. Guests provided multiple points of view on matters related to sex, gender, and sexuality, making the program's mode of address one of constant commentary on norms, viewpoints, and cultural knowledge. By featuring frank discussions about even hot-button topics, the podcasts facilitated a distinct form of political dialogue and civic engagement for audiences that courted diverse sexual minority audiences.

Where Viacom executives cast Logo's business model as signifying a broad cultural acceptance of gay and lesbian people because viewers receive it whether or not they ask for it, Here executives speculated that such a model ultimately does the opposite. In interviews around Logo's launch, Here's CEO charged that an advertiser-supported model required the network to "create programming that's acceptable to advertisers and basic cable but that is also authentic to the community they serve. That's a difficult tightrope to walk."[54] He used the press to highlight differences between Logo and Here, emphasizing how conservative advertisers could deter Logo from adequately serving gay and lesbian audiences. In one interview, he derides Logo as offering audiences little more than "gay lite."[55] In support of Here, the CEO cast the on-demand network as being better suited for gay and lesbian cable because its business model operates free from concerns about advertiser alienation, and is thus able to offer viewers fare with more explicit discussions and sexual themes.[56] He claimed that gay and lesbian viewers will ultimately prefer Here because the network offers more genuine representations of queer life to viewers who "want to see authentic media images of themselves."[57] In discourses on the gay and lesbian cable TV networks, reporters and executives debated which of the networks' business models best serves gay and lesbian audiences, and the differences between them are seen rather plainly in how they produced and distributed news content. Logo's ownership allowed the network to repurpose programming from other Viacom subsidiaries, whereas Here used cheaply made podcasts to produce more informal, budget friendly news content. Q's plans for Logo-like news broadcasts highlighted the difficulties of operating a cable television network with conventional programming but without a corporate parent.

It is possible to isolate these events and chart a particular narrative in which only corporate synergy or inexpensive innovation helps to make news content viable in the gay and lesbian cable TV marketplace. But over time, the impact of corporate ownership and inexpensive production of news content has become less straightforward. In 2009, Logo ended its relationship with CBS News and stopped creating on-air news programming.[58] Consistent with Ng's description of Logo's move toward "gaystreaming," corporate communication describes the change in news programming as a positive development, claiming that the network determined its viewers are better served by news content made available online.[59] Coverage of the events on gay and lesbian blogs unaffiliated with the network has cast the cancellation as a mere matter of finances, worrying about the impact of Logo's bottom line focus on its commitments to gay and lesbian audiences.[60] Furthermore, in 2011, Logo closed down 365gay.com altogether. In interviews, Logo executives characterized the news site as being "successful in its mission," calling attention to the migration of some news content to other sites.[61] Crucially, the network painted this development as "making it easier for readers to find and enjoy all of our original content."[62] After the site's closure, the editor in chief told an interviewer: "The mainstream media is doing such a better job covering a more diverse swath of America. It's about long-term media trends instead of the LGBT market doing something wrong, and as we've become more accepted, we've become more mainstream."[63]

At the end of the network's first decade, news content is much less prominent in Logo's offerings than it was when the network first launched. As of 2016, Logo's news content has been folded into style, entertainment, and fitness coverage on the network's *NewNowNext* website. A handful of reporters write features on current events, where political problems continue to be articulated as personal struggles. For instance, the site covered the legislative and judicial struggles over marriage rights in the United States by publishing stories that focus on the life experiences of gays and lesbians in long-term relationships.[64] In other articles, celebrities offer their personal feelings about sociocultural topics.[65] The network also produces news content for its mobile media application: *NewNowNext Minute* is a series of one- to four-minute videos that feature interviews with celebrities and coverage of industry events like red-carpet premieres mixed in with other features. In these clips, a young, white, gay male reporter offers viewers tips about lifestyle issues like coping with family tension at the holidays. Logo's news content was always intimate in nature, but its framing of public sphere issues for sexual minorities has been replaced by less identity-bound lifestyle coverage.

Logo's website also displays an evasiveness about the network's courtship of gay and lesbian audiences. A question in the Frequently Asked Questions (FAQ) section asks: "Is Logo TV a gay channel?" A programming executive answers: "It depends on what you mean. If you mean TV that appeals to a gay audience, and their friends, and their families, and people who are beyond labels . . . then yes, absolutely. If you mean, like, in a more polarizing sense of a channel only for gay viewers, and that only shows programs that only have gay characters, then no, not so much."[66] Another question asks: "Who watches Logo TV?" The programming executive writes: "People who identify themselves as gay, straight, either, neither, or both. We get pop culture enthusiasts and new culture fanatics, from big cities to college towns, LGBT people, straight people with gay friends and family, or anyone who's open-minded."[67] The website's language highlights transformations in business practices that have changed how the network courts its audience, shifts made manifest in Logo's news programming.

As Logo hedged on its original mission, Here doubled down on serving gay and lesbian audiences, specifically; by 2016, many of Here's advertisements featured the tagline "America's *Only* Gay TV Network." The network also moved from cheaply produced podcasts to more elaborate news content in its appeals to audiences. In 2008, Here acquired the well-known gay and lesbian publications *Out* and the *Advocate*, canceling its podcasts shortly thereafter in favor of creating news programming connected to the magazines.[68] In 2012, Here launched the talk format public affairs show *For & Against* (2012–), which features man-on-the-street interviews conducted in New York City alongside interviews with politicians and elected officials. Jim Morrison, a white gay male politician turned pundit, conducts interviews and provides commentary on issues like the US Supreme Court decisions related to same-sex marriage rights, HIV criminalization, and the separation of church and state in US government. Clips stream on the *Advocate*'s website and full episodes are available on YouTube and Hulu; the program covers issues of interest to sexual minority audiences and demonstrates the kind of corporate synergy more frequently associated with Logo's ownership by Viacom. In addition, the arts and entertainment newsmagazines *OUT: Face to Face* (2010–) and *OUT: Soundcheck* (2010–) collect interviews with performers and musicians. Clips stream on *Out*'s website and, like *For & Against*, full episodes are available on YouTube and Hulu.

News programming on Here also features content made specifically for mobile media. *The Advocate Money Minute* is a branded series made in conjunction with Wells Fargo, where different employees of the financial company appear in scripted clips that stream on the magazine's website to promote wealth management services tailored specifically to gay and lesbian audiences. In four- or five-minute installments created and circulated between 2010 and 2013, *The Advocate Money Minute* advises gay and lesbian audiences on tax issues specific to gay and lesbian couples, retirement plans for long-term yet unwed parents, the financial implications of newly won marriage rights, and incorporating small LGBT-owned businesses. The *Behind the Shoot* video series on *Out*'s website features video interview footage with the celebrities, performers, and musicians featured in the magazine, enticing readers to buy the print version by promoting upcoming issues and features.

By the end of their first decade, both Logo and Here also used news content for the purpose of creating publicity-friendly media events. In 2014, Logo produced *Trailblazers*, a news special devoted to honoring prominent gay and lesbian personalities in popular culture. Press releases characterized the one-hour special as featuring "the celebrities, politicians, activists, and trendsetters who are transforming our cultural landscape—as well as musical performances from some of today's biggest artists."[69] The program honors Edie Windsor and Roberta Kaplan, the lead plaintiff and litigator in *United States v. Windsor,* one of the Supreme Court cases that helped secure same-sex marriage rights in the United States. In addition, *Trailblazers* honors Jason Collins, a professional basketball player, the cast of the Netflix series *Orange Is the New Black*, and John "Longjones" Abdallah Wambere, an LGBT rights advocate in Uganda. The news special is consistent with commodity activism more generally insofar as it generates a media spectacle in honor of gay and lesbian "progress." Similarly, Here produces and circulates short videos related to an annual list compiled by the editorial staff at *Out* called *Out100*, itself a news special that honors prominent personalities involved in gay and lesbian culture.[70] Like *Trailblazers*, *Out100* is an awards show that promotional discourses frame as a celebration of the "progress" made in gay and lesbian politics and culture.

In news specials and across the programming genre as a whole, networks attempt to generate symbolic capital by illustrating their allegiance to gay and lesbian rights, hoping that it is ultimately exchangeable in a marketplace where they must compete for similar demographics.[71] Demonstrating political commitments in these ways are a calculated effort to generate favorable publicity and win over viewers. Yet the exchange value of symbolic capital is difficult to measure. Discourses suggest that Logo's ability to create corporate synergy helps it generate symbolic capital in cost-effective ways, whereas those same discourses suggest Q's closure is the result of an inability to do the same. But identifying such firm links between corporate synergy, symbolic capital, and revenue generation are more difficult in the instance of Here. Over its first decade, the company acquired many different gay and lesbian media outlets and assembled them under one corporate umbrella. The network drew on its holdings to create content partnerships and cross-promotions, which are the kinds of corporate synergy characteristic of Logo.[72]

In trying to avoid Q's fate by taking up Logo-like practices, Here's creation of corporate synergy has proven costly. The company's acquisitions, especially the network's purchase of the *Advocate* and *Out* magazines, may have enticed viewers familiar with the magazines to consume its other content. The network's investment in the magazines also may have lent its news content an air of respectability for audiences, given the history of those publications and their reputation for serving gay and lesbian consumers. But Here's attempts to generate symbolic capital have not translated into exchange value in the marketplace. After purchasing so many different gay and lesbian media outlets in order to build a conglomerate, Here weathered a low return on investment (ROI) and struggled to manage operating costs. By 2010, industry trade journals were reporting that Here was withholding payment from freelance writers and production staff as a result of cash flow problems.[73] Many of these workers were creating and circulating the very news content that the network promoted so heavily.[74] In addition, several legal disputes erupted between Here and former employees, as well as between Here and the investment firms that helped finance the network's acquisitions.[75] Moreover, trade reporters and gay and lesbian bloggers expressed disappointment with the editorial direction of the *Advocate* and *Out* under Here's stewardship, suggesting that a bland corporate sensibility silenced voices and desires on the fringe of sexual minority communities in the interest of generating revenue.[76] Thus, the same kinds of criticisms that Aslinger, Freitas, and Ng make of Logo are made throughout press discourses on Here.

Discourses on gay and lesbian cable point to the corporate synergy seen in its news content as evidence of Logo's financially viability, but those same discourses construct Here's attempts at the creation of corporate synergy as hurting its bottom line. Here's struggles coupled with Q's closure demonstrate the difficulties of entering the cable TV marketplace at all. The tension between the imperatives of revenue generation and the desires for progressive politics is a double bind that structures any and every courtship of minorities on cable TV. To that end, travel programming provides another example of gay and lesbian cable's different funding models. In tracing the development of travel programs over time, the impact of gay and lesbian cable TV's political economy on its content comes into even sharper focus.

Managing Difference on Travel Programs

In the face of increasing audience segmentation and rising prices for the production of fictional programming, travel programs are a relatively cheap schedule filler for television networks and are attractive to advertisers.[77] On these programs, gay and cable networks represent institutions of gay and lesbian life and culture in locations around the world. The programs showcase businesses as sites of interest in each locale and reach across platforms to generate multiple revenue streams. Digital technologies facilitate viewer access to plane tickets and hotel accommodations, which provide advertising opportunities and numerous prospects for the networks to partner with other businesses. Thus, gay and lesbian cable programs like *Q on the Move* (2004–2005), *Round Trip Ticket* (2004–2009), and *Bump!* (2004–2013) court audiences with visions of mobility and promises of connectivity that are simultaneously unique to gay and lesbian cable TV and consistent with less identity-bound travel content.

Travel shows animate a tourist gaze in which a collection of images and ideas signify as "out of the ordinary," where people and customs are depicted as "exemplary" yet also "authentic," constructing places and cultures as signs to be consumed by target audiences, both on- and offscreen.[78] The travel shows on gay and lesbian cable employ narrative strategies that attempt to create a sense of community between on-air talent and viewers in the audience. A host's direct address to the camera helps him or her forge a relationship with viewers, as though he or she is a friend sharing a vacation story. Via this intimate mode of address, the programs attempt to make the differences between the world inhabited by viewers at home and the world depicted in the locale on-screen exciting but also harmless; they are meant to be different enough to be interesting, but not different enough to be off-putting. Such a representational paradigm eases the tensions of cultural differences or leaves them unspoken. On the gay and lesbian travel programs, this management of difference results in modes of address that are rooted in feelings of friendship and mutuality. Segments detail leisure and entertainment opportunities that are available to gay and lesbian people in different locations, suggesting to viewers that the kinds of commodity consumption that punctuate each episode will provide them with feelings of agency and belonging.

Round Trip Ticket constructs locales as sites where gay and lesbian audiences might meet others like themselves. Produced specifically for Logo by a content partner, *Round Trip Ticket* showcases national and international travel destinations popular with gay and lesbian travelers: New York City, Paris, San Francisco, and Berlin. Each episode uses interviews and location footage to highlight a different destination, constructing for audiences a guided tour of businesses and gay and lesbian neighborhoods in each locale. Destinations are almost always urban, and episodes include informal interviews with locals who are often introduced as reporters for local gay and lesbian media. Episodes close with a voice-over in which the program host summarizes the segments and lists lodging and restaurant recommendations. Transitions between segments feature kinetic graphics: animated cityscapes that flash across the screen in black, white, and pink, an aesthetic that unites the program's tropes of leisure, mobility, and sexual identity. Hosted by Will Wikle, a white gay man familiar to many viewers after a stint on a network television reality program, *Round Trip Ticket* opens every episode with a tagline that defines the series as "a passport to how LGBT people are living, loving, and changing the world." Using segments hosted by correspondents Kate Monroe, Gabriel Opoku, and Marc Savoia, *Round Trip Ticket* features television "talk" that is constructed as being spontaneous, in which the host makes the viewer privy to certain, special knowledge.[79] The program also uses interviews to draw on interviewees' direct knowledge, positioning the subjects as experts, as though their opinions are facts. [80]

In *Round Trip Ticket*, multiple segments offer a variety of perspectives, constructing a sense of diversity that underlines the program's claims to authenticity. By including a variety of segments, each episode of *Round Trip Ticket* imagines a diverse audience, easing any tensions between those viewers with a mode of address that emphasizes the merits of distinctiveness and stresses the experiences that sexual minorities share. For instance, *Round Trip Ticket*'s Portland, Oregon, episode begins with a reporter interviewing Gina Daggett and Kathy Belge, writers who pen an advice column in the lesbian magazine *Curve*. During the course of the interview, the program transitions from an office space to a sex shop, where Daggett and Belge discuss historical tensions in lesbian communities related to butch/femme sexual practices and liberal feminism—a conversation that takes place amid racks of vibrators and depilatory creams. The interviewees characterize Portland as being open-minded; at one point, an interviewee tells a reporter: "It's whatever you want." Another segment features Jon Schultz, a Portland-area fashion designer and event planner, who touts the city as a good place for same-sex parents because of the many companies in the area that offer domestic partner benefits. A segment on Thomas Lauderdale, a musician and founder of the Portland-based band Pink Martini, details his involvement in political activism using footage from rights marches and protests, as well as from Pink Martini concert appearances. In the interview, Lauderdale talks about his career while sitting in his home office, sharing that his music career grew out of activism related to an antigay referendum that appeared on Oregon ballots in the mid-1990s.

By describing various gay and lesbian milieus across several different segments, *Round Trip Ticket* offers viewers a range of gay and lesbian experiences, creating a sense of inclusiveness. The head of Portland's Gay Pride organization is featured in one of the closing segments, an interview in which the woman discusses her life as an African American lesbian and sadomasochism (S&M) enthusiast. She identifies her status as a racial minority within a sexual minority as causing her feelings of isolation, but claims to have found a sense of belonging among Portland's leather enthusiasts. The visuals accompanying the interview cut between footage of the woman donning fetish gear and footage of her riding a motorcycle. Of her performance of masculinity, she states that "it's not all about the outfit," describing her life experiences as having fostered a civic-mindedness that transcends any subcultural location. The episode's final segment is a short feature on Voodoo Doughnuts, a local bakery that makes specialty doughnuts with toppings like chocolate fudge and Cocoa Puffs. In an interview with an employee, a reporter reveals for viewers that the store sometimes hosts weddings for its gay and lesbian customers.

The episode is indicative of *Round Trip Ticket* as a whole in that its coverage of gay and lesbian politics becomes enmeshed with its cataloging of commodity pleasures. Similarly, *Round Trip Ticket's* Mexico City episode starts with a sequence in which shots depict people engaging in various activities: shopping, walking down streets, eating in restaurants, and riding bicycles. Yet the voice-over is relatively dissonant in that Wikle tells viewers about the prevalence of poverty in the city, and discusses the antigay sentiments that people in the United States often associate with Latin American cultures. But the voice-over concludes cheerfully; Wikle tells viewers that a new generation of gay and lesbian Mexicans is working "to give people a voice" in civic affairs. The program gestures to socio-economic and cultural issues in Mexico City, but reins in that discussion with optimistic sentiments about gay and lesbian life there. This segment cuts directly to a second segment that introduces a young man through voice-over. Footage of "José, an average Mexican citizen" walking down the street is similar to the clips in the opening montage. In the sequences that follow, sound elements cut between correspondent Marc Savoia's voice-over and an interview with José.[81] Visual elements illustrate the pair as they walk down city streets and into stores and cafés. Via voice-over, Savoia reveals that the area is known as La Zona Rosa, a neighborhood that is home to Mexico City's commercial queer district. Throughout the segment, the reporter discusses US perceptions of Mexico, engaging José in a discussion about the Mexican government's efforts to close La Zona Rosa's gay bars during the early 1990s. He also asks José if he has been victimized by the hypermasculinity that many people in the United States associate with Latin American men. José responds: "You just need to be yourself." Similarly, José answers Savoia's query about the city's cultural climate by telling him that growing up gay in Mexico was "so much fun." In this way, the interview constructs the city as featuring liberal sexual mores by diffusing anxieties that the locale might precipitate among white US audiences.

Couched in feelings of open-mindedness and personal agency, *Round Trip Ticket* simultaneously paints international destinations as commodity pleasures to be consumed and assures US audiences that they will feel safe and welcome there. Additional segments in *Round Trip Ticket's* Mexico City episode feature interviews with lesbian restaurateur Ann Uribe, who discusses her high-end catering business, as well as a tour of a lesbian bar called "Pussy." Here, a reporter mingles with patrons and downs tequila shots with a bartender. The segments represent different elements of gay and lesbian life in Mexico City, paying particular attention to the kinds of commodity consumption unique to the location. The episode's final segment includes an interview with DJ Isaac Escalante in Club Living, a dance club that caters to gay men. Over short clips of sleekly designed dance floors, lounge spaces, and state-of-the-art media equipment, Escalante identifies similarities between the club in Mexico City and gay and lesbian venues in US cities.

Yet Escalante suggests a difference between the United States and Mexico, stating that Mexican media outlets need to pay more attention to issues of interest to gay and lesbian people. It is a telling moment insofar as *Round Trip Ticket* suggests that gay and lesbian tourism is, in some sense, civilizing Mexico.[82]

Episodes of *Round Trip Ticket* strain to manage the friction caused by the program's dialectic between the general and the particular, a tension that becomes most visible in episodes where sexual minorities who live beyond US borders are framed for US-located audiences. As a whole, the program seeks to alleviate white anxieties and soothe middle-class sensibilities with a "can-do" individualistic spirit: that Portland's gay and lesbian culture "is whatever you want," that Mexico City's gay and lesbian people need to "be themselves." But when the program offers viewers an inside look at gay and lesbian cultures abroad, *Round Trip Ticket*'s limited vision often casts locations and the people in them as alluring yet alien: places to be observed, exoticized, and consumed.

While similar in tone to Logo's *Round Trip Ticket*, *Bump!* features formal and financial differences that alter the program's mode of address and thus its management of cultural difference. Produced via a partnership between two Canadian companies—Pink Triangle Press, a gay and lesbian media conglomerate, and Peace Point Entertainment Group, a television production company—*Bump!* began airing on the Canadian gay and lesbian television network OUTtv in 2004, and Here began circulating the program in the United States in 2005. While vernacular used by the hosts alludes to the Canadian production of *Bump!*, episodes do not make explicit references to any single culture. In fact, the program was imagined for international distribution, so episodes seem to actively create a certain amount of transparency.[83] In addition to watching *Bump!* on television, viewers can download individual episodes or watch them streaming online, and many are also available for sale on DVDs that are bundled by geography. For instance, *Bump! American Northeast* collects episodes featuring New York, Philadelphia, and Washington, while *Bump! Great Britain* includes episodes that detail London, Manchester, and Brighton. Furthermore, *Bump!* has a mobile application that allows viewers to download information detailed in episodes directly to their cell phones. Available for use on multiple mobile operating systems, "*Bump!* Mobile Guides" provide links that enable users to access local gay and lesbian websites and publications, find hotels and restaurants, and locate sites of specific interest to sexual minority travelers.

Like *Round Trip Ticket*, *Bump!* uses a range of segments to construct a somewhat varied portrait of queer culture in one locale per half-hour episode. But where *Round Trip Ticket* interviews local business owners, *Bump!* segments are more likely to inform viewers where they can find stores that carry products they buy and use at home. *Bump!* also differs from *Round Trip Ticket* in its use of stock footage rather than location shooting, and it uses voice-over narration more heavily as well. *Bump!* does not use as many interviews as *Round Trip Ticket* does, so *Bump!* episodes do not involve multiple correspondents. Rather than *Round Trip Ticket*'s playful banter between hosts and reporters, *Bump!* episodes focus on the host alone. The Madrid episode is similar to other installations of *Bump!* in that the tensions of cultural difference are raised and then soothed by the host's performance. While touring the gay-owned salon Navarro, host Shannon McDonough gets a manicure and has her hair blown out. McDonough emphasizes her poor mastery of Spanish for the purposes of comedy by miming to the stylist exaggeratedly. Following suit, the stylist laughs on realizing that the host wants a hairstyle akin to the one worn by gay and lesbian icon Cher. This moment epitomizes the show's overall tone: language and ethnic disparities disappear in the host's hammy performance. The segment diffuses still more tension when McDonough is brusquely rebuffed after attempting to flirt with the straight female manicurist, an interaction also played for comedy. It closes with the host turning to the camera in order to perform her embarrassment with a funny face for the benefit of the audience, a gesture that invites the audience to witness queer life in Madrid as the host experiences it. As a whole, the segment resolves ethnic difference via sexuality, and then alleviates those tensions by articulating the host's physical attractions as just another part of her comedic performance.

Bump! dispenses with local perspectives almost completely. In the program's Madrid episode, the host walks through a department store and narration cuts between different shots of signage for international fashion brands, including Diesel, Camper, and Adidas. Such iconography is familiar to viewers and suggests the commodity activism seen across all content on gay and lesbian cable, but it lacks the specificity of *Round Trip Ticket*'s emphasis on gay and lesbian businesses. The episode closes with a series of short sequences that depict McDonough drinking and dancing in different bars and nightclubs. The program cuts between shots of the locations, marking transitions with each business's name and website address. This footage includes some interactions with Madrid's residents, but it overwhelmingly focuses on McDonough as she mugs for the camera, drinks shots with bartenders, and dances with go-go boys and shot girls.

Bump! episodes also showcase gay and lesbian events organized by corporate sponsors and local governments. In its episode on the International Gay Rodeo Association's annual convention in Calgary, segments are narrated in voice-over using primarily stock footage, framing the event as a fund-raiser that benefits charitable organizations in the United States and Canada. Like the series as a whole, the episode raises and then eases the tensions associated with cultural difference. For example, the voice-over narration repeatedly references Calgary's reputation for conservatism, a notion that is then complicated by mentions of Canada's gay-friendly legislation and the city's vibrant fetish communities. At one point in the episode, host Charlie David asks an interviewee why cowboys wear tight jeans. The interview takes place at a store where David buys his own pair of jeans before the rodeo. He suggestively raises his eyebrows after the salesclerk surprises him with a spank, a wink-and-nudge performance consistent with the *Bump!* mode of address.

The fate of travel programming over the course of gay and lesbian cable's first decade highlights the medium's shifting political economy and changing technological makeup. During the brief period it was on the air, Q's travel program *Q on the Move* showcased only US destinations and faced difficulties similar to those it experienced in producing news content. In one episode, production staff used their contacts and the program's Burbank studio location for a Los Angeles episode that included interviews with gay and lesbian—and simply "gay-friendly"—celebrities like Melissa Etheridge, Peter Paige, and Kathy Griffin. In an episode devoted to Miami, the director of a local tourism association presented the program's host with the key to the city of Miami Beach, a destination popular among gay and lesbian tourists. Yet *Q on the Move*'s single-platform mode of address and lack of sponsorship ultimately indicate the difficulties experienced by the Q network as a whole. Half-hour travel programs are central elements in content partnerships and multiplatform modes of address on both Logo and (to a lesser extent) Here; these practices decrease production costs and create revenue opportunities.[84] The limitations of Q's business model were such that the network was not able to benefit from these practices.

Even so, much like it is in the instance of news content, delineating the effects of corporate synergy on the different networks' travel programming is more complicated than it appears at first glance. In 2008, Viacom purchased broadcast rights for *Bump!* and, for a time, the program circulated on Logo and Here simultaneously. Logo stopped producing new episodes of *Round Trip Ticket* in 2009. The network continued to air both programs in reruns for several years and, as of 2016, still streamed *Round Trip Ticket* online. *Bump!* halted production in 2013, though episodes continue to stream on Amazon and circulate on DVD. The different trajectories of travel programs across the period in question demonstrate the diverse effects of various business models on the courtship of gay and lesbian audiences by cable TV.

"Conditions and Constraints"

When the gay and lesbian cable TV networks first launched, their press discourses were remarkable for the passion and commitment expressed by the professionals who worked there. In talking about his employment at Here, CEO Paul Colichmann told a reporter: "I'm fighting the gay culture war on the media front."[85] In the 2005 interview, he describes Here's corporate mission as being an emotionally charged, activist one, stating: "I want those kids who are 13 and 14 now . . . to have a cornucopia of images that empower them and allow them to fully embrace their lives."[86] Just a few years later, press discourses on the network feature backlash about these very same commitments. Critical of the company's attempts to consolidate multiple gay and lesbian media outlets, gay and lesbian bloggers and reporters in the gay and lesbian press have become wary of Here's attempts to compete with Logo via conglomeration. By 2009, a blogger had dubbed Colichmann "the whiny queer version of Rupert Murdoch," and a media industry website called Here "a gay media empire to shove back in the closet."[87] In these sentiments lies the fundamental conundrum in representing and courting minorities on cable TV: the processes of media commerce generate and then contour its civic engagement. In other words, Colichmann's various promises and pledges to gay and lesbian audiences on behalf of Here were never obligations that could trump the imperatives of capital.

Cable TV is a circuit of cultural production in which the requirements of the marketplace shape any and every claim to enact progressive politics. In charting the evolution of news content and travel programming over time, this chapter demonstrates how cable TV that courts minority viewers involves a form of commodity activism hemmed in by funding models and delimited by the tensions that characterize cultural difference. As Ann Pellegrini suggests, "there is nothing new about the intimacy of capital and community formation; to the relay capital-identity-community, we might then reply, 'so what?' This is not the end of politics, homosexual, gay, queer, or otherwise, but among its operating conditions and constraints."[88] It is within those "conditions and constraints" that gay and lesbian cable TV can enact its commodity activism, which, while limited and contradictory, has use values for the people who make and consume it.

I have tried in this chapter to consider the networks and their programming with both generosity and clarity in order to lay out the feelings of agency and belonging they create and to demonstrate how they are shaped by different political, economic, and social forces. The trajectory of these two programming genres over gay and lesbian cable TV's first decade indicates some of the limitations of my critique because the same marketplace dynamics that delimit the scope of the medium's commodity activism also threaten it altogether. When the networks launched, their political commitments were most tangible in their news content and travel programming. While this programming was always consumerist in thrust and limited in scope, it still circulates information about identity and desire to sexual minorities in ways that are important and useful. In the decade since the networks launched, marketplace dynamics have pushed the least likely entrant in the niche off the air completely, and also seem to have curtailed the civic functions that cable TV might perform for its audience.

Even though the networks' political commitments are inevitably limited by the marketplace, a progressive-minded criticism might ask more pointed questions than I do here about the structures and policies that regulate that marketplace. It seems that the dynamics of the media marketplace provide scholars with opportunities to advocate for changes that might alter the shape and tone of what limited activism gay and lesbian cable TV can perform. For instance, how might scholars have advocated on behalf of Q? How could scholars lobby networks for more news content or more programming that is produced locally? Because cable TV operates via the logic of the marketplace, intervening in that marketplace's regulation seems a worthy investment of scholarly time and energy. As gay and lesbian cable TV stretches into its second decade, attempting to alter cable TV policy offers the possibility for a meaningful intervention by academics invested in these issues. Commodity activism presents an inescapably limited mode of politics that can only operate within a set of conditions and constraints. This fact raises an important question: what opportunities exist to change them?

Notes

1. Quoted in David Crary, "Democratic Candidates Address Gay Rights," *Washington Post*, August 8, 2007, http://www.washingtonpost.com/wp-dyn/content/article/2007/08/08/AR2007080801509_pf.html.

2. Quoted in Ted McKenna, "Logo Boosts Awareness with Presidential Forum," *PR Week*, July 12, 2007, http://www.prweek.com/article/logo-boosts-awareness-presidential-forum/1256968.

3. Katherine Sender argues that this "business, not politics" ethos structures the gay and lesbian marketing demographic constructed through niche advertising. "By separating business from politics, marketers appeal to a liberal-utilitarian economic model in which financial decisions can be made free of political motivations or ramifications, and where marketers can reach new consumers and generate increased profits independently of any impact this activity might have on social relations or cultural politics." Katherine Sender, *Business Not Politics: The Making of the Gay Market* (New York: Columbia University Press, 2005), 3.

4. This conceptualization is informed by Stuart Hall's famous description of popular culture as involving a "double movement of freedom and containment." Stuart Hall, "Notes on Deconstructing the 'Popular,'" in *Cultural Theory and Popular Culture: A Reader*, ed. John Storey (New York: Pearson/Prentice Hall, 1998): 443

5. Sarah Banet-Weiser identifies consumer citizenship as an audience appeal used by the cable TV network Nickelodeon to court children. It involves a dialectical relationship between difference and assimilation in which programming and online content is imagined to provide an avenue for viewers to enact group membership as well as individual agency. She emphasizes its limitations, calling consumer citizenship a sign "with no political referent or practice." Sarah Banet-Weiser, *Kids Rule! Nickelodeon and Consumer-Citizenship* (Durham, NC: Duke University Press, 2007): 146.

6. Carolyn Bronstein, "Mission Accomplished? Profits and Programming at the Network for Women," *Camera Obscura* 33–34 (1995): 221.

7. Beretta Smith-Shomade, "Narrowcasting in the New World Information Order," *Television and New Media* 5, no. 1 (February 2004): 73.

8. Lisa Parks, "Flexible Microcasting: Gender, Generation, and Television-Internet Convergence," in *Television after TV: Essays on a Medium in Transition*, ed. Lynn Spigel and Jan Olsson (Durham, NC: Duke University Press, 2004): 141.

9. Ben Aslinger, "Creating a Network for Queer Audiences at LOGO TV," *Popular Communication* 7, no. 2 (June 2009): 112.

10. Anthony Freitas, "Gay Programming, Gay Publics: Public and Private Tensions in Lesbian and Gay Cable Channels," in *Cable Visions: Television beyond Broadcasting*, ed. Sarah Banet-Weiser, Cynthia Chris, and Anthony Freitas (New York: New York University Press, 2006), 225–226.

11. Eve Ng, "A 'Post-Gay' Era? Media Gaystreaming, Homonormativity, and the Politics of LGBT Integration," *Communication, Culture and Critique* 6, no. 2 (June 2013): 259.

12. Ibid.

13. For an in-depth discussion of the relationship between television scholarship and social justice, see chapter 4.

14. Sarah Banet-Weiser and Roopali Mukherjee, *Commodity Activism: Cultural Resistance in Neoliberal Times* (New York: New York University Press, 2012), 2.

15. For an analysis of the relationship between television and neoliberalism, see Laurie Ouellette and James Hay, *Better Living through Reality TV: Television and Post Welfare-Citizenship* (Malden, MA: Wiley-Blackwell, 2008).

16. Banet-Weiser and Mukherjee, *Commodity Activism*, 2.

17. Lisa Henderson, *Love and Money: Queers, Class, and Cultural Production* (New York: New York University Press, 2013): 11–13.

18. Lisa Duggan, *The Twilight of Equality: Neoliberalism, Cultural Politics, and the Attack on Democracy* (Boston: Beacon Press, 2004), xi–xii.

19. Alison Hearn "Brand Me 'Activist,' " in *Commodity Activism: Cultural Resistance in Neoliberal Times*, ed. Sarah Banet-Weiser and Roopali Mukherjee (New York: New York University Press, 2012), 23.

20. John Caldwell calls this "multiplexing," where television networks make use of the multiple streams of content enabled by digital technology to make different kinds of engagement available to viewers. John Thornton Caldwell, "Convergence Television: Aggregating Form and Repurposing Content in the Culture of Conglomeration," in *Television after TV: Essays on a Medium in Transition*, ed. Lynn Spigel and Jan Olsson (Durham, NC: Duke University Press, 2003), 41–74.

21. Rodger Streitmatter, *Unspeakable: The Rise of the Gay and Lesbian Press in America* (New York: Faber and Faber, 1995).

22. The signifiers of news programming condense a particular set of meanings that underscore Bellini's pivotal role in Logo's news content. Margaret Morse characterizes television news anchors as "cohesive cultural fictions" where television, as both sign system and ideological apparatus, constructs its "speaking collective subject," condensing the labors of on- and offscreen media workers into a single persona. She identifies the news anchor as representing "not merely the news per se, or a particular network or corporate conglomerate that owns the network, or television as an institution, or the public interest: rather, he represents the complex nexus of all of them." Margaret Morse, "News as Performance: The Image as Event," in *The Television Studies Reader*, ed. Robert C. Allen and Annette Hill (New York: Routledge, 2004), 213.

23. Mimi White, *Tele-Advising: Therapeutic Discourse in Television* (Chapel Hill: University of North Carolina Press, 1992).

24. Andrew Belonsky, "Logo Getting Half-Hour News Show," *Queerty*, last modified November 5, 2007, http://www.queerty.com/logo-getting-12-hour-news-show-20071105.

25. Ibid.

26. Michael Schudson, *The Power of News* (Cambridge, MA: Harvard University Press, 2000), 62.

27. Quoted in "Logo Won't Be the Only Player in Gay Cable Sweepstakes," *Advocate*, last modified May 27, 2004, http://www.advocate.com/news/2004/05/27/logo-won39t-be-only -player-gay-cable-sweepstakes-12568?page=full.

28. Gail Shister, "Gay Channel Sets a February Start Date," *Philadelphia Inquirer*, May 26, 2004.

29. Ken Parish Perkins, "LOGO Strives to Be Must-See Network for Gay America," *Ft. Worth Star-Telegram*, August 4, 2004.

30. Gary Levin, "What's Going on Here!—and on LOGO and Q?" *USA Today*, June 28, 2005, 4D.

31. Quoted in Preston Turegano, "First Gay, Lesbian Network Prepared for Some Backlash," *Courant*, last modified July 26, 2004, http://articles.courant.com/2004-07-26/features /0407260421_1_gay-issues-gay-cops-big-gay.

32. Quoted in Abbey Klaasen, "Viacom Prepares Coming-Out Party for Its Gay-Targeted Cable Network," *Advertising Age*, May 23, 2005, http://adage.com/article/ad-age-china/viacom -prepares-coming-party-gay-targeted-cable-network/103269/.

33. This avoidance of controversy is best described as animating a "post-gay ideology." Julia Himberg elaborates on this concept with regard to its prevalence on cable programming and the frequency with which professionals use it to describe cable television's business models. Because Himberg's research focuses on networks engaging in multicasting, or the courtship of multiple, finely differentiated target demographics, the discursive labor that "post-gay ideology" performs in that context is different than the labor it performs in a milieu in which sexual minorities are a primary demographic. But there is a strong parallel between these otherwise disparate scenarios insofar as both involve media professionals discussing the content used to court sexual minorities on cable television in guarded, careful ways. "On television, this means that sexual orientation does not define the totality of the character or his or her motivations on a show; rather, he or she 'just happens to be gay.' The interviewees framed this 'post-gay' rhetoric as a popular and progressive form of representation, one that accurately reflects people's lived experiences in early-twenty-first century America." Julia Himberg, "Multicasting: Lesbian Programming and the Changing Landscape of Cable TV," *Television and New Media* 15, no. 4 (April 2014): 299.

34. Quoted in "New Networks Seek Gay, Lesbian Audiences," *USA Today*, last modified May 25, 2004, http://usatoday30.usatoday.com/life/television/news/2005-04-13-gay-networks _x.htm.

35. Julia Himberg argues that the multiplexing of old content is a prominent way in which cable networks court tech-savvy minority audiences. This practice exploits the capacities of digital to court audiences across different delivery technologies without the costs that attend the development of new programming. Himberg, "Multicasting," 294.

36. Quoted in "New Networks Seek Gay, Lesbian Audiences," *USA Today*, last modified May 25, 2004, http://usatoday30.usatoday.com/life/television/news/2005-04-13-gay-networks _x.htm.

37. Logo executive quoted in Jack Egan, "Viacom's LOGO Steps Gingerly into the Unknown," *Variety*, April 28, 2005, 1.

38. Ibid.

39. Quoted in David Bauder, "Three New Television Networks Seeking Gay and Lesbian Audiences," *St. Augustine Record*, April 16, 2005, http://staugustine.com/stories/041605/com _3016271.shtml#.V2h6_rgrl2w.

40. "Q Television Network's *On Q Live* to Begin Airing on Monday, November 15th, 2004," *Business Wire*, November 12, 2004, http://www.allbusiness.com/economy-economic-indicators /economic-news/5583368-1.html.

41. "*On Q Live* Is Gay Pride; Q Television Network's Month-Long Pride Celebration Extravaganza," *Business Wire*, June 3, 2005, http://findarticles.com/p/articles/mi_moEIN/is _2005_June_3/ai_n13794638.

42. John Eggerton, "Good Morning Gay America," *Broadcasting and Cable*, January 7, 2005, http://www.broadcastingcable.com/article/155746-Good_Morning_Gay_America.php.

43. "Josh Fountain Anchors Q Television Network's New Nightly News Show *QTN World-cast*," *Red Orbit*, August 22, 2005, http://www.redorbit.com/news/technology/216043/josh _fountain_anchors_q_television_networks_new_nightly_news_show/.

44. Christopher Lisotta, "Champagne Taste Doomed Tiny Net; Gay-Themed Service Couldn't Match Finances with Ambitions," *Television Week*, June 19, 2006, 18.

45. Ibid.

46. Ibid.

47. Ibid.

48. Neil Thurman and Ben Lupton, "Convergence Calls: Multimedia Storytelling at British News Websites," *Convergence: The International Journal of Research into New Media Technologies* 14 (2008): 440–456, 448–450. The interviews conducted by Thurman and Lupton suggest that news outlets are most successful with their attempts at podcasting when content is designed explicitly for a targeted group of users. It would follow that the inexpensive podcasts enable a range of programs for diverse viewerships.

49. "Here! Lines Up First Talker with Gay Host," *Multichannel News*, September 8, 2008, http://www.multichannel.com/news/cable-operators/here-lines-first-talker-gay-host/334633.

50. John Corner, *Critical Ideas in Television Studies* (New York: Oxford University Press, 2000).

51. Quoted in Kellan Melloy, "Gay Cable Channel Here! Brings 'Josh and Sara' to TV," *Edge on the Net*, September 24, 2008, http://www.edgeonthenet.com/entertainment/television /News//80796/gay_cable_channel_here!_brings_'josh_and_sara'_to_tv.

52. Ibid.

53. Jeffrey Jones, *Entertaining Politics: New Political Television and Civic Culture* (Lanham, MD: Rowman and Littlefield, 2004), 9.

54. Quoted in Suzanne C. Ryan, "MTV Launches Digital Gay Network," *Boston Globe*, June 30, 2005, D1.

55. Quoted in Bauder, "Three New Television Networks."

56. Ibid.

57. Quoted in Levin, "What's Going on Here!?" 4D.

58. Carlos Santoscoy, "Logo Cancels Gay-Themed Newscast," *On Top Magazine*, August 15, 2009, http://www.ontopmag.com/article.aspx?id=4384&MediaType=1&Category=26.

59. Ibid.

60. Ibid.

61. Ibid.

62. Ibid.

63. Quoted in David Badash, "Ins and Outs of Gay News Sites: Here Today, Gone Tomorrow?" *Huffington Post*, October 26, 2011, http://www.huffingtonpost.com/david-badash/gay-news-sites_b_1023212.html.

64. *NewNowNext* covered a US district court's overturning of Indiana's gay marriage ban with a feature on text messages exchanged by a couple who celebrated the decision by getting married. Dan Avery, "Read the Super-Adorable Text Message That Led to Indiana's First Gay Marriage," *NewNowNext*, July 3, 2014, http://www.newnownext.com/read-the-super-adorable-text-message-that-led-to-indianas-first-gay-marriage/07/2014/.

65. For instance, the site featured an interview with country music star Dolly Parton, where she discussed her support of gay marriage rights. "Dolly Parton Supports Marriage Equality: "[Gays] Should Suffer Just Like Us Heterosexuals!" *NewNowNext*, April 30, 2014, http://www.newnownext.com/dolly-parton-supports-marriage-equality-gays-should-suffer-just-like-us-heterosexuals/04/2014/.

66. "Frequently Asked Questions," *LogoTV.com*, http://www.logotv.com/about/faq.jhtml#chan.

67. Ibid.

68. Steven E. F. Brown, "PlanetOut Agrees to Sell Magazine Business for $6 Million," *San Francisco Business Times*, April 9, 2008, http://www.bizjournals.com/sanfrancisco/stories/2008/04/07/daily29.html?jst=b_ln_hl.

69. "About the Show," *LogoTV.com*, http://www.logotv.com/trailblazers/about.jhtml.

70. Sunnive Brydum, "The Other Paul Ryan Wants to Take You Inside Hollywood," *Advocate*, September 21, 2012, http://www.advocate.com/arts-entertainment/television/2012/09/21/legends-here.

71. Pierre Bourdieu, *Language and Symbolic Power* (Cambridge, MA: Harvard University Press, 1983), 66, 171.

72. For more background on how content partnerships and cross-promotions operate in the television industry, see Amanda Lotz, *The Television Will Be Revolutionized* (New York: New York University Press, 2007), 8.

73. Mike Taylor, "Here! Freelance Troubles Keep Popping Up," *MediaBistro* (blog), July 16, 2010, http://www.mediabistro.com/fishbowlny/here-media-freelancer-troubles-keep-popping-up_b15633.

74. Andy Towle, "*Out* Magazine Lays Off Entire Editorial Staff; Editor Plans on Hiring Some Back under His Own Employ," *Towleroad* (blog), April 18, 2012, http://www.towleroad.com/2012/04/out-magazine-lays-off-entire-editorial-staff-editor-plans-on-hiring-some-back-under-his-own-employ.html.

75. Christina Hulen, "Gay Media Empire Regent Accused of Running a $90 Million Scam," *Examiner*, February 9, 2011, http://www.examiner.com/article/gay-media-empire-regent-accused-of-running-a-90-million-scam.

76. Alex Blaze, "Why Are Advocate Columnists So Bad?" *Bilerico Project* (blog), February 4, 2011, http://www.bilerico.com/2011/02/why_are_advocate_columnists_so_bad_1.php; "Regent's Paul Colichman Shoves Gay Website under His Porn Umbrella," *Queerty* (blog), June 24, 2009, http://www.queerty.com/regents-paul-colichman-shoves-gay-website-under-his-porn-umbrella-20090624.

77. Elfreide Fursich, "Packaging Culture: The Potential and Limitations of Travel Programs on Global Television," *Communication Quarterly* 50, no. 2 (Spring 2002): 207.

78. John Urry, *The Tourist Gaze, 2nd Edition* (Thousand Oaks, CA: Sage, 2002), 3.

79. Corner, *Critical Ideas*, 44.

80. Ibid., 43.

81. As Ben Aslinger has written of the program: *Round Trip Ticket* maps "cultural geographies of major cities . . . [by] treat[ing] English as the international . . . lingua franca, and allow[ing] English-speaking elites to define local issues." Aslinger, "Creating a Network for Queer Audiences," 118.

82. Jasbir Puar refers to this combination of US exceptionalism and gay pride as "U.S. sexual exceptionalism," charging that a championing of gay and lesbian rights in the United States often hinges on the demarcation and demonization of a racial ethnic "other" elsewhere around the globe. See Jasbir Puar, *Terrorist Assemblages: Homonationalism in Queer Times* (Durham, NC: Duke University, 2007).

83. In addition to the United States and Canada, *Bump!* has been distributed to gay and lesbian television networks in France, Israel, Germany, and the Netherlands. Scott Olson uses the term "transparency" to refer to the aesthetics and narrative paradigms that media companies employ as they try to create content that is widely accessible to differently located audiences. Charles Acland refers to such aesthetics and narrative paradigms as "degree zero style," characterizing the belief that some aesthetics and narrative paradigms are more suitable for global audiences as a construction of industry discourse and not necessarily a preference among differently located viewers. Scott Olson, *Hollywood Planet: Global Media and the Competitive Advantage of Narrative Transparency* (New York: Routledge, 1999); Charles Acland, *Screen Traffic: Movies, Multiplexes, and Global Culture* (Durham, NC: Duke University Press, 2003).

84. In 2002 and 2003, the travel portal Orbitz announced, in quick succession, a gay and lesbian–themed advertising campaign, the creation of a microsite devoted to serving gay and lesbian travelers, as well as a content partnership with various gay and lesbian media companies.

85. Quoted in "Diverse Voices: Gay Programming Is about More than Sex," *TV Week*, May 4, 2008, http://www.tvweek.com/news/2008/05/diverse_voices_gay_programming.php.

86. Ibid.

87. "All of Gay Media Are Belong to Paul Colichman," *Queerty* (blog), January 9, 2009, http://www.queerty.com/all-of-gay-media-are-belong-to-paul-colichman-20090109; Owen Thomas, "A Gay Media Empire to Shove in the Closet," *Gawker*, January 12, 2009, http://gawker.com/5129853/a-gay-media-empire-to-shove-in-the-closet.

88. Ann Pellegrini, "Consuming Lifestyle: Commodity Capitalism and Transformations in Gay Identity," in *Queer Globalizations*, ed. Arnaldo Cruz-Malave and Martin F. Manalansan IV (New York: New York University Press, 2003), 141.

4 Toward a Queerer Criticism of Television

B<small>Y THE TIME</small> I heard about the sitcom *Normal, Ohio* (Fox, 2000), it had been canceled. Only twelve episodes of the half-hour program were created, but fewer than that ever aired. Audiences could only see the series in its entirety after its streaming rights were licensed to Hulu more than a decade after it was first released. Debuting on network television in the fall of 2000, *Normal, Ohio* narrates the experiences of a man who comes out of the closet, leaves his wife and son, and begins a new life in another city. In the series premiere, the character returns to his hometown to repair the tense relationships he has with his family. *Normal, Ohio* is one of four network TV sitcoms that debuted between 2000 and 2003, were built around a gay or lesbian main character, panned on both style and ideological grounds, and then were canceled shortly thereafter. All signs point to *Normal, Ohio* as well as *The Ellen Show* (CBS, 2001–2002), *Some of My Best Friends* (CBS, 2001), and *It's All Relative* (ABC, 2003–2004) as having "failed"—financially, aesthetically, and politically. Without reclaiming or disdaining the programs, this chapter argues for another understanding of them, one rooted in their affective value.[1] I define *affective value* as the identification that television enables for audiences; in this chapter, I focus specifically on the affective value of television for sexual minorities. At the same time, I demonstrate how such an understanding of television can be obfuscated by ideas about "failure" that circulate in industry settings, trade journals, and the popular press, as well as in media scholarship.

Television's affective value, its potential to engender identification among audiences, differs from other kinds of value attributed to the medium. In industry settings where decisions about programming and distribution are made, value gets coded in financial terms. The duration of a program's production and the methods of its distribution are the result of demands related to generating revenue, and are reached via cost-benefit analyses. Aesthetic judgments also code value. In this context, a program's worth is determined by way of opinion, where some assessments hold more sway than others. When critics and scholars evaluate television programming ideologically, they determine value on political grounds. Here, some texts are deemed "more" or "less" progressive based on ideas about what constitutes "good" or "bad" politics. Television's affective value differs from each of these determinations. This conflict is seen most clearly when programs that viewers identify with get canceled, or when critical opinions clash with popular tastes, as well as when viewers find pleasure in representations that scholars find to be politically problematic. Even as the chapter takes seriously how other value codings operate, it works against reifying the terms by which such determinations are made. Ideas about television's financial, aesthetic, or political "failure" do not always, or even usually relate to the medium's affective value. In fact, such value determinations can cloud a nuanced understanding of how television operates and can prevent a thorough comprehension of the medium's worth for minority audiences.

Television enables audience identification not *in addition to*, but *as part of* its role as a commercial medium. It seems that the conventional way of understanding the difference between minority experiences with television and those of more "mainstream audiences" is to posit a difference in the *identifications*. In contrast, I would suggest that the identifications themselves may actually be similar. Rather, a way of understanding the difference is through attention to identification's *affective* register. The body and flesh may provide a useful site for thinking through the unique experiences that minorities have with media culture.[2] This chapter first examines how television fosters identification among sexual minorities as part of its structural function in capitalism. Using close readings of *Normal, Ohio*, *The Ellen Show*, *Some of My Best Friends*, and *It's All Relative*, the first section also historicizes and contextualizes that process in one prominent network television representational paradigm.[3] The second section examines promotions for the four sitcoms alongside their coverage in trade publications and the popular press to interrogate how value determinations take place in various discourses on television.[4] In doing so, the chapter questions how television is evaluated, where the medium's worth is determined discursively in terms of finances, aesthetics, and politics.

Commonsense ideas about value, especially when television programs are deemed "failures," hinder an understanding of the identification that the medium makes available to sexual minorities. Because affective value has a complicated relationship with more conventional ways of evaluating television, the chapter questions instances when links between financial, aesthetic, and/or political value seem natural. The final section problematizes the relationship between different discourses on television, arguing in favor of television scholarship that troubles connections between the medium, capital, and power. Such a gesture would shift focus away from analysis of television's representations, resulting in scholarship more consistent in its quest for social justice by more self-consciously disconnecting the medium from the processes of capital accumulation that characterize it.[5]

Identification with the Medium

Television encourages identification among audiences, including sexual minorities, in order to circulate capital. A thorough understanding of how this process takes place requires attention to how television functions as a *form*, a medium that operates in service of capital. This process is made manifest in television *content*, programming that courts particular audiences in specific contexts. Broadly speaking, television is a circuit of use and exchange in which users find pleasure in programs that they pay for, sometimes literally (cable connections, subscriptions, downloads), and/or through the attention economy of advertising (commercials, sponsorships, branded content). Theodor Adorno expands this definition by characterizing the medium as smoothing the processes of capitalism. He sees it softening the experience of subjects who labor in the name of capital, blunting the possibility that they might unite in order to alter capitalism's dynamics of power.[6] Amy Villarejo builds on Adorno's definition, stating: "Television's structural function . . . is to promote accommodation to the effects of capitalist subsumption, alienation, and humiliation."[7] As Villarejo highlights, Adorno sees this practice taking place via "pseudorealism,"[8] a logic in which television does not differentiate "between actually repressive social conditions and psychological conformity to them."[9] In pseudorealism, Villarejo identifies a refusal of the boundary between what is real and what is imaginary, casting the audience's identification with television as an identification that takes place with the medium itself.[10] Here, audiences incorporate from television either "an identification with an ego ideal . . . [or] a lesson or punishment following an improper identification."[11] If Villarejo's understanding of pseudorealism defines it as a psychic process, identification has distinctly affective components. To identify with television is to experience feelings of validation, as well as flushes of recognition, bursts of laughter, and surges of tears.[12] Those feelings may vary among differently positioned viewers, even if the identifications are similar.

Television's affective value can be located in its ability to affect its audience; it is a potentiality inherent in the medium that is not influenced by program cancellation or reviewers' critiques in any straightforward way. The experiences viewers have with television can be meaningful to them and are not just evidence of their subordination.[13] But understanding television as a site of identification is to appreciate that the medium functions by the logic of capital, and is part of a larger ensemble of labor and power that animates social hierarchies. Villarejo applies this understanding of television to different historical moments and kinds of programming, casting the medium's representations as functions of the medium itself. She sees television's representations hinging on widely circulating beliefs about identities, desires, and bodies precisely because they offer convenient shorthand that is legible to many different people. Representations of sexual minorities are understood, often negatively, as "stereotypes" wherein television's sign system relies on "abstractions and typology and Manichean divisions and timeless generalizations."[14] For Villarejo, the stereotype is a temporal object in which television conveys information to audiences in units of time: particular scenes, individual episodes, or an entire series.[15] She troubles a liberal progress narrative that casts representations of sexual minorities as improving over television's history by pointing out that the medium always relies on generally understandable images and narratives. According to Villarejo, television's representations of sexual minorities have not "improved" over the medium's history per se, but they did get longer: moving from gestures and moments to characters with histories.[16] These representations may then precipitate varied affective responses among viewers: smirks, laughter, sneers, and so on.

Following Villarejo's notion of the stereotype, I see *Normal, Ohio*, *The Ellen Show*, *Some of My Best Friends*, and *It's All Relative* employing broadly intelligible shorthand in their representations of sexual minorities. They offer evidence of a historically specific trope used to court a specific target audience, of which sexual minorities are a part. On network television in the 1990s, Ron Becker suggests that the broadcast networks frequently courted an audience comprised of socially liberal, urban-minded professionals with programming that demonstrated a distinctly upscale sensibility.[17] He identifies a surfeit of gay and lesbian representations in these programs, where appeals to affluent viewers yoke homosexuality to "good" consumer taste.[18] And because taste can only operate in relief, these representations require a counterpoint, so programs designed to court affluent viewers frequently feature narratives in which viewers are encouraged to disidentify with "bad" consumer taste and, often, close-mindedness about homosexuality. Network television has long courted audiences with taste-stratified appeals, and ongoing changes in how the medium creates and circulates content in the context of digital production and distribution continue to make such class-inflected audience appeals a prominent component of the medium's programming.[19]

The representations of gays and lesbians on *Normal, Ohio*, *The Ellen Show*, *It's All Relative*, and *Some of My Best Friends* are consistent with those that Becker analyzes. They code characters as being gay or lesbian through trenchant associations made in US culture about the relationship between homosexuality and commodity consumption, where same-sex desire is made legible in characters' consumer preferences. Villarejo's understanding of television form highlights how the medium encourages identification as part of its structural function in capitalism. By relating this formulation to Becker's analysis of 1990s-era broadcasting, the identification that sexual minorities make with television can be located in a specific context (network television) in a particular historical moment (the start of the twenty-first century). Becker emphasizes that 1990s-era network television producers and executives did not necessarily imagine a gay and lesbian viewership for such programming.[20] But considering them in light of Villarejo's elaboration of the television apparatus opens up the representations to a different understanding. Here, the representations make available to sexual minorities an identification with television that registers psychically, socially, and/or corporeally.[21]

Normal, Ohio, The Ellen Show, It's All Relative, and *Some of My Best Friends* are sitcoms that use the mise-en-scène of the home and workplace as a vehicle for comedic situations, narrating the interactions that gay and lesbian characters have with their families, friends, and coworkers.[22] The programs make conflicts between gay and straight characters primary narrative problems by playing with the relationship between sexual identity and consumer taste. Each of the sitcoms creates binary oppositions between gay and straight characters by pitting highbrow versus lowbrow cultural tastes, tasteful versus tacky aesthetic sensibilities, and progressive versus conservative political viewpoints. Sometimes the programs use these differentiations to position one identification over and above others, though sometimes the programs place different identifications on equal footing. In both cases, the programs suggest the specifics of network television's business model, which requires the courtship of relatively diverse viewers. At the same time, the representations provide an avenue for sexual minorities to identify with television.

Consistent with the formula of the sitcom, *Normal, Ohio* centers on the relationships that the protagonist has with his family. The main character, "Butch Gamble," is a father in his forties who deserts his family and moves away after coming out of the closet. The series begins when he returns to his hometown, narrating the character's life as he picks up where he left off. While network television's gay male characters are frequently thin, stylish, and effeminate, Butch is the opposite: he is tall and overweight, with a booming voice and hulking presence.[23] Familiar to many different viewers for his role as a hypermasculine father on the long-running sitcom *Roseanne* (ABC, 1988–1997), John Goodman's casting on *Normal, Ohio* also contains some queer in-group humor. The actor embodies the stereotype of the gay male bear, a subcultural identity rooted in body hair and a thick physique.[24] While the program only makes veiled references to Goodman's "bearishness," the actor's physicality makes his *Normal, Ohio* character a marked contrast with other representations of gay men on television.[25] Throughout the series, Butch's conflict with his conservative father is a main narrative tension. Butch's father, Bill, is reminiscent of the cranky, cantankerous character Archie Bunker on the 1970s-era sitcom *All in the Family* (CBS, 1971–1979): both give voice to conservative, often close-minded points of view, and clash with their more progressive children. In *Normal, Ohio,* familial conflicts often devolve to the point of name-calling. In one episode, Bill calls his son "the fruit basket" and, in another, he asks Butch when he "went fluffy." Like all sitcoms, the program eases tensions raised by the homophobic dialogue when Butch matches wits with his father through barbs of his own. In one episode, Butch responds to an insult by shouting, "I'm the best damn showgirl this town has ever seen," delivering the line with a feminine yelp and a flamboyant jump. Goodman's physicality and performance are primary sources of *Normal, Ohio*'s comedy; the program's laugh track amplifies each time the character minces about in order to goad his father.

While *Normal, Ohio* diffuses tensions with humor, the point of identification and lessons about improper identification are made plain in every episode. In keeping with the sitcom's generic conventions, dramatic action often unfolds in the home, where the mise-en-scène underlines how the program connects consumer taste to sexuality. Sets on *Normal, Ohio* feature decor rich in working-class connotations: the living room features mismatched pillows and curtains; clashing wallpaper patterns; fake flowers; and tacky, store-bought art. The kitchen features drab, dilapidated appliances and walls that fade from mustard yellow to sickly gray. The program casts its gay character as an outsider in this setting; episodes draw on cultural associations about homosexuality and upscale commodity preferences. In one episode, Butch has his BMW convertible shipped from Los Angeles to Ohio. On seeing it in the driveway, Bill taunts his son by asking, "What, American cars aren't good enough for you?" and calling him "a tutti-frutti." Later in the episode, Bill develops a fascination with the convertible. Despite his more conventionally masculine taste preferences, Bill experiences a youthful thrill when he drives the BMW. In conflating taste preferences with sexual identity, the episode fosters viewer identification with "good" consumer taste and offers a lesson about proper modes of consumer desire. After all, even Bill likes to drive the BMW.

Like *Normal, Ohio, The Ellen Show* features a lesbian character who moves away from her hometown; it focuses on her relationships with her family members and coworkers after she moves back. Starring comedian Ellen DeGeneres, *The Ellen Show* uses an ironic mode of address to augment the incongruities between the fashionable protagonist and her outdated relatives and coworkers. Supporting characters are quirky and omnipresent; the protagonist cannot escape them. Episodes are routinely interrupted by mundane activities, like the mailman delivering a package or neighbors watering shrubbery. Such plot points set up Ellen's deadpan reactions as she cracks jokes about her unrelentingly friendly community. In the series premiere, Ellen and her mother stand in the protagonist's childhood bedroom. Ellen points to a wall adorned with posters of Billie Jean King and Farrah Fawcett—one a lesbian icon, the other an infamous object of 1970s adolescent heterosexual male fantasy. The character then turns to her mother and asks, "Really, Mom? You had no idea?" Accompanied by a great swell in the laugh track, the scene invites identification with the protagonist in a scene that contains the character's same-sex desire by rendering it as a stereotypical choice in decor. The scene fosters identification with Ellen by characterizing her mother as being simpleminded.

Another example of how the program encourages identification with the lesbian protagonist over and above the heterosexual characters is a recurring conflict she has with a coworker in the high school where she works: the home economics teacher. An older, stereotypically heterosexual female character, the home economics teacher is fond of baking and is routinely outfitted in floral skirts and pastel sweater sets. Ellen's more fashionable costuming and friendlier interactions with characters in their workplace are set against the teacher's dowdy wardrobe and uptight personality. As a result, audience sympathies are supposed to align with the lesbian protagonist and not the heterosexual character, a configuration in which consumer taste and sexual identity become one and the same. *The Ellen Show* uses the protagonist's relationship with another supporting character for similar ends, playing with a well-established stereotype of female gym teachers. In one of the program's recurring plots, the high school's female gym teacher pursues Ellen romantically. Both characters are lesbians, but the narrative encourages identification with the protagonist by way of taste. The gym teacher's aggression is emphasized in her wardrobe and performance: she wears tracksuits and a whistle, and she speaks in a deep, loud voice. In contrast, Ellen is outfitted in tailored suits and designer jeans, and is more conventionally feminine in her demeanor. If the recurring plot's references to butch-femme couples and the perils of lesbian dating offer some in-group humor for sexual minorities, the stereotype of the female gym teacher is widely legible to a heterogeneous audience.

Thus, *Normal, Ohio* and *The Ellen Show* invite identification with protagonists by making strong connections between homosexuality and consumer taste. Both programs augment these binaries through references to cultural geography. As Victoria Johnson has argued, television often imagines the Midwest as a "square" locale that is resistant to change and innovation. When programs are set there, they frequently represent a stronghold of old-fashioned tastes and conservative worldviews. In discussing midwestern-set sitcoms, Johnson states that gay and lesbian characters are "portrayed as a common-sense orientation to good taste, against which déclassé midwesternness serves as comic foil."[26] This opposition between the quaint setting and the main character's urban sensibility is made plain throughout *The Ellen Show*. In the second episode of the series, the protagonist considers her options after the failure of her internet business in Los Angeles. In one scene, Ellen relaxes at a park in her hometown, but she eventually gets bored. So she decides to read a book. Very quickly, she grows tired of reading, as well. By the conclusion of the scene, Ellen has become so bored that she is in dialogue with the voice-over narration. In this conversation with herself—she is the voice-over narrator, as well—the character worries that she may be too restless for life in the leisurely Midwest.[27]

On *The Ellen Show*, the main character's incongruity with her environs is a primary comedic tension, which the program uses to encourage viewer sympathy with the cosmopolitan, out-of-place lesbian. In one episode, Ellen discovers that the town's coffee is much weaker than the coffee she is used to drinking. The episode uses coffee as a metaphor for the town itself; the character wanders around looking for a cup that will satisfy her. She tries coffee at her mother's house, her office, and her sister's workplace, but does not find coffee that she considers suitable. The episode ultimately resolves the problem when Ellen sneaks into a church where the coffee is strong enough to soothe the alcohol cravings of the attendees at a weekly Alcoholics Anonymous meeting. Diffused with humor, such tensions further align viewer sympathies with the lesbian character. *It's All Relative* and *Some of My Best Friends* also play with the signifiers of urban/rural geographic binaries, using their settings in New York's outer boroughs and Boston's South Side to augment taste-based, homo/hetero divides. Like *Normal, Ohio* and *The Ellen Show*, the programs differentiate between gay and straight characters in class-inflected ways, rendering homosexuality by way of the upscale representational paradigm Becker identifies in 1990s network television.

In *It's All Relative* and *Some of My Best Friends*, gay and lesbian identities become legible through characters' chic tastes, in direct opposition to straight characters. The engagement of a young Harvard coed, Liz, and a bartender from south Boston, Bobby O'Neil, provides the comedic tension in *It's All Relative*. An affluent gay male couple raised Liz, while a working-class heterosexual couple raised Bobby. Like *Normal, Ohio*, *It's All Relative* offers differing viewpoints on sexual minorities by showcasing a conservative character with working-class tastes. Bobby's father, Mace O'Neil, has much in common with the protagonist's father on *Normal, Ohio*. Mace often lobs insults at his son's gay in-laws, Simon and Philip, and frequently shares his acerbic, close-minded political views. Thus, episodes of *It's All Relative* foreground conflicts between the in-laws and then alleviate tensions with humor. The program always makes the gay couple sympathetic, but it provides even more compelling evidence of how network television makes gay and lesbian characters potentially pleasurable for diverse viewerships. In one episode, both sets of in-laws support the same local political candidate. But Simon and Philip laud the candidate's support of gay marriage, while the O'Neils find that position offensive. Instead, the O'Neils cheer the politician's assistance to local businesses, like the neighborhood bar they own in working-class south Boston. The episode soothes the contradictions of the couples' divergent politics by focusing on the dishonest, wacky politician. The couples catch him lying about his arrest record and, in the end, witness him killing swans in a local park. The episode thus displaces tensions in favor of a broad joke about the corruption and ineptitude of politicians. Like all television sitcoms, the program diffuses the very tensions it creates. Like *It's All Relative* as a whole, the episode does not warn against identification with the working-class conservative characters. Instead, it softens their homophobia with a narrative that simply warns about the dangers of intractable opinions.

More often than not, the program creates sympathy for Liz and Bobby by warning viewers about the dangers of allowing ideological conflicts to threaten parent-child bonds. *It's All Relative* animates a homo/hetero binary via narrative conflicts that are rendered as parent/child tensions. The program uses these tensions to encourage alignment with both gay and homophobic characters. In another episode, the in-laws fight about plans for Liz and Bobby's engagement party. The young couple becomes so upset with their parents that they sneak out of town for a weekend ski trip to get away from them. But when the O'Neils worry that Liz and Bobby might elope, the in-laws unite to spy on the couple during their romantic getaway. The episode concludes when both sets of in-laws have to be rescued from a snowbound car, and end up sleeping at the inn with Liz and Bobby. At the conclusion of the episode, both couples are relieved to learn that Liz and Bobby have not eloped. *It's All Relative* puts its gay and homophobic characters on equal footing when both sets of in-laws promise to get along better going forward.

Some of My Best Friends is similar to *It's All Relative* in that it equates close-mindedness about homosexuality with bad consumer taste through its representations of upscale gay characters. The program's episodes also paint the sides of this binary as being equivalent rather than cast one or the other as a better or worse identification. Based on the movie *Kiss Me, Guido* (1997), *Some of My Best Friends* centers on disagreements between roommates: Warren, an urbane gay professional, and Frankie, an aspiring actor from a working-class Italian family. As in the other sitcoms, representations of sexual minorities in *Some of My Best Friends* focus on consumer preferences as they differentiate gay and straight characters. In one episode, Frankie invites a group of friends to the apartment he shares with Warren so they can watch a boxing match on television. With thick accents and loud voices, Frankie's friends kid and joke with one another about placing bets and losing money. In their speech and demeanor, the characters function as stereotypes of working-class New York men. This characterization complements a narrative in which Warren's friend Vern visits while the other characters watch the boxing match. Vern is extroverted and animated, a gay male character whose femininity is emphasized by his tight-fitting, pastel-colored wardrobe. At first, Frankie's friends insult and laugh at Vern's queeniness. But when the television breaks, they end up convincing Vern to help them fix it. The episode concludes with the revelation that he could not help them fix anything; Vern pretends he could fix the television because he wants to embarrass Frankie's friends after they insult him. If the episode begins to trouble naturalized connections between masculine gender performance and specialized technical knowledge, the narrative does not follow it through to its expected conclusion. As a result, the episode accommodates, even welcomes, conservative viewpoints on homosexuality that are stereotyped through representations that signify sexual identity via consumer taste. *It's All Relative* and *Some of My Best Friends* cultivate sympathy for gay characters in ways that are similar to *Normal, Ohio* and *The Ellen Show*, but often place that sympathy on equal footing with the one they enable with close-minded characters.

Another similarity between *It's All Relative* and *Some of My Best Friends* is the manner in which they attach homosexuality to whiteness in differentiating between consumer tastes. Scenes from *It's All Relative* cut between different settings: from Simon and Philip's well-decorated house to the O'Neils' crowded bar. Episodes often feature the O'Neils marveling at Simon and Philip's well-stocked cupboard and bevy of high-end kitchen appliances. At the same time, Simon and Philip frequently complain about the dirt and grime of the O'Neils' pub. These narrative elements link the gay couple to upscale consumer taste by associating the Irish family with working-class commodity preferences. While the narratives do not necessarily cast the O'Neils as "other," the program uses widely legible stereotypes about Irishness to make the working-class family "less white" than their gay in-laws.[28]

Similarly, many episodes of *Some of My Best Friends* narrate Frankie's working-class consumer preferences with racial and ethnic connotations. In one episode, Frankie tries to alter his appearance by replacing his undershirt and track pants with a designer suit. A male character dressed in a white tank top is a representation that is rich with significations. Such articles of clothing are frequently called "wife beaters," highlighting how popular vernacular connects them to hyper-, even abusive, masculinity. At the same time, white tank tops have class and ethnic connotations, where entrenched cultural associations connect them to the working class and Italian Americans.[29] When Frankie spends too much money trying to change his appearance, he has to return the merchandise. Frankie's wardrobe update is a class aspiration, an upscale commodity choice that the character cannot afford. If the episode does not necessarily paint this turn of events negatively—the narrative suggests that wearing the suit would ultimately make Frankie uncomfortable—it underlines its working-class characterization with racial and ethnic connotations. Frankie's choice of the white tank undershirt and track pants renders him "less white" than his upscale gay roommate. Thus, both *It's All Relative* and *Some of My Best Friends* mobilize hierarchies related to racial and ethnic differences—an Irish pub, an Italian man wearing a tank undershirt—to encourage viewer identification with various characters. The result is a representational regime that animates a binary in which some characters are "whiter" than other characters as a result of their upscale commodity preferences.[30] By inviting audience identification with various characters, *It's All Relative* and *Some of My Best Friends* link ethnic difference to the working class in order to associate homosexuality with upscale whiteness.

Critics both inside and outside the academy frequently criticize how television renders gays and lesbians normatively in the service of courting straight audiences.[31] As my readings of *Normal, Ohio, The Ellen Show, Some of My Best Friends*, and *It's All Relative* demonstrate, the programs are, if nothing else, highly normative. But that is precisely the nature of the identification that television provides to all of its audiences and is the genesis of the medium's affective value. In that sense, seeing the programs' normativity as evidence of "failure" misconstrues how television operates, maybe especially for sexual minority viewers. As Lauren Berlant argues, a fantasy of normativity is "a felt condition of general belonging and an aspirational site of rest and recognition in and by a social world."[32] For minority audiences, that sort of fantasy can be deeply meaningful. The programs offer evidence of how gay and lesbian representations operate like television does, more generally. These particular sitcoms make sexual identity legible by way of taste, demonstrating television's consumerist thrust and its structural function as a medium. Television can only enable identification within the parameters of its business models, and the business model of network television requires that representations be broadly legible and palatable. If programs that include gays and lesbians foster identification among sexual minority audiences, they also enable identification for viewers hostile to them—hence the development of a stereotype in a particular historical moment that equates sexual identity with consumer taste.[33] This claim is not a defense of the medium nor is it an equivocation about the nature of these four programs. Rather, it is an attempt to establish that all television encourages viewer identification. It is also an effort to demonstrate that the medium's function is made manifest in its content, which does not discriminate against viewers in any uniform way. In these four programs, that process takes place by way of a particular stereotype that offers sexual minority viewers a fantasy of "the good life."

"Failure"

Like *Normal, Ohio, The Ellen Show, Some of My Best Friends*, and *It's All Relative*, the sitcom *Will and Grace* (NBC, 1998–2006) is an extension of the trope that Becker identifies in 1990s-era network television programs, in which "including a gay neighbor, a lesbian sister, or some queer plot twist was not only possible but also lucrative for those networks and producers anxious to differentiate their product in a saturated marketplace."[34] Debuting in 1998, *Will & Grace* featured a mix of upscale gay and straight characters, earned a bevy of critical acclaim, and garnered high Nielsen ratings. *Normal, Ohio, The Ellen Show, Some of My Best Friends*, and *It's All Relative* were imagined by rival networks as marketplace competitors to *Will & Grace*; they debuted after the popular program had been on the air for several seasons. Such a glut, where nearly identical programs premiered in a brief (three-year) period across several competing networks, indicates what John Thornton Caldwell calls the "redundancy and stylistic inertia" of network television in the twenty-first century.[35] Caldwell identifies similarities in programming as one of the primary results of network television's competitive marketplace, where broadcast companies attempt to take one another's audiences amid a limited and shrinking pool of viewers.

None of the four programs discussed here won awards like *Will & Grace*, and none of them had high Nielsen ratings. Moreover, critics maligned them. Even so, a narrative in which *Will & Grace* "succeeds" and *Normal, Ohio*, *The Ellen Show*, *Some of My Best Friends*, and *It's All Relative* "fail" requires some complication. In promotions for the four sitcoms, writers, producers, and executives try to associate the programs with *Will & Grace*. At the same time, promotions attempt to *dis*sociate the programs from *Ellen* (ABC, 1994–1998), another similar sitcom from the same period. In 1997, *Ellen* featured a coming-out episode for its main character as part of a carefully managed, well-publicized media event.[36] In the season that followed, the program featured the female protagonist's relationship with her girlfriend as a regular element of episodes. After that season, it was canceled. Anna McCarthy uses this timeline to argue that network television's representational regime struggles to make sexual minorities recurring elements of programs. Yet McCarthy warns against casting *Ellen* as a "failure," warning: "a 'success-versus-failure' model of gay television obscures more than it reveals."[37] I follow her lead in favor of using *Normal, Ohio*, *The Ellen Show*, *Some of My Best Friends*, and *It's All Relative* to examine the "possibilities . . . and constraints . . . that exist in popular culture and its commercial institutions."[38]

Casting the programs as unproblematic evidence of "failure" performs a retrospective determinism that conflates the different ways television's worth is determined, and it prevents consideration of how those ideas about value shape the production, distribution, and reception of the medium, as well as its criticism both inside and outside the academy. Bracketing such determinations and contextualizing the four sitcoms in their production and reception milieus highlights the discursive struggles involved in network television's representation of sexual minorities. I see careful constructions of meaning in the sitcoms' promotions as industry professionals attempt to frame the programs' representations of homosexuality for diverse audiences. As a result, the marketing efforts are cagey; actors, writers, producers, and network executives attempt to paint the programs as being just like other network television content and thus amenable to the courtship of diverse audiences.

Parsing out how promotions frame the four sitcoms as "normal" and not "edgy" is crucial to understanding how network television operates. In one interview, a writer for *Normal, Ohio* characterizes the program as featuring a gay man who is "not flamboyantly gay. . . . He's a normal man in a normal family, and being gay is not the subject, it's the subtext."[39] The characterization of Butch Gamble's sexual identity as a relatively minor element of a larger, layered depiction of family dynamics on *Normal, Ohio* appears in several different promotional interviews for the program. Producers and writers emphasize that the program focuses on other aspects of the character's life.[40] One writer outlines a story arc in which the protagonist's ex-boyfriend visits, in order to suggest that *Normal, Ohio* represents a gay man but does not underline his homosexuality.[41] The writer stresses that while the story arc foregrounds intimacy between gay characters, "there are ways to access (intimacy) without going to two men kissing."[42] Such rhetorical maneuvering illustrates how *Normal, Ohio*'s writers and producers attempt to characterize the program's representation of sexual minorities as being inoffensive.

The Ellen Show was also publicized carefully. In interviews, the program's star actively distances the program from her 1990s-era sitcom *Ellen*. After the much-ballyhooed, carefully managed coming-out in *Ellen*'s last season, many critics and reviewers charge that the program alienated viewers by becoming "too gay," identifying certain episodes as perhaps being too strident in tone for network television audiences.[43] While it is difficult to draw a causal link between the content of episodes in *Ellen*'s last season and the program's cancellation in 1998, that link is an oft-repeated element in press discourses. In an interview that took place a few years after *Ellen*'s cancellation, DeGeneres carefully differentiates *The Ellen Show* from its predecessor: "I learned that it's really hard to do a sitcom and do very important political issues. . . . [But I] don't think people want to see that. I think people want to sit at home and turn on their TV and just laugh. That's all they want to do, and I understand that now."[44] DeGeneres also downplays *The Ellen Show*'s representation of homosexuality in discussing the program's setting, calling it "a fantasy town that I wish existed. . . . Everybody kind of congratulates her for [being a lesbian]. Nobody is shocked by it."[45] As with *Normal, Ohio*, promotions for *The Ellen Show* emphasize that the protagonist is uninterested in same-sex romance. DeGeneres tells a reporter: "I . . . think we can make the show very funny without worrying about the dating stuff for a while. . . . It's all about funny this time."[46] In interviews, writers and executives also minimize *It's All Relative*'s representation of sexual identity, talking more about the program's homophobic character than they do about the gay characters. They identify homophobia as a programming strategy, casting the sitcom's inclusion of an intolerant character as an "essential tactic" in putting the program together.[47] At the same time, they minimize the program's potential to precipitate controversy, telling the reporter: "It's important for the show to focus on being funny and avoid a political agenda."[48] Thus, the programs' promotional discourses feature a certain evasiveness that becomes most evident when industry professionals cast the programs as "gay," but not "too gay."

In interviews with press outlets, writers, producers, and executives attempt to define the programs as featuring representations of sexual minorities that are comprehensible and accessible to a heterogeneous viewership. As is the very nature of broadcasting, the promotions are evidence of network television's ambiguity about sexual minorities. Programs are formalized attempts to generate revenue. The sitcom in particular has been a mainstay of television for decades because it facilitates the courtship of viewers via a vastly recognizable form: the nuclear family.[49] Press discourses on network television during this period emphasized the proliferation of "multigenerational sitcoms" on network schedules, identifying them as programming imagined to court age-diverse audiences.[50] Yet the sitcom form, a staple of television schedules for decades, was also a topic of considerable debate when these programs debuted. Scores of articles cast the genre as being in a state of decline, framing the cancellations and declining ratings of several 1990s-era sitcoms as evidence of a medium-wide crisis.[51] Reviewing a spate of sitcoms that debuted in the early 2000s, one reporter states that "despite dozens of attempts, the networks have failed to come up with a new hit comedy since the late 1990's."[52] Referring to *I Love Lucy* (CBS, 1951–1957), a beloved sitcom in television history, one reporter states that the broadcast networks "wouldn't know a funny sitcom if Lucille Ball came back from the grave and handed it to them."[53] Another writer asserts: "If you've spent any considerable time watching sitcoms recently, I'm sure you'll agree that the old girl most certainly deserves a nap."[54] In essence, journalists and critics argued that new iterations of network sitcoms were "not as good" as those that had circulated at other points in television history.

Reviews of *Normal, Ohio*, *The Ellen Show*, *Some of My Best Friends*, and *It's All Relative* were informed by critics' distaste for sitcoms in the period when the programs debuted. One writer dismisses *Normal, Ohio* as "join[ing] the bandwagon" of sitcoms built around gay and lesbian characters.[55] In another critique of the program, a reviewer writes: "The idea is obviously to do a show that gay people and straight people can laugh at together, but there's the central problem: Who's laughing?"[56] *The Ellen Show* receives similar disparagements in reviews that highlight the program's status as a sitcom. A writer calls the program "bland and predictable," and too much of "a throwback" to sitcoms in television's past.[57] Reviews of *Some of My Best Friends* are equally critical, with one writer calling the program evidence of a genre that "stinks of stale ideas and comic desperation."[58] Comparably, reviews of *It's All Relative* critique the "obvious setup" of sitcoms,[59] with one reviewer concluding that the program does not have "a voice of its own [because] most of the gags and set-ups are standard sitcom issue."[60]

At the same time, reviews of *Normal, Ohio*, *The Ellen Show*, *Some of My Best Friends*, and *It's All Relative* in trade journals and the popular press involve harsh critiques of the programs' representations of sexual minorities. In one review of

Normal, Ohio, the author requests that audiences not see Goodman's casting as a diverse depiction of gay men on television, stating that "this sorry show . . . has the potential to make everyone cringe, but especially gays. . . . Daring to be stupid is hardly revolutionary television."[61] In a review of *The Ellen Show*, the critic points to the kind yet daft characters from the protagonist's hometown, calling the program element "a glib, ingratiating act that quickly becomes cloying."[62] Reviews of *It's All Relative* feature impatience with the conflation of sexual identity and consumer taste. One critic writes: "The gays live in a palace, worry whether the chardonnay's too woody, and swear by maxims such as 'Don't judge a musical by its road company.' The paint on the blue-collar crew is applied with equally broad strokes."[63] A critic slams *Some of My Best Friends* for representations of gay men designed for broad audiences, calling the characters "completely neutered," stating: "These boys are so asexual, they may not even be anatomically correct."[64]

Coverage of network television in trade journals and the popular press cast the formulaic nature of sitcoms as a "failure" during the time that *Normal, Ohio*, *The Ellen Show*, *Some of My Best Friends*, and *It's All Relative* debuted, seeing the programs as evidence of that "failure." The coverage sees still more "failure" in how the programs represent gays and lesbians. Implicit in these criticisms, I see anxieties about network television's shifting political economy, as well as a palpable disdain for the medium itself. Articles that ridicule sitcoms as a genre and critique representations made legible to and palatable for diverse audiences suggest a desire for network television to be a different kind of medium. In their coverage of the programs, trade publications and the popular press want broadcasting to be less beholden to its regulatory matrix and economic base. In other words, I see in these criticisms a disparagement of network television for being network television. Reporters and journalists cast broadcasting as experiencing a crisis that might be avoided if networks would just circulate different kinds of programs.[65] But the relationships between the waxing and waning of one genre's fashionableness; the cancellation of programs; and network television's broad, historical shifts are correlative, not causal.[66] Although broadcasting's transforming economic base results in particular aesthetic forms and industry practices, programming decisions reveal more about how the medium's various institutions (advertisers, executives, production companies) reach consensus than they do about what viewers like or dislike about particular content.[67]

Treating as definitive and factual the value determinations generated in industry and popular/critical settings—in which sitcoms are "bad" and *Normal, Ohio*, *The Ellen Show*, *Some of My Best Friends*, and *It's All Relative* "fail"—can prevent a nuanced understanding of how television fosters identification among audiences and the means by which it creates feelings of agency and belonging for minority viewers. Even though the equivocations that took place in the programs' promotions suggest "failure" on political grounds, their cancellations suggest "failure" in industry settings, and the harsh reviews suggest "failure" among popular critics, the programs do not then "fail" by every other method of determining value. For instance, the programs do not necessarily "fail" to encourage identification among audiences. While my focus in this chapter is on sexual minorities as an imagined audience for *Normal, Ohio, The Ellen Show, Some of My Best Friends*, and *It's All Relative*, this viewership actually exists. For instance, clips from the programs stream (often illegally) online, where comment sections feature openly gay and lesbian users expressing a great deal of affection for them. Similarly, on the programs' pages at IMDB.com and TV.com, users ask one another where they can find copies of the programs, as they have been circulated unevenly after they were canceled. To these commenters, the programs do not "fail" at all. In that sense, who decides which television programs "fail"? And if audiences ultimately decide "failure," which viewers do that, exactly? Value determinations are discursive, so they are always open for interpretation. Still, ideas about financial, aesthetic, and political value can combine to form commonsense narratives that thwart a nuanced understanding of affective value, the relationship that the medium itself creates with audiences.

In discourses on *Normal, Ohio, The Ellen Show, Some of My Best Friends*, and *It's All Relative*, value determinations could align for a very convenient narrative. Here, industry decisions (cancellations) might be explained with ideological judgments ("stereotypical") and/or aesthetic assessments ("bad programs"). From there, it is but a short jump to use those value determinations as evidence of the programs being uninteresting or lacking affective value. In contrast, this chapter endeavors to explain that television's affective value is a function of the medium itself, and thus not all that determined by other sorts of evaluation. Every network program operates within the bounds of a representational regime animated in service of a specific economic base at a given historical moment. Determinations of financial value that occur in industry settings influence how long a program is on the air and by which mode of distribution it circulates. But the fact that critics brand a program as being low in aesthetic value or understand a program as having no political value does not have a necessary or linear relationship to the program's potential to engender identification among viewers. I hold at arm's length the assessments made in industry and popular/critical discourses on television because it seems that when television scholarship cedes to them, the medium's affective value can fall out of focus. Determinations about television's "success" or "failure," and evaluations of "good" or "bad" programming are provisional and capricious. They are also acts of power, where some evaluations hold more sway than others.[68] As a result, assessments of television's "failure" are never absolute.

And when identification is understood as occurring between audiences and the medium itself, evaluations related to aesthetics and politics often have less to do with the value of television for sexual minorities than they seem to at first glance.

Scholarship frequently evaluates television on ideological grounds. Such criticism often highlights television's transgressions, coding political value negatively in order to elaborate on the differences between representation and reality. I find Villarejo compelling here insofar as she "refuses [a] commonsense model of visual culture in which television has an exterior reality or where it can offer images of others."[69] The media industries produce and distribute television programming for imagined audiences in the interest of generating revenue. So television's representations are always phantasmatic and rendered in the interest of capital.[70] An understanding of the medium that characterizes it as "a buffet of identificatory possibilities" misconstrues television's broader functions.[71] Ideological critique often suggests a profound sense of "failure," where scholars determine that the medium "fails" to engender representations that are as diverse as the audiences it courts. Alas, it seems that seeking representations that demonstrate a certain degree of fidelity to some lived reality can only find failure. In scholarship on sexual minorities, the desires promulgated by television are sometimes dismissed as being "normative" and thus lacking political value. Here, same-sex marriages, fancy houses, professional careers, and designer wardrobes signify all that capitalist democracy might make possible for audiences. As Lauren Berlant writes: "In this version of . . . desire, the subject desires not to feel responsible for inhabiting or policing most social distinctions."[72] Thus, audience identification with television is often rooted in normativity. Yet the fantasies that attend that identification do not often involve the kinds of political value desired most by scholars. Dismissing as normative what television offers to minority audiences misses a chance to unpack exactly what is so comforting and tantalizing about it. In a lot of ways, ideological critiques of television can both discount what the medium actually provides for its audiences and dismiss what people seek from it.

There is a rich tradition of scholarship that critiques television generously by queering texts, using close readings to illustrate a text's moments of rupture.[73] When scholars queer texts, political value and affective value often become co-terminous: a text's defiance of norms is offered as evidence of its capacity to cultivate a subversive identification among viewers in particular social locations. As a critical gesture, queer readings elaborate the capacity for identification with television that is not necessarily imagined in its creation. But such interpretive methods can be difficult to systematize, however rigorous and illuminating they may be. Does the critic's interpretation stand in for all viewers? Which ones? When? Where? In contrast, this chapter shifts the coding of affective value to television as a medium, where sexual minorities are invited to identify with it as a matter of course. In that sense, any television program is open to a queer reading.

Such interpretations can disrupt staid dynamics of power, or trouble conventional understandings of identity and desire. I borrow some of their rhetorical power here in an attempt to disrupt commonsense ideas about "failure," precisely because such assessments about television's "failure" have a complicated relationship with the medium's affective value. At the same time, understanding how television enables identification can slide rather quickly toward apologia. Queer readings are frequently mobilized as evidence of subversion. Given how central the construction of hierarchy is to the function of television, the medium's affective value is necessarily tangled in dynamics of power. When television programming is found to be subversive, it begs larger questions about how radical any reading can be when the medium itself invites identification in service of capital.

Determinations of aesthetic value are regular features of industry and popular/critical discourses on television, where professionals try to generate revenue from programming by promoting it as "art," and reviewers assess a program's stylistic worth relative to others. But aesthetic value is increasingly part of scholarly discourses on the medium as well. At the start of the twenty-first century, certain kinds of television content—often but not always high-budget, hour-long dramas produced and distributed by pay-cable networks—are revered aesthetic objects in academic criticism. Jason Mittell characterizes this sort of evaluation as "an invitation to a dialogue. . . . because debating the merits of cultural works is one of the most enjoyable ways we engage with texts, establish relationships with other consumers, and gain respect for other people's opinions and insights."[74] As such, Mittell suggests that aesthetic questions are always, inevitably central to discussions of the medium, scholarly or otherwise. Even so, a program's aesthetic value does not necessarily have a relationship with how the medium itself engenders identification. Traditionally "low" genres of television like soap operas and talk shows, which are rarely defended on aesthetic grounds, are rather obvious examples of how the medium invites identification among viewers.[75] The sentimentality and emotional display of these genres renders them lowbrow, often on gendered terms.[76] In fact, aesthetic judgments often hinge on bracketing identification altogether, thereby "break[ing] the link between feeling and the faculty of desiring—to make room for a new, disinterested type of pleasure . . . in aesthetic judgment, contemplative pleasure; this pleasure is not linked to desire for the object and, indifferent as to its existence, is solely concerned with representation."[77] As Michael Newman and Elana Levine write, when scholars make value determinations about television aesthetics, they can "perpetuate hierarchies of taste, value, and cultural and social worth" that render the more conventionally lowbrow pleasures of identification as "other."[78] Aesthetic judgments promote, either implicitly or explicitly, some programming as being significant and thus worth the time and effort it would take audiences to consume it. As Jeffrey Sconce suggests, it seems that such evaluations "actively expand the demands and desires of television itself."[79] From that vantage point, finding aesthetic value in television ultimately wants audiences to "lose another 19 hours of their li[ves]" and watch whatever program is found to be interesting or transcendent.[80] Thus, locating aesthetic value in programming can never really subvert television's function.[81]

Understanding television as a medium with structural functions in capitalism poses the question of how evaluation can ever complicate the medium's relationship to power. In some sense, the very act of television scholarship can be looped into a social formation that maintains hierarchies. In that regard, Michael Newman and Elana Levine ponder how television scholars "are—wittingly or not—complicit in the very discursive formation [they] intend to critique."[82] I focus on *Normal, Ohio*, *The Ellen Show*, *Some of My Best Friends*, and *It's All Relative* in this chapter precisely because they are "bad" objects, not valued on financial, aesthetic, or political grounds. They are not more interesting than other representations of gays and lesbians on television, nor are they "better." They are not necessarily even "more revelatory" than more widely consumed representations of gays and lesbians on television like *Ellen* or *Will & Grace*. Nevertheless, I analyze them in depth to demonstrate how the affective experiences that television makes available to sexual minorities confound common ways of explaining the medium vis-à-vis value and "failure."

If identification with television is a normative fantasy embedded in hierarchical relations, the question remains how scholarship might ever trouble such a framework. When television scholarship finds political value in certain interpretations or locates aesthetic value in particular content, there seems to be profound risk that the critic's attention to programming will occlude questions about the nature of the medium. If rebellious readings and championing aesthetics suggest that some programs invite audience identification more than others, however provisional such determinations are, is that really fortuitous? In many ways, such evaluations want audiences to identify more with the very circuits of capital and dynamics of power that subordinate some people for the benefit of others. While such evaluations can be (and often are) thoughtful and careful, considering television in the broader context of capitalism makes it difficult to reconcile the medium's politics with a scholar's quest for social justice. At what point does the consideration of an object obscure an understanding of the implications of consuming it? As this chapter demonstrates, the fantasies of normativity that television provides for minority audiences are essentially fantasies of power and capital. When assessments conclude that certain programs are "better" than others, they seem to be rather easily folded back into television's structural functions. If media scholars are invested in complicating or even just highlighting the relationship between television and cultural power, the content that is most valuable for such an endeavor might be that which prompts audiences to turn the television off.

Television Criticism Queered

I should admit that, despite my liberal guilt and hand-wringing, I am an ardent television watcher. As I state at the opening of this chapter, television's use values are not limited to the medium's pacification of audiences. Viewers find information and meaning in television's programming and the methods by which they consume it. Even so, it seems that considering television as a medium can make critiques about its ruptural moments and transcendent programs rather cruel optimism.[83] Scholarship is itself a mode of cultural production where reading, writing, and teaching produce knowledge. The remainder of this chapter thinks through two critical gestures that might problematize television's relationship to capital and power. This list is by no means exhaustive, and my goal is not to valorize some scholarship over other scholarship—I am not so deluded that I think academic criticism of television is ever going to topple capitalism. Even so, I want to elaborate on some ways that television scholars might queer their interactions with the medium. In academic criticism, the term "queer" typically signifies a labile identity or desire, as well as an interpretive practice that moves connotative meanings to the foreground. I want to queer television in a different way, by mobilizing modes of critique that question, make strange, or throw shade at television's relationship to capital and power.

The gay and lesbian press has devoted much attention to the recirculation of older television programming on various delivery technologies: reruns, DVD box sets, and streaming services. In reviews, writers cast the programs as objects that illuminate gay and lesbian history, constructing reading strategies that position the texts as enabling cultural knowledge and facilitating membership in sexual minority communities. These reviews often draw reader attention to programs' "special" episodes on gay and lesbian themes, making television representations that are frequently understood as "bad stereotypes" important elements of gay and lesbian history. In such reviews, two different modes of understanding television emerge: derision and contextualization. One such review of a reissue of the 1970s and 1980s sitcom *The Facts of Life* uses the derisive mode to examine the series premiere. *The Facts of Life* narrates the lives of teen girls at a boarding school, and it debuted with a "lesbian panic" episode in which one of the girls is accused of being overly masculine and too affectionate with other students. The narrative resolves with the character proving her heterosexuality by wearing a dress to a school dance and flirting with a boy. The reviewer calls the episode "fairly astounding and astoundingly offensive," casting the program as a "bad object" in a way that constructs a comforting liberal progress narrative, as though "television is better now, so the world is better now."[84]

In contrast, another writer uses the contextualizing mode to direct readers to the boxed set of *Soap*, the racy 1970s sitcom that satirized daytime dramas.

Famously, comedian Billy Crystal was featured in a gay role. The reviewer credits Crystal by saying that the role "broke down some barriers, but not before having to stumble through issues of cross-dressing, gender reassignment and even heterosexual experimentation," calling the series' frequent use of homophobic jokes "cringe-worthy."[85] The reviewer frames the jokes as an essential element of gay and lesbian history, calling the humor "part of the price that had to be paid on network television more than 30 years ago."[86] In the two reviews, I see different understandings of television's capacity to engender identification among sexual minorities. The first review sees in television evidence of close-mindedness about homosexuality, implying that such representations foreclose on the possibility of minority identification with the medium. Tacitly, it suggests that such events are less likely to occur in the contemporary moment. It also suggests that sexual minority viewers are more likely to identify with contemporary programming than they are to identify with content from the past. The second review makes a different interpretive gesture, suggesting that the queeny gay male character is how television rendered sexual minorities legible for diverse viewerships at a certain point in time. I want to read the *Soap* review as understanding the faulty logic at work in presentist ideological critiques of television's past. Rereading past television can provide more nuanced understandings of how the medium has fostered identification among sexual minorities at different points in its history.

Contextualized understandings of television interpret programming as historically specific, widely legible shorthand that fostered identification among audiences in different ways at specific moments in time. From that vantage point, representations of minorities are not "good" or "bad," but are evidence of a shorthand that transforms in the interest of courting an imagined audience in a given moment. More than hairsplitting, such an interpretive method complicates the binary logics that can be animated by ideological critique. Television has not "gotten better" over the course of its history; rather, its shorthand has changed. In all cases, television engendered identification among sexual minorities. Moreover, the attention that such reviews pay to programs and representations that are scorned and disavowed in liberal progress narratives complicate what exactly is valuable about television for sexual minorities. And elaborating on how such audiences might consume television complicates the discourse that McCarthy sees in *Ellen*, where industry executives, trade reporters, and reviewers in the popular press promote programs about sexual minorities as new and groundbreaking when, in so many ways, they are neither.

When I first started writing about *Normal, Ohio*, *The Ellen Show*, *Some of My Best Friends*, and *It's All Relative*, all of the programs had already been canceled and only *The Ellen Show* had circulated on DVD. I found copies of the other three programs among fans trading illegal recordings on the internet. In 2011, Carsey Werner, the production company that created *Normal, Ohio*, sold the program's licensing rights to Hulu. As of this writing, the series run—including the episodes that never aired—streams there. In determining which programs get redistributed for new delivery technologies, industry discourses can serve implicit agenda-setting functions for television scholars. While the value determinations that take place in industry discourses do not always have a linear relationship with television's affective value, programs only recirculate when television's institutions identify adequate potential for them to generate revenue. As a result, questions of archive demonstrate even further how television tangles not just identification but also scholarship with capital and power.

File sharing is a prominent way that both television audiences and scholars try to circumvent the industry's attempts to generate revenue.[87] On BitTorrent and other online sites, people trade programming outside many of the industry's attempts to exact payment from audiences. But as Michael Newman points out, file sharing generates its own hierarchies, operating by way of "a set of downloading distinctions keyed not only to ideas about media economics but also about the relative value of genres and formats depending on placement in the cultural hierarchy." [88] As a practice, torrenting television frequently values some content—often high-concept, big-budget programming constructed as "quality" in various discourses on television—over and above other kinds of content. As a result, there is a vast swath of television programming that is deemed so worthless that a lot of it simply cannot be found after it airs.

If the variety of programs available to audiences via streaming platforms, DVD boxed sets, and online file sharing suggests perpetual, continuous access to television, that fantasy is mitigated by the vast array of content, like *Some of My Best Friends* and *It's All Relative*, that falls out of circulation as a result of its complicated relationship to questions of value. Mimi White uses the term "apparitional television" to describe programs

> whose appeal and conditions of access are narrow and precarious. . . . [Apparitional television is] an analytic concept for assembling and thinking about different kinds of television programs that are unlike the categories that attract considerably more critical attention. . . . Some examples are television programs that air on small, local broadcast stations, stations that do not even get picked up by regional cable systems; shows produced for local access cable channels; primetime network programs that fade from view because they are not widely redistributed . . . ; programs that are not readily available on DVD or on sites such as iTunes, YouTube, or Hulu.[89]

Television programs that do not build a viewership in ways that can be monetized have limited exchange value for the industry, but they could be rather useful for queering television scholarship. In apparitional television, the ways that the medium fosters identification among viewers come into focus via programming that makes very few claims to value of any kind. As this chapter demonstrates, identification is always a function of aesthetics with political consequences, although locating value in programming can hinder a scrupulous understanding of how the medium itself engenders identification. It would be silly to valorize apparitional television as more interesting, revelatory, or "better" than other more celebrated, more acclaimed programming. It also risks a vanguardism where content that is difficult to locate becomes the most desirable object of analysis. Those caveats aside, apparitional television allows attention to the medium in ways that can be difficult with more conventional objects of analysis.

Thus, my vision of queer television scholarship would involve, first, an attention to the politics of representation and identification that willfully troubles standard ideological critiques of programming. This critical gesture does not have to descend into crankiness that sees subordination in every element of television, but it would question the terms by which scholars understand the relationship between sexual minority representations and sexual minority viewers. By doing that, scholars could circumvent a tendency to make small, subjective differentiations among similar appeals to audiences. Furthermore, my vision of queer television scholarship involves employing objects of analysis that are less likely to reify evaluations of television that take place in industry settings and popular discourses. Doing that can push "big picture" issues related to the medium's structural functions in capitalism out of focus. In episodes of *Normal, Ohio, The Ellen Show, Some of My Best Friends*, and *It's All Relative*, the bourgeois gay and lesbian characters would not think twice about how their consumption solidifies relations of power and flows of capital. And the identification that such characters provide for audiences hinges on bracketing such concerns, as well. I believe this is precisely why television scholarship should differ. If identification with television as a medium hinges on a refusal of the binary between the real and the imagined, it seems as though there is much to be gained when academic criticism of the medium can refuse the terms and prerogatives of the industry that creates it. Then, in some small way, scholarship might complicate what television is and does.

Notes

1. My understanding of failure follows the one put forth by Jack Halberstam. It upends standard notions of worth for the purposes of queer critique. See Judith [Jack] Halberstam, *The Queer Art of Failure* (Durham, NC: Duke University Press, 2011).

2. I make this claim to underscore the complex role of the body in the processes of identification. I do not define that role as a set of uniform reactions among different groups of television viewers. For a discussion of how issues related to biology and essentialism are taken up in scholarship on affect and emotion see the introduction herein.

3. This section draws on an analysis of sixty half-hour episodes, the sum of all four series runs.

4. This section draws on an analysis of over a hundred articles that were published in industry trade publications and the popular press dealing with both sitcoms as a genre and these four programs specifically.

5. For a different take on these issues, one less connected to issues in queer criticism and more firmly rooted in ongoing debates in television studies, see Hollis Griffin, "Television, Affect, and Evaluation," *Cinema Journal*, forthcoming.

6. This idea recurs in many of Adorno's writings. See Theodor Adorno, *The Culture Industry*, 2nd ed., ed. J. M. Bernstein (New York: Routledge, 2001).

7. Amy Villarejo is particularly in dialogue with Theodor Adorno, "How to Look at Television," *Quarterly Review of Film, Radio, and Television* 8, no. 3 (1954): 213–235. Amy Villarejo, *Ethereal Queer: Television, Historicity, Desire* (Durham, NC: Duke University Press, 2014), 42.

8. Ibid., 20.

9. Ibid., 41.

10. Her analysis is more involved than I have room to elaborate on here, but Villarejo likens the audience's identification with television to Freud's notion of melancholia. Ibid., 47–49.

11. Ibid., 52.

12. For more analysis on the relationship between affect and television, see Misha Kavka, *Reality Television, Affect and Intimacy: Reality Matters* (New York: Palgrave Macmillan, 2008).

13. With mordant wit, Villarejo criticizes this claim: "Alleging that hidden messages of . . . unreflecting obedience emanate from a monolithic culture industry . . . [is] a reductive and juvenile model of interpretation for mass-cultural texts, one I like to call 'the secret decoder ring' theory of media (whereby a message is hidden in a given text, and it wends its way nefariously toward an unwitting receiver: the astute cultural critic knows better, decodes the hidden message, and exposes the lurking evil)." Villarejo, *Ethereal Queer*, 43.

14. Ibid., 56.

15. Ibid.

16. Ibid., 22.

17. Becker identifies this upscale audience appeal as an attempt among the broadcast networks to court the affluent demographics that were increasingly migrating to cable television and the internet during the period in question. Ron Becker, *Gay TV and Straight America* (New Brunswick, NJ: Rutgers University Press, 2006), 80–107.

18. Becker discusses representations of gay and lesbian life as offering television networks the means to demonstrate an alliance with socially liberal sensibilities in a commerce-friendly way. Representational tropes related to affluent, educated gays and lesbians allowed network programming to sidestep the issues of inequality and differentials of power that would attend self-conscious representation of racial and ethnic minorities. Ibid., 108–135.

19. Television's courtship of upscale audiences, and a programming emphasis on upmarket audience appeals have been features of the medium since the 1970s. Julie D'Acci outlines this process and its history at length in her attention to "the woman's audience" on network television in the 1980s. Julie D'Acci, *Defining Women: The Case of* Cagney & Lacey (Chapel Hill: University of North Carolina Press, 1994).

20. Becker, *Gay TV and Straight America*, 176–177.

21. The four programs discussed in this chapter were also reported on rather widely in the gay and lesbian press, suggesting that even though they were circulated so briefly, they had

some sexual minority viewership. Becker self-consciously brackets this question, but points to the utility of examining it: "For lesbian, gay, bisexual, and queer viewers who [have] long lived with a television universe that usually ignored their existence, the increase of gay material on TV . . . [is] no doubt moving, affirming, frustrating, entertaining, and insulting. . . . It is important not to erase that activity. . . . As I focus on the ways gay-themed programming reflected the anxieties of Straight America, it is important to keep in mind that such programming was important for many viewers, often for very different reasons." Ibid., 11.

22. For a discussion of the ideological limitations of LGBT representations in sitcoms, see Kathleen Battles and Wendy Hilton-Morrow, "Gay Characters in Conventional Spaces: *Will and Grace* and the Situation Comedy Genre," *Critical Studies in Media Communication* 19, no. 1 (March 2002): 87–105.

23. Andrew J. Douglas discusses the centrality of John Goodman's physicality to his star persona in "The B.M.O.C.—Big Men on Celluloid: Images of Masculine Obesity in Popular American Film and Television" (PhD diss., Northwestern University, 2005).

24. Peter Hennen, *Faeries, Bears, and Leathermen: Men in Community Queering the Masculine* (Chicago: University of Chicago Press, 2008).

25. In the episode "Caught on Tape," Butch and his mother end up at a bar that caters to gay bears after their car breaks down.

26. Victoria Johnson, *Heartland TV: Prime Time Television and the Struggle for U.S. Identity* (New York: New York University Press, 2008), 148.

27. The hip queer character out of place in her midwestern environs points to a well-established trope in television sitcoms, "the fish out of water." Here, writers "strike a narrative balance between repetition of premise and differentiation of plot. If a series is to succeed for hundreds of episodes, it must feature an appealingly familiar and yet ultimately repetitive foundation of premise and character relations. . . . 'Fish out of water' stories generate endless difference within repetition as writers simply insert the consistently incongruous character(s) into a new 'stock plot' each week." Jeffrey Sconce, "What If? Charting the New Textual Boundaries of Television," in *Television after TV: Essays on a Medium in Transition*, ed. Lynn Spigel and Jan Olsson (Durham, NC: Duke University Press, 2003), 100–101.

28. Diane Negra, *The Irish in Us: Irishness, Performativity, and Popular Culture* (Durham, NC: Duke University Press, 2006).

29. Jonathan J. Cavallero, "Gangsters, Fessos, Tricksters, and Sopranos," *Journal of Popular Film and Television* 32, no. 2 (2004): 50–63.

30. For further analysis of how differences in whiteness are used to mobilize racial hierarchies, see Linda Williams, *Playing the Race Card: Melodramas of Black and White from Uncle Tom to O.J. Simpson* (Princeton: Princeton University Press, 2002).

31. This criticism is so common that I have argued it myself. Hollis Griffin, "Queerness, the Quality Audience, and Comedy Central's *Reno 911!*" *Television and New Media* 9, no. 5 (September 2008): 355–370.

32. Lauren Berlant, *The Female Complaint: The Unfinished Business of Sentimentality in American Culture* (Durham, NC: Duke University Press, 2008), 5.

33. Becker refers to this phenomenon as the "straight panic" prompted by gay and lesbian content on television. Becker, *Gay TV and Straight America*, 13–36.

34. Ibid., 158.

35. John Thornton Caldwell, "Convergence Television: Aggregating Form and Repurposing Content in the Culture of Conglomeration," in *Television after TV: Essays on a Medium in Transition*, ed. Lynn Spigel and Jan Olsson (Durham, NC: Duke University Press, 2003), 58.

36. Bonnie Dow, "*Ellen*, Television, and the Politics of Gay and Lesbian Visibility," *Critical Studies in Media Communication* 18 (June 2001): 123–140.

37. Anna McCarthy, "*Ellen*: Making Queer Television History," *GLQ: A Journal of Lesbian and Gay Studies* 7, no. 4 (2001): 596.

38. Ibid.

39. Quoted in "Producers Went Back to Ohio to Find Show's Humor," *USA Today*, November 1, 2000, 5D.

40. Quoted in Eric Deggans, "The Long Road to 'Normal, Ohio,'" *St. Petersburg Times*, October 31, 2000, 1D.

41. Ibid.

42. Ibid.

43. This is Anna McCarthy's central argument in "*Ellen*: Making Queer Television History," where she points out that the last season of the program moved into a reflexive mode of address that questioned the terms of sexual representation in the medium and examined the show's place in television history.

44. Quoted in Eric Mink, "Ellen Wants Last Laugh: Back in Fall with Sitcom," *New York Daily News*, July 26, 2001, 92.

45. Quoted in Ed Bark, "Ellen DeGeneres Goes Back to Humor Home Base," *Dallas Morning News*, July 27, 2001.

46. Ibid.

47. Ibid.

48. Quoted in Bill Keveney, "Taking a Page from 'Birdcage,'" *USA Today*, August 13, 2003, 4D.

49. A great deal of the research on television in postwar America emphasizes how the medium was advertised as a technology for familial consumption, and how sitcom programming in particular played a crucial role in educating consumer tastes and normalizing suburban living. See Lynn Spigel, *Make Room for TV: Television and the Family Ideal in Postwar America* (Chicago: University of Chicago Press, 1992).

50. Several articles in both trade publications and the popular press discuss this development in network television schedules at the end of the 1990s. For more thorough discussions, see Josef Adalian, "Sitcoms Shop for Mom and Pop," *Variety*, August 16–22, 1999, 21–23; and John Consoli, "Fall TV Report: Network TV—Situation Critical," *Mediaweek*, September 13, 2003.

51. Popular 1990s-era sitcoms that were canceled during this period include *Seinfeld* (NBC, 1989–1998), *Friends* (NBC, 1994–2004), *Mad About You* (NBC, 1992–1999), *3rd Rock from the Sun* (NBC, 1996–2001), *Dharma & Greg* (ABC, 1997–2002), and *The Drew Carey Show* (ABC, 1995–2004).

52. Jim Rutenberg, "No Laughing Matter for Networks: A Dearth of Successful Sitcoms," *New York Times*, May 12, 2003, E1.

53. Robert Bianco, "Is One Good Sitcom Too Much to Ask?" *USA Today*, January 22, 2003, 4D.

54. Peter Tolan, "Reason for Optimism," *Variety*, August 31, 2001, A1.

55. Phil Gallo, "Review: *Normal, Ohio*," *Variety*, October 31, 2001, 10.

56. Tom Shales, "'Normal, Ohio': No Place Like Home," *Washington Post*, November 1, 2000, C1.

57. Julie Salamon, "Back from the Big City, Just Hangin' Out with the Rubes," *New York Times* September 24, 2001, E6.

58. David Bianculli, "'My,' This Is a Sad Sitcom," *New York Daily News*, February 28, 2001, 73.

59. Virginia Heffernan, "Class-Blind Lovebirds and Hidebound Parents," *New York Times*, October 1, 2003, E1.

60. Kevin Thompson, "*It's All Relative* really should be called 'It's Only So-So,'" *Cox News Service*, September 30, 2003.

61. Julie Salamon, "Gay and Crude? Whatever Happened to 'Faaabulous'?" *New York Times*, November 1, 2000, E5.

62. Salamon, "Back from the Big City," E6.

63. Jonathan Storm, "Good-Looking Tough Gal: A Gal with Two Gay Dads," *Philadelphia Inquirer*, October 1, 2003, E1.

64. Robert Bianco, "'Some of My Best Friends' Sounds Insincere, Unfunny Gays and Italians Get Stereotypical Sitcom Treatment," *USA Today*, February 28, 2001, 4D.

65. I have discussed industry reactions to US broadcasting's "crisis" elsewhere. See Hollis Griffin, "Manufacturing Massness: Aesthetic Form and Industry Practice in the Reality Television Contest," in *A Companion to Reality Television*, ed. Laurie Ouellette (Malden, MA: Wiley-Blackwell, 2014), 155–170.

66. Horace Newcomb criticizes how discourses on 1960s television framed the waning popularity of the Western in this manner. Horace Newcomb, "From Old Frontier to New Frontier," in *The Revolution Wasn't Televised: Sixties Television and Social Conflict*, ed. Lynn Spigel and Michael Curtin (New York: Routledge, 1997), 287–304.

67. Ien Ang, "Understanding Television Audiencehood," in *Television: A Critical View, 5th Edition* (New York: Oxford University Press, 1994), 367–386.

68. Denise Bielby, "Who's to Say? Why Television Criticism Is Complicated," *FLOW: A Critical Forum on Television and Media Culture*, May 5, 2014, http://flowtv.org/2014/05/who's-to-say-why-television-criticism-is-complicated-denise-bielby-university-of-california-santa-barbara/.

69. Villarejo, *Ethereal Queer*, 49.

70. In her critique of queer television criticism, Villarejo uses Theodor Adorno's concept of "pseudorealism" to argue that television constructs a sense of the real as part of its ideological function that, despite the medium's claims to the contrary, bears only a tenuous relationship to a lived reality. Ibid., 41–49.

71. Ibid., 49.

72. Berlant, *Female Complaint*, 9.

73. Alexander Doty, *Making Things Perfectly Queer: Interpreting Mass Culture* (Minneapolis: University of Minnesota Press, 1993).

74. Jason Mittell, *Complex TV: The Poetics of Contemporary Television Storytelling* (New York: New York University Press, 2015), 207.

75. Tania Modleski, *Loving with a Vengeance: Mass Produced Fantasies for Women*, 2nd ed. (New York: Routledge, 2007); Jane Shattuc, *The Talking Cure: TV Talk Shows and Women*, 1st ed. (New York: Routledge, 1997).

76. Linda Williams, "Film Bodies: Gender, Genre, and Excess," *Film Quarterly* 44, no. 4 (Summer 1991): 2–13.

77. Pierre Bourdieu, *Distinction: A Social Critique of the Judgment of Taste* (Cambridge, MA: Harvard University Press, 1987), 595.

78. Michael Newman and Elana Levine, *Legitimating Television: Media Convergence and Cultural Status* (New York: Routledge, 2011), 154.

79. In a moment of youthful arrogance, I posted a critical comment about this article on the Flow website when it was first published. To Jeffrey Sconce, I issue a humble apology. Many rereads later, I think it is rather spot-on. Jeffrey Sconce, "A Spectre Is Haunting Television Studies," *FLOW: A Critical Forum on Television and Media Culture*, October 31, 2008, http://flowtv.org/2008/10/a-specter-is-haunting-television-studies-jeffrey-sconce-northwestern-university/.

80. Ibid. Mark Andrejevic makes a similar claim in his analysis of communication between television creators and television viewers on the website *Television without Pity*. Andrejevic underscores how audience interactivity with television precipitates a sense of shared control over content even as it off-loads labor onto the very people who are already paying for it. Where Gayatri Spivak's notion of producer as consumer opens the possibility of agency in the form of affective labor, Andrejevic's take on that relationship is more pessimistic. For a discussion of Gayatri Spivak and affective labor, see the introduction herein. See also Mark Andrejevic, "Watching Television without Pity: The Productivity of Online Fans," *Television and New Media* 9, no. 1 (January 2008): 24–46.

81. One caveat here would be analyses that consider aesthetic value the product of social relations, where such evaluations are understood as being discursive. When aesthetic value is understood as being inherent in a text, it can operate as a powerful claim to truth. But when aesthetic value is framed as a determination arrived at by way of a cultural process, its relation to power comes into sharper focus. While not a necessary outcome of aesthetic evaluation, analyzing television's aesthetics can willfully bracket the social in ways that disregard power dynamics. For a sustained dialogue about such concerns, see Mittell, *Complex TV*, 206–232; and Sudeep Dasgupta, "Policing the People: Television Studies and the Problem of 'Quality,'" *NECSUS: European Journal of Media Studies*, accessed August 12, 2015, http://www.necsus-ejms .org/policing-the-people-television-studies-and-the-problem-of-quality-by-sudeep -dasgupta/

82. Newman and Levine, *Legitimating Television*, 154.

83. Lauren Berlant, *Cruel Optimism* (Durham, NC: Duke University Press, 2011).

84. Christian McLaughlin, "You Take the Good, You Take the Bad, *Advocate*, May 8, 2006, http://www.advocate.com/2006/05/08/you-take-good-you-take-bad.

85. Gregg Shapiro, "DVDiva: As Seen on TV," *Chicago Free Press*, accessed March 4, 2010, www.chicagofreepress.com/node/2326.

86. Ibid.

87. This practice has a longer history in the trading of VHS tapes. Kim Bjarkman, "To Have and to Hold: The Video Collector's Relationship with an Ethereal Medium," *Television and New Media* 5 (2004): 217–246.

88. Michael Newman, "Free TV: File-Sharing and the Value of Television," *Television and New Media* 13, no. 6 (November 2012): 474.

89. Mimi White, "Barry Chappell's Fine Art Showcase: Apparitional TV, Aesthetic Value, and the Art Market," in *After the Break: Television Theory Today*, ed. Marijke de Valck and Jan Teurlings (Amsterdam: University of Amsterdam Press, 2013), 185, 189.

5 Wanting Something Online

Dᴜʀɪɴɢ ᴛʜᴇ ᴛɪᴍᴇ I was writing this book, a friend forwarded me an internet meme about Grindr, one of several geosocial networking applications ("apps") marketed to sexual minorities via the smartphone.[1] This particular meme communicates sarcasm using an image from a scene in *Willy Wonka & the Chocolate Factory* (1971). Known colloquially as a "Wonka meme," the graphic features text superimposed on a picture of the character Willy Wonka (figure 5.1). The text makes fun of people who look for sexual partners on the internet but pretend otherwise, and the image is taken from a scene in which Wonka condescends to a group of children. Ostensibly, Willy Wonka stands in for Grindr users as they encounter others claiming to be "looking for friends" on the app. Because the pursuit of sexual encounters is such a common practice among gay and lesbian app users, the joke is: no one is ever just "looking for friends" on Grindr. From that vantage point, users who imply otherwise appear deceitful and/or coy. Wonka's facial expression is a reaction to this experience, and it is a relatively enigmatic one; it could signify disbelief, amusement, or maybe even scorn. The possibility of multiple interpretations highlights the bevy of feelings—disdain, embarrassment, or amusement—that users might experience on gay and lesbian apps. The meme's humor is the wry commentary it offers on the pursuit of desire on the internet. In its arch yet deadpan tone, the meme points to the cultural norms that shape desire, as well as the norms that inform the pursuit of desire via these particular technologies.[2]

Gay and lesbian apps involve a tension in which database designs, the desires that users pursue in online environments, and the cultural norms related to sexuality rub up against and inform one another. Because users consume apps in an attempt to realize their desires, the technologies always involve a sense of lack. That is the very nature of desire: when the subject desires, he or she wants something that can only be found externally.[3] By consuming gay and lesbian apps, users pursue any number of desires: love, sex, or sometimes little more than relief from boredom.[4] But all desires, in some sense, take users outside of themselves. Fundamentally, desire is the experience of being nonsovereign.[5] At the same time, apps put users in relation to technology because the desires that users pursue online do not always have firm objects. Frequently, users consume the apps merely to pass time, with few expectations about the outcome of the minutes or hours they spend scrolling through profiles and/or chatting with other users. As a result, the

Figure 5.1. This Wonka meme pokes fun at Grindr users who act coy online.

apps do not necessarily put users in relation to something beyond the screen itself.[6]

This chapter examines the discursive limits of the gay and lesbian apps, or the space beyond their affordances, in order to observe how the lack at the heart of all desire dovetails with the difficulties associated with communicating in online environments.[7] To seek interpersonal connections via mobile media is to be burdened with the precarious feelings that attend desiring others.[8] Thus, the apps require a considerable amount of emotional negotiation by users. By analyzing the database designs and marketing discourses of gay and lesbian apps, the chapter illustrates how mobile media companies suggest that some arrangement of pull-down menus and text boxes will allow users to fully express themselves and find precisely what they seek. In doing so, the companies make the pursuit of desire a civic issue, promoting the "success stories" of users who have found particular sorts of interpersonal connections on the apps as evidence of the political work that the technologies undertake.[9] These stories construct the apps as technologies of agency, tools that users might employ to achieve happiness and fulfillment. Even though desire is rarely that simple, and the desires of users shift and change shape over time, mobile media companies foreground the allure of romantic love in marketing themselves to users and advertisers.

Romance is but one form of interpersonal connection that users seek on the apps, where identifications and modes of relation are arranged via taxonomies that users draw on in order to communicate who they are and what they want.[10] In their profiles, users employ vernacular terms in an effort to articulate themselves and their desires in ways that are familiar to others. Interactions between users require legibility and precipitate expectation; words, phrases, and images signify particular ideas about bodies, identities, and intimacies as they flow between users via the profiles they construct, as well as in the conversations they have with one another.[11] The marketing discourses of the gay and lesbian mobile media companies use these categories to promote themselves as being politically progressive. Such discourses work within stable institutions like the electoral processes of the nation-state to cast the apps as fostering social change. Marketing discourses on the apps are thus evidence of a mode of sexual politics that operates within existing systems and frameworks by drawing on established language like the categories of identity politics used in database designs. As is alluded to in the Wonka meme, app users are often disenchanted by the experiences they have on the apps. In memes, blog posts, and other user-generated content, app users manage their feelings about the difficulties of realizing desire, and they contend with the hardships inflicted on them by the social norms they experience while pursuing desire online. In doing so, app users make desire strange: sometimes they laugh about the limitations of the technologies or the actions of other users, though they convey sadness and anger about them too. The bevy of emotions that users express about their experiences on the apps are more numerous and complicated than the apps suggest at first glance.[12]

Gay and lesbian apps are technologies that feature both territorialization, a politics that reifies prevailing practices, and deterritorialization, a politics that undermines established systems in order to reimagine them.[13] This chapter sees the apps encompassing both modes of politics: while one is evident in the rights claims put forth by the mobile media companies in their marketing discourses, a second can be seen in the user-generated content in which people discuss the feelings they experience when consuming the technologies.[14] To parse out the differences between these modes of politics, the first section examines different understandings of interfaces. The term "database design" connotes the organization of information via pull-down menus and text boxes, whereas "interface" refers more broadly to the relationship that the apps forge between human and machine.[15] The two genres of politics at work on the apps—territorialization and deterritorialization—involve disparate understandings of the interface. Where the former stresses the role of database design in shaping user interactions with information, the latter highlights the role of users' embodied responses to that information. More than semantic, the contrast between these disparate understandings of the interface opens the apps to different modes of critique: a territorialized politics that emphasizes the relationship between users and the objects of their desire, and a deterritorialized politics that stresses the relationship between users and the mediation of desire by technology.[16]

The second section of the chapter examines the apps' marketing discourses alongside an analysis of how they arrange information. Adjustments to database features—additions to pull-down menus, changes in text boxes—are constructed discursively as matters of social justice. Here, industry attempts to serve diverse consumers are cast as evidence of ideological commitments in trade publications and the popular press, efforts that are supplemented by corporate communications that foreground the life stories of mobile media executives as app users. These personal stories are framed as an impetus for corporate missions, where marketing discourses characterize the apps as avenues for civic engagement and thus tools for achieving social change. In doing so, the apps and their marketing discourses generate ideas of hierarchy by emphasizing particular desires and forms of intimacy, creating a set of power dynamics that imply some ways of being and wanting are more valuable than others.

Yet, as the Wonka meme suggests, users are often well aware of attempts to make respectable the disreputable desires and intimacies that people seek on the apps. Thus, the third section of this chapter looks to user-generated content related to gay and lesbian apps—blog posts, viral videos, and posts to social media networks—as evidence of the strains inherent in the mediation of desire by technology. By examining the ways that users discuss their experiences with the apps, the section highlights the range of emotions that they express about desire and the use of technology in pursuing it. User-generated content expresses the humor, embarrassment, and disgust that users experience when they consume the apps. In expressing these feelings, users negotiate the lack at the heart of all desire, as well as the difficulties inherent in communicating desire via technology. More complicated than the range of options available to them via database designs, these emotions highlight the disjoint between user experiences and the affordances of technology. The laughter, anger, and sadness that people experience while using the apps demonstrates the range of feelings they have about desire, as well as the variety in their experiences with technology.

Interfaces

App users make themselves legible to one another by constructing profiles, a process that is both enabled and hemmed in by the design of a given database. Images are integral to that process because they function as testaments to the identity claims that users make on the internet.[17] In fact, images carry so much weight in online interactions that users frequently upload several different pictures, and/or share additional photos while chatting with one another. These photos are often close-ups or medium close-ups that essentially ground disembodied information in a knowable body.[18] The sharing of pictures, especially face pics, facilitates that process. Users sometimes limit their pictures to images of torsos, especially on the apps that target gay men. This practice simultaneously makes bodies available for perusal by others and provides a modicum of anonymity. Such photos often have the explicit purpose of performing the nuances of sex, gender, and sexuality: athleticism through musculature, masculinity by way of body hair, or femininity via attire. Yet when users conceal their identities by not including face pics, they can run afoul of app norms. A user's failure to share a face pic is frequently cited as grounds for blocking profiles and/or not responding to messages. For many users, the publicness inherent in sharing a face pic is a necessary precursor for all interactions online.[19]

Mark Hansen offers two ways of understanding the relationship between such images and users' interactions with them: a functionalist model called the "human-computer interface" (HCI), and an affective model called the "digital facial image" (DFI). In the HCI, which is the functionalist model of the interface, the range of users' experiences with information is equated with the aesthetics of the database, or how it arranges text and image via menus and boxes. In this understanding of the user's interaction with data, Hansen sees the notion of faciality that Gilles Deleuze and Felix Guattari put forth in *A Thousand Plateaus*.[20] Here, facialization names the process by which capitalism subsumes intensities of experience, where matter moves "from the organic strata to the strata of signifiance and subjectification."[21] In this account, the face becomes overcoded with bodily information, operating as both a "white wall," where the social order inscribes itself, and the "black hole" into which potentiality is reined in via representation.[22] This sublimation of body into face is, in essence, an abbreviation in which Deleuze and Guattari see a taming of potentiality via the processes of signification.[23] In this understanding of the interface, pics reconceive bodily information as representation, making the apps a window to some object beyond the screen. It is an indexical relationship that acts as a filter, limiting the possibilities for users to interact with digital information to the representations available to them in the database. This model of the interface limits the range of experiences that the apps enable, binding them to the sign system that animates the database.[24] According to this logic, technology drives the interface.

What is happening around the technology determines how the interface functions just as much as the technology itself.[25] Hansen's second model, the DFI, addresses these factors by emphasizing the multiplicity of bodily responses to information. In contrast with the functionalist model, the DFI is an affective model of the interface that "transfers the site of [the] interface from computer-embodied functions to the open-ended, positive feedback loop linking information to the entire affective register operative in the embodied viewer-participant."[26] In this conceptual shift, Hansen prevents the "channeling [of] the body's contribution through the narrow frame of pre-constituted software options," opting instead to reconceive the interface as a site defined by "the richness of the bodily processing of information."[27] An affective model of the interface involves a different understanding of faciality, one that is consonant with the definition of the close-up Deleuze puts forth in *Cinema 1*. Unlike the definition of faciality in *A Thousand Plateaus*, the close-up of *Cinema 1* liberates affect from the face, rendering it an expression of the body that does not eliminate the body. The characterization of faciality put forth in *Cinema 1* releases the image from its spatiotemporal context, imbuing it with excessive properties that prompt a bodily response in the person viewing it.[28] Hansen builds on this definition of the close-up to suggest that in this version of faciality, "the face does not so much *express* the body, as *catalyze* the production of a *supplementary* sensorimotor connection between the body and a domain (informatics) that is fundamentally heterogeneous to it."[29] Characterizing this process as an "affective attunement," Hansen uses it to imagine an interface structured by the dynamic interaction between human and technology. In this affective model of the interface, the body affects and is affected by something outside of it—digital information—in ways that can be identified by terms not wholly dictated by the arrangement of signifiers in the database. According to this logic, the representational system that organizes the database can only ever be a synecdoche, making humans the driving force of the interface. Their reactions to information they encounter in the database—laughter, anger, disgust, and so on—shape how the interface operates.

In the functionalist model, I see an understanding of the interface that places users in relation to something beyond the screen, which gives short shrift to technology's necessarily imperfect mediation of that relation.[30] In the affective model, I see an understanding of the interface that is more process oriented; it is a loop where technology's inability to ever seamlessly mediate the relationship between users and the objects of their desire comes into sharper focus. Insofar as the apps are used in search of something specific, where users scroll through images of people as they seek love, sex, friendship, or some other kind of intimacy, the functionalist model offers a straightforward avenue for understanding the apps as conduits to objects of desire. In this view, a database redesign that, for example, features more inclusive pull-down menus is an important development: it increases the scope of bodies, identities, and desires accommodated by a given technology. Corporate discourses on mobile media promote such developments with ideas about freedom and belonging that can be found in all rights claims made in the name of identity politics. According to this logic, a database with more finely conceived sexual identities and desires marks a step toward achieving social justice. Even so, a functionalist understanding of the interface cannot fully account for the difficulties of desire, especially as those difficulties relate to the nature of digital technology's mediation.

But like the inscrutability of Willy Wonka's facial expression in the meme described at the opening of this chapter, users often experience multiple, conflicting emotions when they encounter information online. What I like about Hansen's notion of the affective interface is its emphasis on the gap between human and machine, like the ways that people struggle to navigate information, and/or are otherwise affected by the experience of using technology. The users of gay and lesbian apps do not always know what they seek when they are online, and they are not often certain they have found the objects of their desires when they encounter them. An affective model of the interface highlights the difficulties of pursuing desire on the apps. Users calibrate and recalibrate the needs, wants, and disclosures they make to others in concert with the feelings they experience on the apps. "Long-term relationship" and "casual sex" are frequent menu options on the technologies, but users' experiences when looking for those relations often involve laughter and tears, featuring as many funny moments as they do painful and disappointing ones. The functionalist model enables an understanding of how gay and lesbian apps are influenced by the politics of identity and desire that characterize the contemporary moment. But the affective model opens the apps to an analysis of the feelings that users have about those politics. It shifts attention to the person in front of the screen, as opposed to limiting analysis to the contents therein.

The Functionalist Interface and Territorialized Politics

Consuming the apps requires that users submit to the logic of search; in their profiles, users must articulate their identities and desires in ways that are legible to others. But in announcing the debut of Mesh, a mobile media company that serves queer women, cofounder Yeni Sleidi proclaims: "Mesh doesn't put anyone in a box," because unlike many other gay and lesbian apps, Mesh's database design includes pull-down menus with inclusive categories like "queer" and "transgender."[31] This tension between the structure of database design and the agency of individual users highlights rhetorical maneuvering seen across the applications that gay and lesbian mobile media companies make available. In order to be "included," user profiles have to be searchable, and in order to be searchable, users have to be "put in boxes." When filling out their profiles, people pick from a range of preconstituted options on pull-down menus. Eric Freedman characterizes the design of dating websites as animating categories that operate as "containers for particular outpourings of identity, [with] subdivisions . . . driven by both the architecture of site engines and those desiring engines attached to particular formations of identity."[32] Users describe who they are and what they want from their time online, a process that is informed by the terms made available to them in database designs.

The terminology of a given database precipitates expectations about the people behind the profiles that users encounter online. For example, profiles require that users pick from a range of options when characterizing their romantic entanglements. Wing Ma'am, another app that caters to women, features a pull-down menu that offers users a variety of potential relationship statuses to pick from: "single," "in a relationship," "poly," and "it's complicated." Similarly, Growlr, an app that targets gay men who participate in bear subcultures, offers its users a detailed relationship status menu that includes the standard varieties of "single," "in a relationship," and "married," but adds the categories "it's complicated," "open relationship," and "triad." The categories collected in pull-down menus provide users with terms for self-definition that are widely legible, both online and off. When users pursue desire online, their identities and desires are delimited and contoured by the terminology that organizes a given database.

In their attempts to be inclusive and cater to a wide variety of users, app pull-down menus present considerable variety. For example, Wing Ma'am allows users to pick from a dozen sexual identities: lesbian, bisexual, trans, transman, transwoman, queer, questioning, intersex, genderqueer, pansexual, asexual, and polyamorous. On all of the gay and lesbian mobile media apps, users traverse "looking for" menus that they use to state the kinds of interpersonal connections they seek online. On Grindr, this function allows users to tag multiple desires; an individual can state that he is looking for "chat," "dates," "friends," "networking," or a "relationship"—or any combination therein. On Scruff, another app that caters to gay men, the "looking for" menu adds the category "random play/NSA [no strings attached]." The Growlr "looking for" menu adds terms that circulate among bear communities like "cubs" and "otters," where "cubs" are younger hairy men and "otters" are thinner hairy men. Growlr's pull-down menu also allows users to pick from "polar bears" for older hirsute men, "chub" for fuller-figured men, and "chasers" for their admirers. Thus, pull-down menus allow users to articulate with some specificity what they seek and whom they wish to meet. The specificity of these features demonstrates the fine differentiations that databases make in parsing out categories of identification and desire for users.

Crucially, the variety that databases attempt to construct is never limitless. While commitments to inclusion via design are a central element of marketing discourses on the gay and lesbian apps, they are necessarily hemmed in by the functionality of digital technology. Race and ethnicity menus provide a case in point. While all of the apps make a variety of identity options available in their pull-down menus, the menus cannot accommodate all of the permutations that racial and ethnic identifications might involve.[33] The limits of database design can also be seen in how apps allow users to articulate HIV status. While some (though not all) of the gay male apps have pull-down menus for such disclosures, these categories have become far more complex in light of treatment developments and evolving sexual practices related to managing the virus. Users may identify as being HIV-positive on the apps, but many HIV-positive people take medications that make their viral loads undetectable.[34] As a result, "HIV-positive" is a multiple category. Other users identify as being HIV-negative, but also take pre-exposure prophylaxis, a pharmaceutical preventative used to decrease the risk for contracting HIV.[35] So "HIV-negative" is a multiple category too. At the same time, variations in serostatus lead to a set of sexual practices related to condom use: always safe, usually safe, sometimes safe, never safe, and so on. Pull-down menus do not accommodate such variety, gesturing to some of the tensions between the features that organize databases and the off-line bodies and practices to which they refer.[36]

Many of the apps include text boxes, which mitigate the limitations of pull-down menus and allow users to refine the selections they make when filling out their profiles. The architecture of Lesarion, another app that caters to women, features more text boxes than pull-down menus. The result is a profile with more spaces in which users may employ their own language. One section of the Lesarion profile includes a series of prompts that users swipe through and answer. The categories include: "In my free time I—," "I should do more—," "I like—," "I don't like—," "My dream woman—," "How I came out," "In a relationship, it's important to me—," "I dream about—," "My motto/life philosophy is—," and "A perfect day for me is—." In the text boxes, users type a few sentences to give others a better sense of the person behind the profile. Lesarion also includes several blank text boxes in which users can pose and answer questions of their own. Similarly, a section of the Wing Ma'am profile provides a list of five talking points regarding "when you meet me in person," providing users with a blueprint for what the person behind the profile would like to do upon meeting off-line. These categories are also followed by text boxes that users fill in with their own words: "Buy me a—," "Talk to me about—," "Never mention—," "Make sure you have—," and "Icebreaker idea." While such interface elements can only accommodate a limited number of characters, they are still more open-ended than pull-down menus.

Nevertheless, language is always somewhat opaque, and desire can defy easy representation. Apps demand that users consciously self-present, an interpellation that requires a performance of self that can be a difficult, sometimes even unbearable task.[37] In the text that users type into free-form text boxes, they grasp for legible terminology when communicating information about their bodies, identifications, and desires to other users. Sometimes users employ the text boxes to draw boundaries that delineate desirable interactions. On all of the apps, users employ the text boxes to refine the options available to them in pull-down menus, like when users specify their ethnic identifications: Irish, Italian, Puerto Rican, or Dominican. The term "FWB" is also a common feature in text boxes on the apps, referring to "friends with benefits," or friends who sometimes engage in casual sex. Users also often use the text boxes to identify as "tops" or "bottoms," terms that refer to insertive or receptive partners for the purposes of sexual penetration, as well as dominant or submissive partners more generally. On the apps that target men, users often use the text boxes to clarify HIV status and elaborate on their safer sex practices. On the male apps, users also employ text boxes to screen other users' interests (or lack thereof) in "partying," a term that refers to the practice of coupling sexual activity with recreational drug use. In those profiles, "partying" is often spelled "parTying," where the capital "T" connotes "Tina," a vernacular term used by gay men that refers to methamphetamine. A quick perusal of profiles on the apps that target women reveals that users often employ text boxes to dismiss "bi-curious" users. Here, "curiosity" signifies an interest in sexual experimentation that defies established identity categories. Although the apps accommodate considerable variety, users do not welcome fluidity with the same gusto. In these ways, users attempt to state up front the kinds of interactions they seek, and to be explicit in identifying the practices in which they will and will not engage.

Although text boxes allow users greater leeway in self-expression than pull-down menus, users can struggle to convey the subtleties and nuances of identity and desire there too. Pull-down menus relieve users from the pressure of having to describe their wants and needs in their own words, if only because of the menus' finitude. As the examples illustrate, negotiating desire on the apps requires a considerable amount of explanation and elaboration, and the potential for miscommunication runs high. In marketing discourses on gay and lesbian mobile media, those obstacles are framed as political issues, presenting the communication of desire as a problem that company executives have experienced themselves. Part of the promotional work undertaken in these discourses is the characterization of the mobile media industry generally, and the courtship of gay and lesbian app users specifically, as a personal, political passion for media professionals. The founders of gay and lesbian mobile media companies cast their labor as being informed by their own struggles as sexual minorities, particularly their challenges related to love and romance. For instance, in press discourses on Grindr, founder Joel Simkhai emphasizes the isolation he felt growing up as a closeted gay man, mobilizing it as an impetus for his professional labor. To one reporter, he states: "The question I think every gay man starts asking, from the moment he realizes he's gay [is]. . . . 'Who else here, right now, is gay?' You are looking around, you are constantly wondering. . . . And every gay man who asks himself that question also thinks 'Wouldn't it be good if there was some way for me to tell? Some way for me to know?'"[38] He states: "Every gay man has had the idea for Grindr"; the social media network transforms a potentially hostile space into a gay-friendly place.[39] According to Simkhai, the technology realizes this fantasy by identifying other gay men in a user's immediate vicinity. He positions the app as solving the problem of users feeling lonely, ostensibly helping them find others like themselves.

As in the instance of Grindr, marketing discourses on Scruff articulate the app as solving the problem of gay men who find it difficult to locate others like themselves, a desire for community that masks the operations of power on which it is predicated. In interviews, Scruff founder Johnny Skandros differentiates his app from Grindr by pointing to differences in who the apps target, identifying "scruffy" men as "look[ing] more masculine, [men who] look more rugged."[40] Using conventional ideas about masculine gender performance, Skandros draws a distinct typology in identifying Scruff's target market, suggesting that such users find it difficult to meet one another without the app.[41] In marketing discourses on Growlr, founder Coley Cummiskey parses out the app's target demographic by making fine differentiations in the bodies, identifications, and desires of gay men. He states: "The apps I found seemed more twink-based, there were none aimed solely at the bear community. . . . I think a lot of the bigger guys didn't feel comfortable developing an app for this specific market."[42] Cummiskey casts himself and the communities to which he belongs as minorities within minorities, identifying "twinks," a term that refers to young, athletic gay men with smooth torsos, as occupying a higher position in the social hierarchy of gay male identities than do "bears," a term that refers to hirsute gay men with thick builds. On the one hand, Skandros's and Cummiskey's statements indicate the multiplicity of identity formations, erotic tastes, and presentational styles that comprise the target demographics for the apps. On the other hand, their comments gesture to the complications that occur when commingling in digital spaces, where users segregate each other and express their distaste for the categorizations employed by databases and other users. The beleagueredness of gay men who perform relatively conventional forms of masculinity is debatable. But in their insistence that their professional labor is informed by their personal difficulties meeting people like themselves, Skandros's and Cummiskey's comments point to the frictions that occur between users and the hierarchies at work in any taxonomy of bodies, identities, and desires.

In marketing discourses on the apps that cater to women, the personal investments of media professionals are often located in the gender-specific perils of pursuing desire on the internet. Mesh's founders explain that the app's database features were prompted by the surfeit of "creepy messages" that queer women receive from heterosexual men.[43] These features include specific blocking functions in which users identify "dealbreaker questions" to siphon out unwanted interactions. Many women report male harassment in online environments, where men either masquerade as women or seek threesomes with bi-curious female partners.[44] In interviews, the company's CEO claims that the impetus for the app was women's happiness and safety: "Harassment and undesirable vulgarity runs unchecked . . . leaving many women with a negative experience."[45] In 2015, the app Daatch (a neologism that combines "date" with "match") rebranded itself as HER, emphasizing its female owners and designers as key elements of its appeal to female users. To help protect its users, Daatch/HER includes a gender verification process that requires users to sign up via their Facebook or Twitter accounts. Yet, in their attempts to protect female app users from predatory behavior, the apps can naturalize assumptions about sex, gender, and desire. For instance, in the rules that govern photo uploads on Wapa, the company warns: "Most genuine girls don't say filthy things on their profile, if you do it'll make us look at it twice. We're very good at telling the difference between the things a man pretending to be female would say as opposed to a real female."[46] In its efforts to protect women, the company insists on a binary understanding of gender and delimits a set of "proper" behaviors for its female users, constructing "right" and "wrong" ways for women to identify and behave.

The ideological work performed by database designs and marketing discourses creates tacit dynamics of power. In casting themselves as victims of cultural hierarchies, Skandros's and Cummiskey's stated investments in the mobile media companies value some modes of desire and identity over and above others. Perhaps to a lesser extent, Wapa's photo policy suggests that some users may not feel welcome on the app. In all cases, marketing discourses create a set of norms about proper ways of being and wanting, demonstrating some of the tensions that operate between the apps and the people who use them. These dynamics of power are particularly evident in the testimonials of app users. Grindr publishes testimonials on its website, where users report finding love and community on the app in ways that denigrate other modes of relation available there. In one such testimonial, a user from a rural area in Canada writes: "I had always thought of Grindr as a hook-up app. It wasn't until I found out that men in ultra conservative areas were using it to find each other for social calls and real [long-term] dating that I decided that it was ok and [downloaded] it. Now, I am an avid supporter of this app. It is an awesome tool that I have met many friends on and helped many other[s] come out."[47] In gesturing to the search for love as a primary reason why users consume Grindr, the testimonial highlights the users' discomfort with the notion that the apps might be used for "hooking up," or interpersonal connections of the purely sexual sort.

Throughout the testimonials published on Grindr's website, a politics of respectability shapes how people talk about apps and the intimacies found on them.[48] In recognizing Grindr for helping him come out of the closet, a user in Massachusetts thanks Grindr by animating the same hierarchy: "I was using Grindr to explore my sexuality and help build self-confidence as I discovered my most comfortable self. And out of nowhere I met someone who has changed me forever. I'm in a healthy happy loving and strong relationship with a beautiful person. We met on Grindr. I am forever grateful."[49] The user's testimonial points to the ways in which he emerged from the closet into a welcoming, accepting community. But here, too, the user constructs that community through language that champions certain modes of intimacy over and above others. According to this user, conventional romance is better than casual sex. He reports that Grindr helped him create attachments that were difficult to forge in real time but frames those attachments in terms that are consistent with conservative bourgeois norms about intimacy and sexuality.

In fact, most of the user testimonials published on Grindr's website champion romantic connections over and above sexual ones. A Grindr fan from Australia writes:

> I personally haven't had anything to do with Grindr, but I thought I would come here and discuss the positive experience my best friend has had. My best friend only came out at the end of 2009, after leaving high school. He joined Grindr as a way to get in contact with more gays in the area and met his now boyfriend of more than a year. They met on here, and are inseparable. Talking about marriage, children etc. Just wanted to come here and tell you my story, thank you so much for giving this to people out there. Hope more people have had a positive experience like my best friend![50]

Wholly complicit with the company's bottom line, the testimonial gestures to user investments in the app by emphasizing how the technology fosters feelings of agency and connection among those who use it. In doing so, the testimonial exhibits traditional beliefs about which desires and modes of relation are most valuable.

All of the apps self-consciously exploit their user base for political ends, providing more evidence of the ideological balancing act required of their corporate communications.[51] Because the apps are often discursively connected to crime and drug abuse, their coverage in the popular press often pathologizes same-sex desire.[52] As a result, the companies' promotional efforts are more complicated than simple attempts at creating respectability. Many of the apps that target female users have calendar functions that allow users to share information about community meetings and events.[53] Both Grindr and Scruff distribute information about sexually transmitted diseases to their users, and all of the apps periodically release advertisements related to political and cultural issues. After Hurricane Sandy struck the northeastern United States in October 2012, an advertisement circulated on Growlr that declared support for those displaced and injured by the storm, and provided "click-thru" links that allowed users to make donations to storm relief efforts. A similar advertisement circulated on Scruff after the March 2011 Tohoku earthquake and tsunami. Like the Growlr advertisement, it provided users with "click-thru" links that allowed them to make donations to relief efforts. Press releases for all of the companies highlight their political commitments, generating a discourse in which there is a discernible anxiety about how users and advertisers understand the cultural functions of the apps.[54]

Most of the activism that takes place on the apps focuses on issues specific to sexual minorities. When the US Supreme Court heard opening arguments on cases related to gay marriage in 2011, Grindr distributed a pop-up advertisement that declared support for marriage-minded queer people, but also featured "click-thru" links connecting users to local rallies in their areas. Similarly, a pop-up advertisement on Growlr after Barack Obama's second inauguration in January 2013 made users aware of the US president's statements related to lesbian, gay, bisexual, transgender (LGBT) rights and issues. Around the same time, Scruff issued a message in support of gay, lesbian, and bisexual people working in the military. It made users aware of the Military Acceptance Project, and included "click-thru" links for users to sign petitions and offer financial support. While these ads gesture to the apps' reach in amassing support and assistance for global and national issues, the technologies also feature hyperlocal political advertising. When I lived in New England between 2010 and 2012, Grindr advertisements repeatedly made Maine residents aware of local politicians' support for LGBT people and issues. One prompted users to contact the state's US senators about LGBT rights issues being debated on the congressional floor. Another issued a statement of support for two state Democratic candidates, urging network users to vote for the candidates on Election Day. Through such political advertisements, mobile media companies emphasize their participation in the electoral process as well as their potential to foster civic engagement.

The apps' civic potentialities are not often their primary appeal to users, and the fundamentally destabilizing experience of desire can be anathema to the communitarian impulses that mobile media companies attempt to associate with the technologies. Considering the apps as sites where identity and desire function generically underscores how rarely contemporary culture affords equal status to different ways of being and wanting. Where monogamy and hegemonic masculinity operate in some proximity to respectability, polyamorous relationships and genderqueer identities rarely involve fantasies of centrality or cultural dominance. As such, genre offers a rubric for thinking through the power relations that are embedded in sexuality and is thus always operative on gay and lesbian apps, be it the desire for self-definition amid many different methods for defining the self, or the desire for a mind-blowing orgasm amid many different methods for achieving it. The genres that operate on mobile media involve a tension between the structure of databases and the agency of users, as well as the fixedness of community and the flux of desire. These tensions are made manifest in user attempts to refine the staid functions of databases in text boxes, as well as the ideas about romantic happiness and civic engagement that mobile media companies use for the purposes of marketing and promotion. The desires that users seek on the apps are often mundane and prurient, like relief from boredom or the possibility of casual sex. When the mobile media companies promote themselves as resources for community-building and finding a romantic partner, they champion certain ways of being and wanting over and above others. Not only does this phenomenon seem to run counter to the spirit in which the apps have been conceived but it is a phenomenon that can slip by unnoticed when the focus of inquiry is the technology itself.

The Affective Interface and Deterritorialized Politics

As a sometime user myself, I can report that the gay and lesbian apps involve as much disappointment as they do pleasure, a fact that has as much to do with the nature of desire as it does with the nature of digital technologies. Users often ignore each other or use the "block" feature to break off contact. Sometimes they will communicate for a few minutes and then move on to someone else, though sometimes users just disappear altogether, either by signing off or deleting their profiles. Interactions can be tense and harsh because users frequently send messages with dismissive, imperious, or just plain offensive language. Interactions of this sort underscore the operation of a panoptic regime on the gay and lesbian apps wherein users police each other even as they regulate themselves. The connections enabled by the apps are policed by a set of in-group norms related to "proper" identities and "appropriate" desires. Of course, what is "proper" and "appropriate" is subjective. As such, using the apps to forge interpersonal connections requires the navigation of a complicated regulatory matrix in disclosing personal information. If the severity of some of these asocial behaviors can be explained by the lack of accountability that attends the physical remove of online interactions, I also see them indicating the precariousness precipitated by users making themselves vulnerable to others. In their pursuit of desire, people do things they might not do otherwise.

The range of feelings that users experience on the apps is far more nuanced and varied than the terms that the databases put forth. The reactions that people have to the difficulties of desire are legend, resulting in as many love songs and romantic comedies as they do self-help books and therapy sessions. Of the feelings that such experiences precipitate, Lauren Berlant writes: "Subjects are not usually shocked to discover their incoherence or the incoherence of the world; they often find it comic, feel a little ashamed of it, or are interested in it, excited by it, and exhausted by it too."[55] While the apps can only mobilize a limited set of terms for defining identity and desire, users have a much more varied vocabulary for discussing them. User-generated content provides evidence of the emotional negotiations that people engage in when using the apps. Blog posts, viral videos, and activity on social media networks underline the array of feelings that users experience when consuming mobile media. For instance, the website Douchebags of Grindr provides evidence of the anger that app interactions can precipitate among users. On this website, administrators collect and publish Grindr profiles in order to express their distaste for the racist and ethnocentric language commonly found in user profiles, and chastise users for behaviors that construct hierarchies of gender performance and socioeconomic class.

Douchebags of Grindr's administrators tag profiles by offense, like racism and hypermaterialism. They publish screen grabs of Grindr profiles, overlay the image with a Douchebags of Grindr watermark, and then offer commentary on the users' transgressions. The site's "hypermaterialism" tag criticizes Grindr users for being tacky and ostentatious in their profiles. In the text box on one profile, Grindr user "Steven" cites a preference for "fast cars, masculine muscle men and money," warning other Grindr users that "if you live off mom and dad I'm not interested."[56] Grindr user "Pilot!" tells other network subscribers, "less than 6figs move on," delimiting the kinds of people he wants to meet along economic lines. This desire causes site administrators to label him with the derisive tagline "High Flying Douche."[57] Similarly, Grindr user "A" lists his annual salary in his profile, prompting site administrators to call him "60K Douche."[58] On May 19, 2015, Douchebags of Grindr published the profile of Grindr user "Rob," tagging it as racist. The profile headline reads: "I'm rob love life be happy," followed by a text box in which the user writes: "I'm attracted to ozzy boys and middle eastern. I'm sorry not into Asian or Indian or no pic get blocked."[59] Douchebags of Grindr administrators dub this user "Loves Life + Specific Races Only Douche." Site administrators lob a similar criticism at Grindr user "Jaymez," whose profile text box reads: "Risk it to get the Biscuit. Sup guy!! I'm a lil more into Vanilla and Spice than chocolate or rice."[60] For citing racial and ethnic preferences that exclude black and Asian men, Douchebags of Grindr labels "Jaymez" a "Limp Biscuit."

Yet Douchebags of Grindr is not just straightforward evidence of app users' hurt feelings and attempts at political correctness. The blog suggests ongoing-ness, the ways that users contend with and manage their feelings related to social forces that impinge on their happiness. It is a sarcastic compendium that demonstrates the humor, anger, and maybe even hope that coexist with anger and injury that users often experience when using the apps. In his discussion of the insults suffered by queer black men in online spaces, Shaka McGlotten suggests that these wounds have parallels with other, older wrongs even as they point to emerging formations of collective hurt. He stops just short of labeling them "trauma," suggesting instead that these forms of insult "nestl[e] alongside other feelings, including a vulnerability less certain than trauma, and the hard to pin down incipience that is an always already beginning, an ongoing process of becoming."[61] In the snarky critiques that *Douchebags of Grindr* lob at the racist invective of some Grindr users, I see traces of the optimism McGlotten locates in black men navigating intimacy online.[62] Tan Hoang Nguyen reconceives the hurt feelings that users experience as a result of racism on the apps in a different way, looking to the surfeit of posts devoted to Asian men on Douchebags of Grindr as containing the potential for an oppositional politics. Nguyen sees a chance to reconfigure "bottomhood," the penetrated position in sex between men, in the failed masculinity and sexual passivity frequently associated with queer Asian men. He writes: "Instead of shoring up our sovereignty by conflating agency with mastery, adopting a view from the bottom reveals an inescapable vulnerability, exposure, and receptiveness in our reaching out to other people."[63] Rather than battle racist assumptions about Asian male sexuality with strategies of masculinization, Nguyen wants instead to think about embracing "bottomhood" as an affective connection that offers new ways of imagining ethics and relationality. For Nguyen, Douchebags of Grindr is more than just a critique of the racialized dynamics of power at work in queer sexual practices. In his characterization, the blog also allows for the imagination of new connections between the arrangements of bodies and the making of worlds.

If anger and injury contain the possibility that users might employ them to forge new ways of being and wanting, feelings of doubt and insecurity are more difficult to conceive of as potentially agentic. Enjoying a conversation with another user on the network can be undergirded by the trepidation of: "Does this person like this as much as I do?" Interactions frequently precipitate thoughts like: "Does he or she like me too?" The apps bind intimacy and regulation in ways that can create feelings of precariousness among users. When users run afoul of each other's ideas about what constitutes proper comportment and/or suitable identifications, the connection is often severed: sometimes they block each other, though sometimes they just ignore each other and stop interacting. Users sometimes prefer these outcomes, of course; when they are not compatible, parting ways can be a relief for both of them. Nevertheless, such events can also be painful, especially when the needs and wants of two users diverge.

Apps provide users with opportunities for both embodied and disembodied exchange, so some users see trading messages and pictures as pleasures in and of themselves, while other users see the interpersonal interactions that take shape on the networks as eventually leading to off-line encounters. These connections also shift and morph over time; users do not always know what they want from particular interactions when they begin. Sometimes chat between users evolves into the desire to meet in person. Other times, one user wants a face-to-face meeting and the other user does not. Desire is never an easy proposition. And because the apps provide users with a menu of possibilities, the technologies can make desire that much more uncertain.

Contrasting goals and a bevy of options can leave users feeling unsure and unsettled, shaping interactions between them in ways that precipitate negative feelings, which can then strip users of their agency. *The Grindr Guide* is an eight-episode YouTube series that chronicles some of these experiences. The episodes feature interviews with users in which they express the anxiety they experience when engaging in the various practices that take place on the apps: picking a profile picture, waiting for another user to respond to a message, and planning a meeting in person. In episode 3, a Grindr user named Jack discusses the decisions he made in selecting a picture for his profile. Via direct address, Jack shares with viewers his suspicion that his picture was turning off other users because it does not show his face clearly, prompting them to ignore his profile. Jack shares his hesitation in uploading a picture that shows his body, admitting that he is embarrassed that he is not as physically fit as other users he has seen online. When he uploads a new photo, a clearer face pic, Jack does not receive more messages than he had before. The episode closes with him expressing his disappointment that more Grindr users were not telling him he looked attractive. Also featured in the seventh episode of *The Grindr Guide*, Jack tells viewers about his lifelong insecurity regarding people not finding him physically appealing. Shot in medium close-up, he tells viewers that seeing pictures of naked torsos in the Grindr profiles of other users makes him feel as though he is in a competition. Jack confesses that the app makes him so insecure about his appearance that he rarely contacts users who upload torso pictures, stating: "Why would I ever bother messaging that person, they [sic] would never to talk to me." Jack is chatty and upbeat at the beginning of the seventh episode, but becomes plaintive and sad by its close, disclosing to viewers that scrolling through Grindr profiles makes him feel undesirable.

In episodes of *The Grindr Guide*, the apps are technologies of incapacitation more than they are technologies of agency. Episode 6 is called "The Aftermath," in which a Grindr user named Joel has a real-time meeting with another user he met online. Joel wants the meeting to result in an ongoing relationship, and the episode details his experience waiting for the other user to get back in touch with him. The episode is organized as a series of vignettes that unfold over several days, as Joel obsessively checks Grindr while waiting for the other user to send him a message. The episode becomes difficult to watch as Joel realizes that the other user does not reciprocate his romantic feelings. Joel's demeanor moves from nervous excitement after the encounter to sadness and dejection when he does not hear from his paramour. Roland Barthes characterizes love as a collection of such experiences, writing: "All of love's 'failures' resemble one another. . . . And yet X and Y are incomparable; it is in their difference, the model of an infinitely pursued difference, that I find the energy to begin all over again."[64] In centering on the lived, felt dimensions of devotion and infatuation, Barthes emphasizes how love is often rooted in hurt and pain; he stresses that it is often characterized by deficit, disappointment, and decline. He suggests that we love, lose, and love again; love is enthralling but episodic. These intermittent affinities are rapturous and engulfing, but by their very nature are never wholly mutual or constant. Characterizing love as a fleeting series of encounters organized by injury and pain seems especially apt when considered in the context of app-enabled intimacies. Users do not always agree on what sort of relationship they want from one another. As intimacies change shape and form, they generate a whole series of feelings that can overlap, conflict, and transform into other feelings entirely.

The apps structure how users communicate who they are and what they want, allowing them to tag themselves as looking for a range of interpersonal connections: love, sex, or nothing beyond a conversation. Yet the way that users feel about the interactions that characterize those pursuits determines how they interact with the apps as well as with the other users they meet there. Users calibrate their disclosures according to how interactions make them feel, processes that are necessarily shaped and influenced by social mores related to bodies and identities, as well as the desires and intimacies that circulate both online and off. For many users, the experience of deciding what is "too much" information to disclose to another user or determining when is "too soon" to share it results in amusement and laughter. On Twitter and Instagram, app users share screen grabs of the awkward, humorous interactions they have with other users while chatting online. Accompanied by the hashtags #awkwardgrindr and #grindrfail, the screen grabs point to the comedy of manners that sometimes results from two people negotiating their needs and wants. The hashtags are metadata that make the thousands of these images that get posted to the networks a searchable archive of strained online courtship and clumsy internet innuendo.

Much of the humor in the screen grabs shared on Twitter and Instagram can be traced back to the contrasting rates at which different users move from introductory banter to sex talk because the speed with which users segue from perfunctory greetings to erotic exchange can differ considerably. When users interact with someone who is "moving faster than they are," they often make light of the hasty sexual overtures and poke fun at the disdain the other user will often lob back. In one such interaction shared on social media, a user initiates a conversation by requesting forceful oral sex, to which the second user responds by saying he prefers "warm hugs." When the first user insults the second user for being coy about his request, the second user ends the conversation by calling the first user, derisively, "a little charmer."[65] The spatial remove involved in user exchanges on the apps is another frequent topic of screen grabs shared on Twitter and Instagram. In one such interaction, a user initiates a chat by telling the second user that he is visiting a friend at the hospital and is looking for casual sex from the waiting room in the cancer ward.[66] On Twitter and Instagram, screen grabs shared by app users get layered with additional dialogue as other users find humor in the ways that people interact on the apps. Like Douchebags of Grindr, some of the laughter precipitated by #awkwardgrindr and #grindrfail comes at the expense of others, of course, but some of that laughter also results from users recognizing their own experiences in the content that circulates there.

The disconnects between the needs and wants of different users—and the inability of the databases to signify such disparities—are integral components of users' experiences with the apps. Although database designs attempt to mitigate that disconnect, an affective view of the interface keeps in focus the fact that the apps can never fully transcend it.[67] An overly neat equation of database functionality with the user's experience of it cannot account for the range of feelings that users experience online, nor can it accommodate the ways in which those feelings ebb, flow, and change shape. When users find the apps frustrating, dispiriting, or acerbically amusing, it underlines the seam between human and technology, bringing into focus the tensions implicit in mediating desire. Some users flout the apps' intended functions, as well as their regulations and guidelines, by creating fake profiles. When they construct profiles for people real and imagined, app users play with database designs in ways unimagined by the people who created them, and prohibited by the companies that operate them. I have seen app profiles for the pope, Jesus Christ, various pop stars, and an assortment of characters from cinema and television.

Fake profiles are funny; they move beyond the apps as screen grabs that circulate via text message and social media, gesturing to the range of feelings that users have about pursuing desire on the apps. One Grindr user created a profile with a face pic of Alex Forrest, the villainess from *Fatal Attraction* (1987). The user fills in the text box as though he is the character from the movie, a scorned lover who seeks revenge from the paramour who wronged her: "Pick me. You won't regret it" (figure 5.2). As a joke, the fake Grindr profile functions on two different levels. On the one hand, the face pic resurrects an infamous movie character for the purposes of camp, rearticulating the murderous mistress as a bitch goddess looking for Mr. Right. On the other hand, the profile points to the array of emotional

Figure 5.2. A fake Grindr profile depicting the famously "scorned woman" in *Fatal Attraction* (1987) suggests the difficult feelings that can attend online courtship.

experiences users have when they consume the apps. If the fake profile creates humor by placing the picture of a famously scorned woman on an app that targets gay men, it also points to the feelings of rage and despair that can attend desire. Neither "spurned lover" nor "angry rage" are options available to users in app pull-down menus, but at one point or another, many users will likely have identified with such categories. Thus, the experiences that users have with technology do not match up neatly with the terms put forth in database designs. An affective model of the interface opens the apps to an examination of the feelings that users have about their experiences in online environments. In its oblique consideration of technology, such a model of the interface casts desire as the complicated object of analysis that it is. From that perspective, the ways that users experience the mediation of desire are far more nuanced than the options available to them in a pull-down menu, and are decidedly more complicated than text boxes and user testimonials would often have us believe.

Gender, Grindr, and Same-Sex Marriage

Because cruising for sex is a practice more likely to be associated with gay men, the apps marketed to them are more often discussed in press discourses on the apps than are the apps marketed to women, and they are more often the subject of user-generated content, as well.[68] The mobile media companies that operate apps for women promote themselves as correctives for an inequality of the marketplace, as though such consumer recognition bestows on women the power of sexual agency.[69] Yet the introduction of apps that target women can never ameliorate the structural differences in how cultures organize male versus female desire. Not only are men more likely than women to be identified as a target market, but men in general are more likely than women to have access to—and feel safe and comfortable in—public space.[70] So while the apps that enable women to make interpersonal connections are a welcome addition to the media marketplace, they cannot undo the limitations and eliminate the blind spots of gender and sexuality as cultural formations. Moreover, the fact that the app marketplace is predicated on a male/female binary further highlights the deficiencies of consumer culture as an arena for the enactment of progressive politics.[71] Even if the database designs accommodate identity categories that blur the male/female binary, the bodies that inhabit those categories are still subject to the scorn and ridicule of other users.

Nevertheless, it is too easy to look at gay and lesbian apps and lament their considerable shortcomings. I am impatient with that mode of critique, if only because it assumes from the outset that desire is a trajectory with definite resolution. At the same time, it seeks a justice that media commerce cannot provide. To that end, I see the limitations of the apps as potentially beneficial to progressive politics in terms of the discourse they generate. User-generated content about the apps often makes explicit the power dynamics that are implicit in "the romance of community" that attends media culture's courtship of sexual minorities.[72] Instances when mobile media users negotiate clashing needs and wants reveal the tensions at work when queer bodies come into contact with mechanisms of cultural power. Desire is a tricky business. Alas, it is often an ugly one too. An affective view of the interface allows for the consideration of desire as a phenomenon that people experience as bewildering, upsetting, and funny. Attention to how arduous it can be to relate to and find sustenance in others is a useful rejoinder to the romance of same-sex marriage rhetoric, where long-term commitments are too frequently painted as the best way for sexual minorities to desire. Love and romance have complex relationships with the variety of relations that users seek online. In this context, the more casual, decidedly more carnal forms of intimacy that users seek on the apps become "other" to more conventional, more respectable modes of relation. Moreover, even with the establishment of same-sex marriage as a right of citizenship, people can find such intimacies disheartening and exasperating. Sometimes they even find them hilarious. Considering the range of emotions that people have when online allows for more careful consideration of the connections they forge with one another, as well as the thorny relationships that humans have with machines.

Notes

1. An internet meme is a piece of culture that circulates between users online; it is typically a joke told via image, phrase, sound file, and/or video clip. Internet memes are replicable and malleable: users modify and then share them, so memes morph as they circulate by way of text message, e-mail, or social media. Patrick Davison, "The Language of Internet Memes," in *The Social Media Reader*, ed. Michael Mandiberg (New York: New York University Press, 2012), 120–136.

2. Another interpretation of the meme might see in it a critique of online intimacies more generally. Contemporary culture often looks down on the forms of attachment available on the internet, as though such intimacies are somehow "less than" those found off-line. In that sense, the meme is consonant with prevalent beliefs about desire and the internet, which often feature disdain for people who look for meaningful connections with others online. In discussing the development of online spaces that facilitate intimacy, Shaka McGlotten writes: "These new freedoms and possibilities picked up anxieties like Velcro. Virtual intimacies signaled new possibilities even as they foregrounded the perceived failures of intimate belonging. Virtual intimacies were failures before the fact. If you had to get online to get it, it couldn't be the real thing." Shaka McGlotten, *Virtual Intimacies: Media, Affect, and Queer Sociality* (Albany: State University of New York Press, 2013), 2.

3. Jacques Lacan refers to this phenomenon as the "*objet petit a*," the object cause of desire. It is a structuring absence more than a positive entity, giving shape to desire as a force that is always, in some way, "without." Jacques Lacan, *The Four Fundamental Concepts of Psycho-Analysis* (New York: W. W. Norton, 1981). See also Todd MacGowan, *Real Gaze: Film Theory after Lacan* (Albany: State University of New York Press, 2007).

4. Scott Richmond offers boredom as a mode of spectatorship characterized by detachment rather than immersion. He defines boredom as a modality rooted in neoliberal capitalism, where the subject's attention is distributed across his or her different roles, responsibilities, and engagements. "Boredom helps us understand some of the affective postures and aesthetic dispositions that make damaged, precarious life bearable in our current economic, social, cultural, and technical milieux." Scott Richmond, "Vulgar Boredom, or What Andy Warhol Can Teach Us about *Candy Crush*," *Journal of Visual Culture* 14, no. 1 (April 2015): 3.

5. I borrow this term from Lauren Berlant and Lee Edelman and use it to refer to the notion that desire makes one less than autonomous, or not always "in control." See Lauren Berlant and Lee Edelman, *Sex, or the Unbearable* (Durham, NC: Duke University Press, 2013).

6. Kane Race suggests that the term "checking in" is a useful metaphor for describing a primary use of these technologies. "'Checking in' has become a key element in the enactment of an erotically-invested gay identity, in which online browsing and random chat takes the form of a compelling mode of everyday distraction, personal validation and social recognition." Kane Race, "Speculative Pragmatism and Intimate Arrangements: Online Hook-Up Devices in Gay Life," *Culture, Health and Sexuality* 17, no. 4 (July 3, 2014): 3–4, doi: 10.1080/13691058.2014.930181.

7. Robert Payne identifies a similar set of links between the affordances of digital technologies, the financial imperatives of media industries, and the moral economies of individual agency that characterize contemporary culture. We differ in how we conceptualize our objects of analysis but our projects overlap considerably in taking up questions of affect in relation to sexuality and social media. See Robert Payne, *The Promiscuity of Network Culture: Queer Theory and Digital Media* (New York: Routledge, 2014).

8. Berlant and Edelman, *Sex, or the Unbearable*, 6.

9. Tarleton Gillespie uses the term "platform" to connote the tensions at work in technology companies' different functions and publics. "The term 'platform' helps reveal how YouTube and others stage themselves for these constituencies, allowing them to make a broadly progressive sales pitch while also eliding the tensions inherent in their service: between user-generated and commercially-produced content, between cultivating community and serving up advertising, between intervening in the delivery of content and remaining neutral. In the process, it is offering up a trope by which others will come to understand and judge them." Tarleton Gillespie, "The Politics of 'Platforms,'" *New Media and Society* 12, no. 3 (September 2010): 348.

10. For an overview of the intellectual genealogies that inform the study of user identities in online environments, see Alice Marwick, "Online Identity," in *Companion to New Media Dynamics,* ed. John Hartley, Jean Burgess, and Axel Bruns (Malden, MA: Blackwell, 2013), 355–364. For a brief overview of the literature on queerness as it relates to communication technologies, see Adrienne Shaw and Katherine Sender, "Queer Technologies: Affordances, Affect, Ambivalence," *Critical Studies in Media Communication* 33, no. 1 (March 10, 2016): 1–5, doi: 10.1080/15295036.2015.1129429.

11. I see these typologies of bodies, identities, and desires operating as genres, where genre can be understood as "a conventional habitus entailing understandings and agreements that don't need to be specifically negotiated concerning the 'kinds' of social interaction that are possible under the aegis of that culture. . . . What genres regulate, with varying degrees of rigidity and flexibility, is the social appropriateness of discursive behavior." Quoted in David Halperin, *How to Be Gay* (Cambridge, MA: Belknap, Harvard University Press, 2012), 131.

12. My aims here are similar to Kane Race's aims in describing the relationship between technological devices, information infrastructures, and the desires of mobile app users. He calls his approach "speculative pragmatism," which "entails the analysis and description of design features and functions of smartphone and interfaces as these features are—or may be—used and put into practice. A key concern is to situate digital devices as active elements in the shaping of sexual practices; to trace how digital devices interfere with, transform or otherwise impact given practices and relations. As such, this approach has both empirical and speculative dimensions: it is concerned not only with what happens, but also what might happen, the possible." Race, "Speculative Pragmatism and Intimate Arrangements," 5.

13. Manuel DeLanda differentiates assemblages from other sorts of categorization, seeing in them the potential to reimagine the ways in which cultures function: "Taxonomists reify the general categories produced by their classifications. . . . Assemblage theory does not presuppose the existence of reified generalities." Furthermore, Alex Galloway's ideas about the different regimes of signification at work in the interface overlap with DeLanda's insofar as both

argue that different political results follow from different aesthetic arrangements. See Manuel DeLanda, *A New Philosophy of Society: Assemblage Theory and Social Complexity* (New York: Continuum, 2006), 26; and Alexander R. Galloway, *The Interface Effect* (Malden, MA: Polity, 2012), 46–53.

14. Lauren Berlant uses this dual definition of genre: "Genre stands as something like a conventionalized symbolic, an institution whose modern translation through the commodity form affixes it with both genericness and a uniqueness derived from the particularity of its distinguishing details. Genre also figures the nameable aspiration for discursive order though which particular life narratives and modes of being become normalized as the real." Lauren Berlant, *The Female Complaint: The Unfinished Business of Sentimentality in American Culture* (Durham, NC: Duke University Press, 2008), 259.

15. Lev Manovich, *The Language of New Media* (Cambridge, MA: MIT Press, 2002).

16. In parsing out these different understandings of the interface, I follow Kane Race's lead in problematizing impasses in modes of thought used to describe queer desires in online environments. I take a slightly different tack, though, insofar as Race is interested in how criticism of these issues often "bifurcates gay sex into two distinct, discrete and directly juxtaposed figures: the self-interested, competitive, neoliberal, market subject, who frequents the spaces and venues of casual sex, and the romantic subject of regular domestic partnership, who enjoys special access to spaces of care and intimacy." But like Race, I am interested in the space between oft-generated critical categories in order to better understand the experience of pursuing desire via mobile apps. Race, "Speculative Pragmatism and Intimate Arrangements," 3.

17. "We take pictures of ourselves knowing the paths they will take . . . , or we repurpose (and edit) pictures taken for other occasions and carefully attempt to reinscribe them, as we try to massage . . . what we perceive to be our likeness. Perhaps as an attempt at self-narration, many online daters include multiple images, showing themselves in varied contexts . . . and from varied perspectives, as a storyboard of sorts, creating a bare-bones plotline that also yields a greater assurance of authentic communication." Eric Freedman, *Transient Images: Personal Media in Public Frameworks* (Philadelphia: Temple University Press, 2011), 121.

18. "Consciousness and memory are not produced by an accumulation of signifiers; rather, they are the products of narrative. As we approach the [profile], we may add up the formal cues and the site's specific forms of data, but we do so in order to construct a different type of portrait. Beyond the literal image found on the page, we create a projection by narrativizing the subject, or pulling the subject out of its immediate context and repurposing it." Ibid.

19. In his analysis of Gaydar, a UK-based online network for gay men, Sharif Mowlabocus emphasizes that a user's reluctance to self-present can cast doubt on his claims to truthfulness and genuineness among other users. Sharif Mowlabocus, *Gaydar Culture: Gay Men, Technology, and Embodiment in the Digital Age* (Burlington, VT: Ashgate, 2012).

20. Faciality and face pics are not one and the same. "Faciality" refers to the process of signification, broadly conceived. I apply it here to images that circulate on the apps, pointing out that app norms require users to share pictures of themselves, often face pics.

21. Gilles Deleuze and Felix Guattari, *A Thousand Plateaus: Capitalism and Schizophrenia* (Minneapolis: University of Minnesota Press, 1987), as quoted in Mark Hansen, *A New Philosophy for New Media* (Cambridge, MA: MIT Press, 2006), 131.

22. Deleuze and Guattari, *Thousand Plateaus*, 167.

23. "The deterritorialization of the body implies a reterritorialization on the face; the collapse of corporeal coordinates or milieus implies the constitution of a landscape. The semiotic of the signifier and the subjective never operates through bodies. It is absurd to claim to relate

the signifier to the body." Deleuze and Guattari, as quoted by Hansen, *New Philosophy for New Media*, 131.

24. Alex Galloway stresses that new media are often understood as relaying undistorted facts in ways that elide the role of technology in shaping information. For Galloway, that phenomenon makes an understanding of an interface as a "specific communicative artifice" all the more crucial. Galloway, *Interface Effect*, 9.

25. The call to move analysis of online media toward modes of criticism and objects of analysis that can shed more light on the embodied experience of users is a frequent one in scholarship on the internet. For instance, Michele White complicates the frequent framing of the internet user as being either an "active" agent or a "passive" receptacle for ideology by looking to representations of users and their devices in order to "theorize the fleshy position of the body in front of a computer screen." Similarly, Jason Farman stresses the need for scholars who study mobile media to consider the ways in which "devices work in tandem with bodies and locales in a process of inscribing meaning into our . . . social interactions." See Michele White, *The Body and the Screen: Theories of Internet Spectatorship* (Cambridge, MA: MIT Press, 2006), 177; and Jason Farman, *Mobile Interface Theory: Embodied Space and Locative Media* (New York: Routledge, 2011), 1.

26. Hansen, *New Philosophy for New Media*, 130.

27. Ibid.

28. "The face is this organ-carrying plate of nerves which has sacrificed most of its global mobility and which gathers or expresses in a free way all kinds of tiny local movements which the rest of the body usually keeps hidden. Each time we discover these two poles in something—reflecting surface and intensive micro-movements—we can say that this thing has been treated as a face . . . even if it does not resemble a face. There is no close-up *of* the face, the face is in itself close-up, the close-up is by itself face and both are affect, affection-image." Emphasis in the original. Gilles Deleuze, *Cinema 1: The Movement Image* (Minneapolis: University of Minnesota Press, 1986), as quoted in Hansen, *New Philosophy for New Media*, 132.

29. Emphasis in the original. Hansen, *New Philosophy for New Media*, 133.

30. Galloway characterizes digital interfaces as always, in some sense, "unworkable": "What you see is not what you get. Software is the medium that is not a medium. . . . Code is never viewed as it is. Instead, code must be compiled, interpreted, parsed, and otherwise driven into hiding by larger globs of code." Ibid., 69.

31. Quoted in Kate Dries, "Meet Mesh, a Dating Site That Sifts Out Spammers and Harassers," *Jezebel*, April 25, 2014, http://jezebel.com/meet-mesh-a-dating-site-that-sifts-out -spammers-and-ha-1567634724.

32. Freedman, *Transient Images*, 126.

33. As Lisa Nakamura points out, the expression of racial subjectivity via menu options in digital environments naturalizes certain assumptions about race and ethnicity. She charges that new media platforms frequently "forc[e] reductive, often archaic means of defining race upon the user." Lisa Nakamura, *Cybertypes: Race, Ethnicity, and Identity on the Internet* (New York: Routledge, 2002), 101.

34. Kane Race, *Pleasure Consuming Medicine: The Queer Politics of Drugs* (Durham, NC: Duke University Press, 2009).

35. Jonathan S. Jay and Lawrence O. Gostin, "Ethical Challenges of Preexposure Prophylaxis for HIV," *Journal of the American Medical Association Online*, July 27, 2012, http://jama .jamanetwork.com/article.aspx?articleid=1262682.

36. In 2014, Scruff added a category in one of its pull-down menus that allows for HIV-positive app users to tag themselves as members of a "Poz" community. The company promoted

the change to the pull-down menu by framing it as an act of social justice that aims to combat the stigma of HIV. So while the companies are well aware that HIV status is a matter of import to their users, the affordances of the technology do not allow for the fine differentiations that characterize the virus off-line. See Jason Marchant, "Beyond 'HIV Status': Interface Design Is Personal at Scruff," *Huffington Post*, December 1, 2014, http://www.huffingtonpost .com/jason-marchant/beyond-hiv-status-interfa_b_6227964.html.

37. Many thanks to Ben Aslinger for helping me clarify this point.

38. Quoted in Polly Vernon, "The New Sexual Revolution," *Observer*, July 4, 2010, 34.

39. Ibid.

40. Doug Rule, "Bear Necessity," *MetroWeekly*, July 28, 2011, www.metroweekly.com /nightlife/clublife/?ak=6457.

41. Yael Roth, "Locating the 'Scruff Guy': Theorizing Body and Space in Gay Geosocial Media," *International Journal of Communication* 8 (July 2014), http://ijoc.org/index.php/ijoc /article/view/2286/1192.

42. Jon Dunn, "We Love Growlr—More Bears in More Places," *Outlook*, April 2011, http:// outlook.columbus/2011/04/we-9/.

43. Caitlin Dewey, "A Wave of New Dating Sites Attempts the Impossible: Getting Rid of All the Creeps," *Washington Post Online*, September 30, 2014, http://www.washingtonpost.com /news/the-intersect/wp/2014/09/30/a-wave-of-new-dating-sites-attempts-the-impossible -getting-rid-of-all-the-creeps/.

44. In their marketing discourses, mobile media companies reference this phenomenon frequently, citing it as an impetus for the creation of apps geared for women.

45. Quoted in Dries, "Meet Mesh."

46. All of the gay and lesbian apps have strict guidelines about what kinds of nudity can and cannot be included in user photos, pointing to a regulatory regime that seeks to harness desire for a variety of reasons. On the apps that cater to women, photos are scrutinized in order to ensure that a user's visage is consistent with the claims made in her profile. For an example of one such policy, see Wapa's user agreement at "What Are the Rules?" http://wapa-app.com /photo_rules_wapa.htm. For more information on the regulatory nature of photo policies in online spaces catering to gay men, see Yael Roth, "'No Overly Suggestive Photos of Any Kind': Content Management and the Policing of Self in Gay Digital Communities," *Communication, Culture and Critique* 8, no. 3–4 (September 2015): 414–432.

47. "Stories," Grindr.com, Accessed July 30, 2013.

48. Matthew Tinkcom suggests that online intimacies are rarely considered anything other than pathological or failed "because such digital sexualities make possible the idea of a heteronormative monogamous sexuality, in which all other sexualities are excluded." Matthew Tinkcom, "You've Got to Get on to Get Off": *Shortbus* and the Circuits of the Erotic," *South Atlantic Quarterly* 110, no. 3 (Summer 2011): 695.

49. "Stories," Grindr.com.

50. Ibid.

51. While users can respond to the pop-up advertisements distributed on the apps, they cannot easily distribute political information themselves. As John Edward Campbell has written about the online portal Gay.com: "All [new media technologies] purporting to serve politically marginalized groups beg the question of whether there can be a harmonious balance between the interests of community and the drives of commerce." John Edward Campbell, "Virtual Citizens or Dream Consumers: Looking for Civic Community on Gay.com," in *Queer Online: Media, Technology, and Sexuality*, ed. David Phillips and Kate O'Riordan (New York: Peter Lang, 2007), 213.

52. This phenomenon is part of a longer legacy related to sex panic. See Lauren Berlant and Michael Warner, "Sex in Public," *Critical Inquiry* 24, no. 2 (Winter 1998): 547–566. Kane Race connects this legacy to the apps that target gay men, in "'Party and Play': Online Hook-Up Devices and the Emergence of PNP Practices among Gay Men," *Sexualities* 18 (March 2015): 253–275.

53. In their research on queer women and intimacy online, Megan Sapnar Ankerson and Sarah Murray suggest that the emphasis on temporality marks an important difference in the technologies targeted to females. See Megan Sapnar Ankerson and Sarah Murray, "Lez Takes Time: Designing Lesbian Contact in Geosocial Networking Apps," *Critical Studies in Media Communication* 33, no. 1 (April 11, 2016): 53–69, doi:10.1080/15295036.2015.1133921.

54. For instance, Grindr became involved in same-sex marriage activism by launching "Grindr for Equality." In promoting these efforts in the press, Simkhai stated: "'Grindr for Equality' is looking to continue our involvement in the political process by tapping into our engaged community in order to update them on GLBT issues on a local, national, and international scale." My point is less to question the authenticity of these efforts than to point out that the activist efforts offer a veneer of respectability for a company that, in no small part, generates revenue by facilitating gay male sexuality. Simkhai quoted in David Duran, "Grindr Joins with Courage in Marriage Equality Project," *East Bay Reporter*, March 1, 2012, http://www.ebar.com/news/article.php?sec=news&article=67471.

55. Berlant and Edelman, *Sex, or the Unbearable*, 6.

56. "A Material Douche," Douchebags of Grindr, February 2, 2016, http://www.douchebagsofgrindr.com/2016/02/a-material-douche/.

57. "High Flying Douche," Douchebags of Grindr, August 19, 2011, http://www.douchebagsofgrindr.com/2011/08/high-flying-douche/.

58. "60K Douche," Douchebags of Grindr, August 13, 2011, http://www.douchebagsofgrindr.com/2011/08/60k-douche/.

59. "Loves Life + Specific Races Only Douche," Douchebags of Grindr, May 19, 2015, http://www.douchebagsofgrindr.com/2015/05/love-life-specific-races-only-douche/.

60. "Limp Biscuit," Douchebags of Grindr, August 9, 2011, http://www.douchebagsofgrindr.com/2011/08/limp-biscuit/.

61. McGlotten, *Virtual Intimacies*, 63.

62. While Douchebags of Grindr effectively renders them equivalent, modes of injury like racism, femmephobia, and classism are not interchangeable. I do not want to erase the specificities that McGlotten locates in the black male experiences of queer spaces online. In linking different modes of injury, my aim is more to highlight how the experiences of the apps are multiple, operating on planes that differ considerably from the options available to users in databases.

63. Tan Hoang Nguyen, *A View from the Bottom: Asian American Masculinity and Sexual Representation* (Durham, NC: Duke University Press, 2014), 2.

64. Roland Barthes, *A Lover's Discourse: Fragments* (New York: Hill and Wang, 1979), 10.

65. Users collect these interactions and share them on Tumblr as well. See www.grindrlol.com and www.grindrlulz.com. Accessed November 21, 2015.

66. This interaction was featured in a *Buzzfeed* article. Matt Ortile, "27 Grindr Users Who Failed So Hard They Almost Won," *Buzzfeed*, June 16, 2014.

67. "An interface is not a thing, an interface is always an effect. It is always a process or a translation." Galloway, *Interface Effect*, 33.

68. Most of the scholarly literature on gay men and mobile media connects the apps to a longer history of cruising for sex, suggesting that the apps mark a historical development in

the practices of gay male desire. I see them more as symptomatic of the same impulse, making them practices that now coexist. See Roderic N. Crooks, "The Rainbow Flag and the Green Carnation: Grindr in the Gay Village," *First Monday* 18, no. 11 (November 4, 2013), http://firstmonday.org/ojs/index.php/fm/article/view/4958/3790.

69. Eleanor Margolis, "Online Dating for Lesbians: Has Daatch Rewritten the Rules?" *Guardian*, March 24, 2014, http://www.theguardian.com/lifeandstyle/womens-blog/2014/mar/24/online-dating-lesbians-app-dattch-women.

70. While the media marketplace imagines technologies targeted to men and women as being equivalent, the reality is that the experience of desire is shaped by gendered mechanisms of power. "The study of sexuality is not coextensive with the study of gender; correspondingly, antihomophobic inquiry is not coextensive with feminist inquiry. But we can't know in advance how they will be different." Eve Kosofsky Sedgwick, *The Epistemology of the Closet* (Berkeley: University of California Press, 1990), 27.

71. For example, the blog *Trans Men of Grindr* circulates screen grabs of the painful conversations that trans men endure on the apps, where they weather invective and mistreatment at the hands of cisgender men as a matter of course.

72. Miranda Joseph, *Against the Romance of Community* (Minneapolis: University of Minnesota Press, 2002).

Afterword
#LoveWins

As I was writing this book, there were developments in the legal rights afforded sexual minorities by the government of the United States, which then precipitated phenomena in media culture akin to those discussed in these pages. The 2015 Supreme Court decision in *Obergefell v. Hodges* requires that states license marriages between two people of the same sex, identifying one mode of intimacy between a pair of consenting adults as being protected by the due process and equal protection clauses of the Fourteenth Amendment to the Constitution. Millions of Twitter users celebrated the decision with the hashtag "#LoveWins." These nine characters operate as an abbreviation that invokes more intimacies than it can contain, a feat it accomplishes by charting a narrative in which the politics of sexuality get reduced to a binary between those who are "for" this thing called "love" and those who are "against" it. The force of "winning" versus "losing" pushes the question of what "love" is or includes out of focus. The entrenchment of the culture wars in the twenty-first-century United States, where every issue of culture and power becomes organized around the poles of "liberal" and "conservative," augments the hashtag's sensibility. In this context, conversations about matters of identity and desire are crippled by broad generalizations and faulty assumptions. So the "love" of #LoveWins remains undefined, but whatever it is or includes is somehow "better" than it used to be.

#LoveWins is a frozen narrative, one that locks sexual politics into a recently finished battle defined on binary terms. Just like the hashtag leaves aside exactly what the battle was about, it never addresses the costs of winning it. Over the last few decades, some of the most energizing critiques of this limited thinking have emerged from queer theory circles in the academy. Like the appraisal of #LoveWins I offer here, queer theory worries about the margins of gay and lesbian liberation, where the right to privacy and the ability to amass wealth get fetishized in ways that empower some people at the expense of others. For queer theory, the "love" of #LoveWins is not that "liberal" at all. But I worry that this criticism can become its own frozen narrative, one in which the "progress" celebrated by LGBT liberation—the "love" of #LoveWins—is then followed immediately by a queer critique that points to its constraints. The potential for identifying overlap between seemingly opposing positions or forging coalition across otherwise conflicting viewpoints gets supplanted by "either/or" thinking and "this, not that" assessment. However provisional and fleeting it might be, the potential for a "both/and" consideration of gay and lesbian media and queer politics—one that might chart moments of overlap or locate points of intersection—ends before it can develop.

In the days after the *Obergefell v. Hodges* decision, one such critique appeared in the op-ed section of the *New York Times*. The author underlines the affective reasoning of the majority opinion, where "marriage . . . embodies the highest ideals of love, fidelity, devotion, sacrifice, and family," in order to criticize the enfranchisement of the romantic dyad as US policy.[1] He argues that "old questions remain: Why can't I put a good friend on my health care plan? Why can't my neighbor and I file our taxes together so we could save some money, as my parents do? If I failed to make a will, why is it unlikely a dear friend would inherit my estate?"[2] Rightfully, the author worries about the material impact of encoding one mode of intimacy as law, where marriage becomes the hinge on which so many rights and freedoms pivot. As the op-ed circulated across my various social media networks, some of my friends and acquaintances accused the author of being too cranky or overly radical. In exchanges punctuated by the #LoveWins hashtag, many of them wondered: couldn't the op-ed just let "us" have this win? Others, like me, defended the critique because it identifies in the pinning of citizenship rights to marriage a rather profound double-edged sword. Why should the federal government connect any form of intimacy to the rights of citizenship in the first place? In this dialogue, we all—me included—animated a depressingly familiar conversation. I became bored with that debate even as I was having it because it was essentially over before it ever began.

This book considers how scholarship might push past impasses like this one. How might the force of the op-ed's critique coexist with, maybe even invigorate, the intensity of optimism and relief captured in the hashtag #LoveWins? In other words: how might a queer critique of gay and lesbian media be transformative? It is a question without a clear answer, and it is a more interesting proposition than can be found in the declarative, which goes something like: gay and lesbian media and queer critique are diametrically opposed, and ne'er the twain shall meet. There is a wide body of scholarship on these matters that questions the logics underpinning liberation's "progress," and is attuned to the contradictions presented in the tangle of consumption and citizenship that structures gay and lesbian media— and the lives of all sexual minorities—in the twenty-first-century United States. In addition to pointing to the restrictions of #LoveWins, scholars might also look to redirect the hashtag's energy, where its suggestion of "progress" could be reconfigured as a beginning rather than an end. A heteronormative cultural mainstream now welcomes certain same-sex desires in ways that it had not previously. Its reasoning in doing so is not always liberatory and the benefits provided therein are not universally accessible. Those facts suggest an interesting starting point more than they point to a compelling finish line.

Like the media forms examined in this book, the use value of #LoveWins is the affective function it serves: it provides comfort to the battle weary because "progress" is important to people. The hashtag suggests to marriage-minded sexual minorities and the people who support them that they have the moral high ground in ongoing cultural struggles about how people should live, want, and be. This suggestion is no small victory in the twenty-first-century United States, a period during which vast income inequality and growing racial unrest continue to fray the social contract of the American welfare state. The proliferation of new myths about the American Dream erase history and particularity according to free market reasoning, as though every individual is an equal agent and all issues can be resolved by the marketplace. As a category, citizenship reduces to a mode of self-reliance animated by way of sentiment, one in which systemic inequalities provide nothing but the motivation for individual triumphs. When one cannot surmount these inequalities, it is understood to be a personal failure, not a structural problem. In this line of thinking, the nation-state bears increasingly fewer responsibilities to protect its people from forces more powerful than they are. The messy contradictions of privilege and power that occur in this milieu fracture coalitions more often than they offer the means to forge new ones.[3] As a narrative, #LoveWins is normative and limited, as are the feelings of freedom and belonging it engenders. Nevertheless, #LoveWins also suggests that something good has happened. For many people, such events are all too rare.

As the preceding chapters demonstrate, the texts that circulate in gay and lesbian media culture provide evidence of the tensions at work in the contemporary United States, where identity is thought to be a personal choice more than a structural location. In this context, identity is a commodity orientation in which the best ways to enact the rights of US citizenship are buying things and falling in love, and then accumulating capital and getting married. Alongside this critique, the chapters suggest that scholarship on media and sexuality can counter these seemingly ubiquitous rationales with some concerted effort. A scholarship that seeks transformation would unfreeze the binary thinking at work in and around phenomena like #LoveWins without dismissing their affective resonances. A scholarship that seeks transformation would recognize that the power of normativity provided by media culture is located in how cinema, television, and online media can make people feel, because people just need to "feel normal" sometimes, if only so they can continue from one moment to the next. Finally, a scholarship that seeks transformation would never be content to simply apologize for that need and conclude with it.

In bringing an analysis of feeling, emotion, and affect to bear on media created by and for sexual minorities, *Feeling Normal* attempts this sort of scholarship.

It problematizes the historical and political narratives that circulate about digital technology and sexual minorities in the twenty-first century. A rejoinder to the tyranny of the new, it is a *longue durée* that reconceives the oft-identified break between an analog past and a digital present by identifying a parallel between urban centers and digital media in terms of the relationship they forge between capital and sociality, which the book defines as an affective phenomenon. From there, the book recalibrates the critique of normativity that prevails in scholarship on media and sexuality. Gay and lesbian movies, television programs, and online media invite disparate individuals into intimate publics, suggesting commonalities of experience by bracketing their limitations. By addressing sexual minorities in this way, these movies, television programs, and online media often reinvest in many of the same ideologies they initially questioned. Crucially, though, that is often why so many people find comfort in them in the first place. Moreover, the book worries about how complicit scholarship can become with the logics that govern media commerce. In identifying friction between the mandates of industry and the aims of scholarship, the book demonstrates how scholars invested in social justice might employ strategic choices of object and method to operate at least somewhat outside industry rationales. By using feeling, emotion, and affect to shed new light on these perennial questions, I aim for self-reflexivity in considering the difficulties and possibilities of scholarship on media and sexuality in this particular historical moment.

When I presented this research at conferences, I was often asked to defend my archive and method. The objects examined in these pages are as disposable as a Twitter hashtag: cheap magazines, direct-to-video movies, quickly canceled sitcoms, and screen grabs from mobile technologies. They are not easily defensible in and of themselves. People wanted me to tell them: why look at these objects at all, if not to reclaim or disparage them? Rather than defend or dismiss the archive for this book, I use it as a wager: if an emotional resonance can be identified in objects often thought to have none at all, it must say something about the process of producing and consuming minority media more generally. Reading media forms for feeling, emotion, and affect is easy in the instance of beloved objects because they are renowned for providing the very sensations of interest to such criticism.[4] Moreover, it can be easy to forgive cherished texts for their ideological transgressions.

In place of evaluations that can only be subjective and apologia that are never all that warranted, I argue that reading for feeling, emotion, and affect in gay and lesbian cinema, television, and online media underlines something more fundamental about the nature of media forms made by and for sexual minorities: because minority media help consumers "feel normal," their affectivity is rarely outside of the power dynamics that they attempt to deconstruct. Rather, much of their affective resonances can be attributed to those very constraints. But as I wrote, the necessity of not apologizing for the transgressions and limitations of my archive became more difficult. In researching the production and distribution contexts of gay and lesbian media, I discovered how fervently the media professionals who labor in them believe in the importance and righteousness of the very objects in which I could not help but locate so many shortcomings. Doing justice to the workers' investments resulted in a method that reads gay and lesbian media by way of a double movement that simultaneously examines how media forms shoehorn bodies into confining norms and emphasizes the mix of relief and despair that those norms provide.

In the question I often received when presenting this work—"Why look at these objects at all?"—I see hierarchies of aesthetics and politics that I frequently shared with my interlocutors. Scholars do not occupy a single habitus, and their tastes are frequently contradictory; aesthetic sensibilities can dovetail with political leanings in ways that sometimes place avant-garde cinema on par with lowbrow internet memes. In assembling my archive, I bracketed my own habitus as much as possible in an effort to approach texts with detached generosity. Alas, I am not confident that my own tastes would foster much critical remove or clarity of purpose. Yet I see in these pages the traces of a younger me, the kid who grew up in a suburban subdivision and looked for gay and lesbian people where he knew he could find them: online, on TV, and at the video store. This younger me turned to media culture for the feelings of freedom and belonging that I can now be quick to dismiss as bland and false. The younger me was not naïve, but he was hopeful; in many ways, he was a more careful media consumer than I am now because he was still willing to be surprised. I tend now to be a paranoid consumer who struggles to see beyond the ideological complicity of gay and lesbian media.[5] With that reflection, I put the archive for this book together with the younger me in mind, and I tried to let his perspective nuance my method too. The result is a consideration of cinema, television, and online media through close readings, where a mix of hopefulness and skepticism takes seriously the desire for a livable life shared by so many sexual minorities yet remains wary of the ways media forms offer that to their audiences. My goal was a "both/and" criticism that allows for an analysis of gay and lesbian media that illuminates them as the multivalent objects they are. From that vantage point, #LoveWins is like the rest of my archive in that it features an optimism with limitations that are uncomfortable. But like the rest of the objects in this book, if its hopefulness is shortsighted, disdain for that hopefulness is too.

Notes

1. Michael Cobb, "The Supreme Court's Lonely Hearts Club," *New York Times*, June 30, 2015, http://www.nytimes.com/2015/06/30/opinion/the-supreme-courts-lonely-hearts-club .html?_r=0.

2. Ibid.

3. Online activism places new tensions on old coalitions, for better and worse. While tensions between white and black feminists predate the advent of digital technology, recent conflicts that have erupted on Twitter underline how social justice in the contemporary milieu can be a difficult endeavor. See Michelle Goldberg, "Feminism's Toxic Twitter Wars," *Nation*, January 29, 2014, http://www.thenation.com/article/feminisms-toxic-twitter-wars/.

4. For instance, Herbert Schwaab criticizes scholars' attention to "quality" television, identifying circular reasoning when academic criticism looks to media content that is branded as being "quality" in production and distribution contexts: "It is too easy to write about characters which, due to the exigencies of this genre, are branded to be complex, contradictory or self-reflexive. It feels like repeating something self-evident, like affirming a status that had already been gained." It seems to me that reading for feeling, emotion, and affect has the same potential pitfall. Herbert Schwaab, " 'Unreading' Contemporary Television," *After the Break: Television Theory Today* (Amsterdam: Amsterdam University Press, 2013), 24.

5. This differentiation is what Eve Sedgwick characterizes as "paranoid reading" versus "reparative reading." Eve Sedgwick, *Touching Feeling: Affect, Pedagogy, Performativity* (Durham, NC: Duke University Press, 2002): 123–151.

Selected Bibliography

Acland, Charles. *Screen Traffic: Movies, Multiplexes, and Global Culture*. Durham, NC: Duke University Press, 2003.

Adorno, Theodor. *The Culture Industry*, 2nd ed. Edited with an introduction by J. M. Bernstein. New York: Routledge, 2001.

Ahmed, Sarah. *The Cultural Politics of Emotion*. New York: Routledge, 2004.

Andrejevic, Mark. "Watching *Television without Pity*: The Productivity of Online Fans." *Television and New Media* 9, no. 1 (January 2008): 24–46.

Ang, Ien. "Understanding Television Audiencehood." In *Television: A Critical View, 5th Edition*, edited by Horace Newcomb, 367–386. New York: Oxford University Press, 1994.

Aslinger, Ben. "Creating a Network for Queer Audiences at LOGO TV." *Popular Communication* 7, no. 2 (June 2009): 107–121.

Banet-Weiser, Sarah. *Kids Rule! Nickelodeon and Consumer-Citizenship*. Durham, NC: Duke University Press, 2007.

Banet-Weiser, Sarah, and Roopali Mukherjee. *Commodity Activism: Cultural Resistance in Neoliberal Times*. New York: New York University Press, 2012.

Barthes, Roland. *A Lover's Discourse: Fragments*. New York: Hill and Wang, 1979.

Becker, Ron. *Gay TV and Straight America*. New Brunswick, NJ: Rutgers University Press, 2006.

Bell, David, and Gill Valentine, eds. *Mapping Desire: Geographies of Sexualities*. New York: Routledge, 1995.

Benson-Allott, Caetlin. *Killer Tapes and Shattered Screens: Video Spectatorship from VHS to File-Sharing*. Berkeley: University of California Press, 2013.

Berlant, Lauren. *Anatomy of a National Fantasy: Hawthorne, Utopia, and Everyday Life*. Chicago: University of Chicago Press, 1991.

———. *Cruel Optimism*. Durham, NC: Duke University Press, 2011.

———. *The Female Complaint: The Unfinished Business of Sentimentality in American Culture*. Durham, NC: Duke University Press, 2008.

———. *The Queen of America Goes to Washington City: Essays on Sex and Citizenship*. Durham, NC: Duke University Press, 1997.

Berlant, Lauren, and Lee Edelman. *Sex, or the Unbearable*. Durham, NC: Duke University Press, 2013.

Berlant, Lauren, and Michael Warner. "Sex in Public." *Critical Inquiry* 24 (Winter 1998): 547–566.

Binnie, Jon. "Trading Places: Consumption, Sexuality, and the Production of Queer Space." In *Mapping Desire: Geographies of Sexualities*, edited by David Bell and Gill Valentine, 166–181. New York: Routledge, 1995.

Bordwell, David. "Intensified Continuity: Visual Style in Contemporary American Film." *Film Quarterly* 55, no. 3 (2002): 24.

———. *Narration in the Fiction Film*. Madison: University of Wisconsin Press, 1985.

Bordwell, David, Janet Staiger, and Kristin Thompson. *The Classical Hollywood Cinema*. New York: Columbia University Press, 1985.

Boyd, Nan Alamilla. *Wide-Open Town: A History of Queer San Francisco to 1965*. Berkeley: University of California Press, 2003.

Brinkema, Eugenie. *The Forms of the Affects*. Durham, NC: Duke University Press, 2014.

Bronski, Michael. *Culture Clash: The Making of Gay Sensibility*. Boston: South End, 1984.

Bronstein, Carolyn. "Mission Accomplished? Profits and Programming at the Network for Women." *Camera Obscura* 33–34 (1995): 213–242.

Butler, Judith. *Undoing Gender*. New York: Routledge, 2004.

Caldwell, John Thornton. "Convergence Television: Aggregating Form and Repurposing Content in the Culture of Conglomeration." In *Television after TV: Essays on a Medium in Transition*, edited by Lynn Spigel and Jan Olsson, 41–74. Durham, NC: Duke University Press, 2003.

Campbell, John Edward. "Virtual Citizens or Dream Consumers: Looking for Civic Community on Gay.com." In *Queer Online: Media, Technology, and Sexuality*, edited by David Phillips and Kate O'Riordan, 123–138. New York: Peter Lang, 2007.

Clarke, Eric. *Virtuous Vice: Homoeroticism and the Public Sphere*. Durham, NC: Duke University Press, 2000.

D'Acci, Julie. *Defining Women: The Case of Cagney and Lacey*. Chapel Hill: University of North Carolina Press, 1994.

Davis, Glyn. "A Taste for *Leeches!* DVDs, Audience Configurations, and Generic Hybridity." *Film and Television after DVD*, edited by James Bennett and Tony Brown, 45–62. Routledge: New York, 2008.

Davis, Nick. *The Desiring-Image: Gilles Deleuze and Contemporary Queer Cinema*. New York: Oxford University Press, 2013.

Davison, Patrick. "The Language of Internet Memes." In *The Social Media Reader*, edited by Michael Mandiberg, 120–136. New York: New York University Press, 2012.

DeLanda, Manuel. *A New Philosophy of Society: Assemblage Theory and Social Complexity*. New York: Continuum, 2006.

Delany, Samuel. *Times Square Red, Times Square Blue*. New York: New York University Press, 2001.

Deleuze, Gilles. *Cinema 1: The Movement Image*. Minneapolis: University of Minnesota Press, 1986.

Deleuze, Gilles, and Felix Guattari. *A Thousand Plateaus: Capitalism and Schizophrenia*. Minneapolis: University of Minnesota Press, 1987.

D'Emilio, John. "Capitalism and Gay Identity." In *The Lesbian and Gay Studies Reader*, edited by Henry Abelove, Michele Aine Barale, and David M. Halperin, 467–476. New York: Routledge, 1993.

Dow, Bonnie. "Ellen, Television, and the Politics of Gay and Lesbian Visibility." *Critical Studies in Media Communication* 18 (June 2001): 123–140.

Duggan, Lisa. *The Twilight of Equality: Neoliberalism, Cultural Politics, and the Attack on Democracy*. Boston: Beacon, 2004.

Elleström, Lars. "The Modalities of Media: A Model for Understanding Intermedial Relations." *Media Borders, Multimodality, and Intermediality*, edited by Lars Elleström, 11–50. New York: Palgrave MacMillan, 2010.

Farman, Jason. *Mobile Interface Theory: Embodied Space and Locative Media*. New York: Routledge, 2011.

Freedman, Eric. *Transient Images: Personal Media in Public Frameworks*. Philadelphia: Temple University Press, 2011.

Freitas, Anthony. "Gay Programming, Gay Publics: Public and Private Tensions in Lesbian and Gay Cable Channels." In *Cable Visions: Television beyond Broadcasting*, edited by Sarah Banet-Weiser, Cynthia Chris, and Anthony Freitas, 215–233. New York: New York University Press, 2006.

Galloway, Alexander R. *The Interface Effect*. Malden, MA: Polity, 2012.

Gillespie, Tarleton. "The Politics of 'Platforms.'" *New Media and Society* 12 (September 2010): 347–367.

Gray, Herman. *Cultural Moves: African Americans and the Politics of Representation*. Berkeley: University of California Press, 2005.

Griffin, Hollis. "Manufacturing Massness: Aesthetic Form and Industry Practice in the Reality Television Contest." In *The Companion to Reality Television*, edited by Laurie Ouellette, 155–170. Malden, MA: Wiley-Blackwell, 2014.

———. "Queerness, the Quality Audience, and Comedy Central's *Reno 911!*" *Television and New Media* 9, no. 5 (September 2008): 355–370.

———. "Your Favorite Stars, Live on Our Screens: Media Culture, Queer Publics, and Commercial Space." *Velvet Light Trap* 62, no. 2 (Fall 2008): 15–28.

Halberstam, Judith [Jack]. *The Queer Art of Failure*. Durham, NC: Duke University Press, 2011.

———. *In a Queer Time and Place: Transgender Bodies, Subcultural Lives*. New York: New York University Press, 2005.

Halperin, David. *How to Be Gay*. Cambridge, MA: Belknap, Harvard University Press, 2012.

Hanhardt, Christina. *Safe Space: Gay Neighborhood History and the Politics of Violence*. Durham, NC: Duke University Press, 2013.

Hansen, Mark B. N. *A New Philosophy for New Media*. Cambridge, MA: MIT Press, 2006.

Hearn, Alison. "Brand Me 'Activist.'" In *Commodity Activism: Cultural Resistance in Neoliberal Times*, edited by Sarah Banet-Weiser and Roopali Mukherjee, 23–38. New York: New York University Press, 2012.

Henderson, Lisa. *Love and Money: Queers, Class, and Cultural Production*. New York: New York University Press, 2013.

Hilderbrand, Lucas. *Inherent Vice: Bootleg Histories of Videotape and Copyright*. Durham, NC: Duke University Press, 2009.

Himberg, Julia. "Multicasting: Lesbian Programming and the Changing Landscape of Cable TV." *Television and New Media* 15, no. 4 (April 2014): 289–304.

Holt, Jennifer, and Kevin Sanson. *Connected Viewing: Selling, Streaming, and Sharing Media in the Digital Age*. New York: Routledge, 2013.

Howard, John. *Men like That: A Southern Queer History*. Chicago: University of Chicago Press, 2001.

Jenkins, Henry. *Convergence Culture: Where Old and New Media Collide*. New York: New York University Press, 2006.

Johnson, Victoria. *Heartland TV: Prime Time Television and the Struggle for U.S. Identity*. New York: New York University Press, 2008.

Joseph, Miranda. *Against the Romance of Community*. Minneapolis: University of Minnesota Press, 2002.

Joyrich, Lynne. "Epistemology of the Console." *Critical Inquiry* 27, no. 3 (Spring 2001): 439–467.

Keeling, Kara. *The Witch's Flight: The Cinematic, the Black Femme, and the Image of Common Sense*. Durham, NC: Duke University Press, 2007.

Lefebvre, Henri. *The Production of Space*. Translated by Donald Nicholson-Smith. Cambridge: Blackwell, 1991.

Leys, Ruth. "The Turn to Affect: A Critique." *Critical Inquiry* 37, no. 3 (Spring 2011): 434–472.

Lipsitz, George. *Time Passages: Collective Memory and American Popular Culture*. Minneapolis: University of Minnesota Press, 2001.

Lotz, Amanda. *The Television Will Be Revolutionized*. New York: New York University Press, 2007.

Manovich, Lev. *The Language of New Media*. Cambridge, MA: MIT Press, 2002.

Marwick, Alice, Mary Gray, and Mike Annany. "'Dolphins Are Just Gay Sharks': *Glee* and the Queer Case of Transmedia as Text and Object." *Television and New Media*. doi: 10.1177/1527476413478493.

Massumi, Brian. *Parables for the Virtual: Movement, Affect, Sensation*. Durham, NC: Duke University Press, 2002.

McCarthy, Anna. *Ambient Television: Visual Culture and Public Space*. Durham, NC: Duke University Press, 2001.

——. "Ellen: Making Queer Television History." *GLQ: A Journal of Lesbian and Gay Studies* 7 (2001): 593–620.

McGlotten, Shaka. *Virtual Intimacies: Media, Affect, and Queer Sociality*. Albany, NY: SUNY Press, 2013.

Meeker, Martin. *Contacts Desired: Gay and Lesbian Communications and Community, 1940s–1970s*. Chicago: University of Chicago Press, 2003.

Mittell, Jason. *Complex TV: The Poetics of Contemporary Television Storytelling*. New York: New York University Press, 2015.

——. *Television and Genre: From Cop Shows to Cartoons in American Culture*. New York: Routledge, 2004.

Moore, Candace. "Distribution Is Queen: LGBTQ Media on Demand." *Cinema Journal* 53, no. 1 (Fall 2013): 137–144.

Mowlabocus, Sharif. *Gaydar Culture: Gay Men, Technology, and Embodiment in the Digital Age*. Burlington, VT: Ashgate, 2012.

Nakamura, Lisa. *Cybertypes: Race, Ethnicity, and Identity on the Internet*. New York: Routledge, 2002.

Newcomb, Horace. *TV: The Most Popular Art*. New York: Anchor, 1974.

Newman, Michael. "Free TV: File-Sharing and the Value of Television." *Television and New Media* 13, no. 6 (November 2012): 463–479.

Newman, Michael, and Elana Levine. *Legitimating Television: Media Convergence and Cultural Status*. New York: Routledge, 2011.

Ng, Eve. "A 'Post-Gay' Era? Media Gaystreaming, Homonormativity, and the Politics of LGBT Integration." *Communication, Culture and Critique* 6, no. 2 (June 2013): 258–283.

Ngai, Sianne. *Ugly Feelings*. Cambridge, MA: Harvard University Press, 2005.

Nguyen, Tan Hoang. *A View from the Bottom: Asian American Masculinity and Sexual Representation*. Durham, NC: Duke University Press, 2014.

Nye, David. *American Technological Sublime*. Cambridge, MA: MIT Press, 1994.

Olson, Scott. *Hollywood Planet: Global Media and the Competitive Advantage of Narrative Transparency*. New York: Routledge, 1999.

Ouellette, Laurie, and James Hay. *Better Living through Reality TV: Television and Post-Welfare Citizenship*. Malden, MA: Wiley-Blackwell, 2008.

Parks, Lisa. "Flexible Microcasting: Gender, Generation, and Television-Internet Convergence." In *Television after TV: Essays on a Medium in Transition*, edited by Lynn Spigel and Jan Olsson, 133–162. Durham, NC: Duke University Press, 2004.

Payne, Robert. *The Promiscuity of Network Culture: Queer Theory and Digital Media*. New York: Routledge, 2014.

Pellegrini, Ann. "Consuming Lifestyle: Commodity Capitalism and Transformations in Gay Identity." In *Queer Globalizations*, edited by Arnaldo Cruz-Malave and Martin F. Manalansan, 4:134–148. New York: New York University Press, 2003.

Puar, Jasbir. *Terrorist Assemblages: Homonationalism in Queer Times*. Durham, NC: Duke University Press, 2007.

Race, Kane. " 'Party and Play': Online Hook-Up Devices and the Emergence of PNP Practices among Gay Men." *Sexualities* 18 (March 2015): 253–275.

———. *Pleasure Consuming Medicine: The Queer Politics of Drugs*. Durham, NC: Duke University Press, 2009.

———. "Speculative Pragmatism and Intimate Arrangements: Online Hook-Up Devices in Gay Life." *Culture, Health and Sexuality*, 2014. doi: 10.1080/13691058.2014.930181.

Rand, Erica. *The Ellis Island Snow Globe*. Durham, NC: Duke University Press, 2005.

Rich, B. Ruby. *New Queer Cinema: The Director's Cut*. Durham, NC: Duke University Press, 2013.

Roth, Yael. "Locating the 'Scruff Guy': Theorizing Body and Space in Gay Geosocial Media." *International Journal of Communication* 8 (July 2014). http://ijoc.org /index.php/ijoc/article/view/2286/1192.

———. " 'No Overly Suggestive Photos of Any Kind': Content Management and the Policing of Self in Gay Digital Communities." *Communication, Culture and Critique* 8, nos. 3–4 (September 2015): 414–432.

Schleier, Merill. *Skyscraper Cinema: Architecture and Gender in American Film*. Minneapolis: University of Minnesota Press, 2009.

Schudson, Michael. *The Power of News*. Cambridge, MA: Harvard University Press, 2000.

Sconce, Jeffrey. "A Specter Is Haunting Television Studies." *FLOW: A Critical Forum on Television and Media Culture*, October 31, 2008. http://flowtv.org/2008/10/a -specter-is-haunting-television-studies-jeffrey-sconce-northwestern-university/.

———. "What If? Charting the New Textual Boundaries of Television." In *Television after TV: Essays on a Medium in Transition*, edited by Lynn Spigel and Jan Olsson, 93–112. Durham, NC: Duke University Press, 2003.

Sedgwick, Eve Kosofsky. *The Epistemology of the Closet*. Berkeley: University of California Press, 1990.

———. *Touching Feeling: Affect, Performativity, Pedagogy*. Durham, NC: Duke University Press, 2003.

Sender, Katherine. *Business Not Politics: The Making of the Gay Market.* New York: Columbia University Press, 2005.

———. "Gay Readers, Consumers, and a Dominant Gay Habitus: 25 years of the *Advocate* Magazine." *Journal of Communication* 51, no.1 (March 2001): 73–99.

Shaviro, Steven. *The Cinematic Body.* Minneapolis: University of Minnesota Press, 1993.

———. *Post Cinematic Affect.* London: Zero Books, 2010.

Shouse, Eric. "Feeling Emotion Affect." *M/C: A Journal of Media and Culture* 8 (December 2005). http://journal.media-culture.org.au/0512/03-shouse.php.

Simmel, Georg. "The Metropolis and Mental Life." In *The Blackwell City Reader,* edited by Gary Bridge and Sophie Watson, 103–110. Oxford and Malden, MA: Wiley-Blackwell, 1903/2002.

Skeggs, Beverly. "The Appearance of Class: Challenges in Gay Space." In *Cultural Studies and the Working Class: Subject to Change,* edited by Sally Munt, 129–151. London: Cassell, 2000.

Smith-Shomade, Beretta. "Narrowcasting in the New World Information Order." *Television and New Media* 5 (February 2004): 69–81.

Snediker, Michael. *Queer Optimism: Lyric Personhood and Other Felicitous Persuasions.* Minneapolis: University of Minnesota Press, 2008.

Spigel, Lynn. "From the Dark Ages to the Golden Age: Women's Memories and Television Reruns." *Screen* 36, no. 1 (Spring 1995): 16–33.

Spinoza, Baruch. *Ethics.* New York: Penguin, 2005.

Spivak, Gayatri Chakravorty. "Scattered Speculations on the Question of Value." *Diacritics* 15, no. 4, Marx after Derrida (Winter 1985): 73–93.

Streitmatter, Rodger. *Unspeakable: The Rise of the Gay and Lesbian Press in America.* New York: Faber and Faber, 1995.

Thrift, Nigel. "Intensities of Feeling: Towards a Spatial Politics of Affect." *Geografiska Annaler* 86, no. 1 (2004): 57–78.

———. *Non-Representational Theory: Space, Politics, Affect.* New York: Routledge, 2007.

Tinkcom, Matthew. "You've Got to Get On to Get Off": *Shortbus* and the Circuits of the Erotic." *South Atlantic Quarterly* 110 (Summer 2011): 693–713.

Tryon, Chuck. *On-Demand Culture: Digital Delivery and the Future of Movies.* New Brunswick, NJ: Rutgers University Press, 2013.

———. *Reinventing Cinema: Movies in the Age of Media Convergence.* New Brunswick, NJ: Rutgers University Press, 2009.

Urry, John. *The Tourist Gaze, 2nd Edition.* Thousand Oaks, CA: Sage, 2002.

Villarejo, Amy. *Ethereal Queer: Television, Historicity, Desire.* Durham, NC: Duke University Press, 2014.

———. *Lesbian Rule: Cultural Criticism and the Value of Desire.* Durham, NC: Duke University Press, 2003.

Wallace, Lee. *The Sexual Life of Apartments: Lesbianism, Sex, and Cinema.* New York: Routledge, 2009.

Warner, Michael, ed. *Fear of a Queer Planet: Queer Politics and Social Theory.* Minneapolis: University of Minnesota Press, 1993.

———. *Publics and Counterpublics.* Cambridge, MA: Zone Books, 2002.

White, Michele. *The Body and the Screen: Theories of Internet Spectatorship.* Cambridge, MA: MIT Press, 2006.

White, Mimi. "Barry Chappell's Fine Art Showcase: Apparitional TV, Aesthetic Value, and the Art Market." In *After the Break: Television Theory Today*, edited by Marijke de Valck and Jan Teurlings, 179–192. Amsterdam: University of Amsterdam Press, 2013.

——. *Tele-Advising: Therapeutic Discourse in Television*. Chapel Hill: University of North Carolina Press, 1992.

Wood, Gregory. " 'Something for Everyone': Lesbian and Gay 'Magazine' Programming on British Television, 1980–2000." In *Queer TV: Theories, Histories, Politics*, edited by Glyn Davis and Gary Needham, 108–120. New York: Routledge, 2009.

Index

Page numbers in italics refer to figures.

Adorno, Theodor, 114, 138n70

advertisements, 27–28, 32, 34–35, 37, 39, 40, 48

advertisers, 90–91, 94, 98

Advocate, 27, 96, 97, 98

Advocate Classifieds, 27

Advocate Money Minute, The, 96

aesthetic value, 129–130, 139n81

affect, 3, 10, 11–12, 19n8, 19n9, 21n33, 24. *See also* feeling/emotion/affect

affective interfaces (apps), 145–146, 154–161

affective value, 13–16, 112–113, 114, 127, 128–129, 130

aggregation, 23–24, 37–42, 47

Ahmed, Sara, 3, 19n10

AIDS. *See* HIV/AIDS

Allison, Dorothy, 6

Amazon, 53, 59, 104

American Dream, 5, 8, 9, 20n15, 76, 171

And Then Came Lola (2009), 65–66

Andersonville (Chicago), 34

Andrejevic, Mark, 139n80

Angels in America (Kushner), 7–9

antisemitism, 7, 9

Antoine, Chagmion, 89–90

apparitional television, 133–134

apps, 140–162; affective interfaces and, 145–146, 154–161; aggregation and, 42; bodies and, 144–146, 149, 150–151, 157, 164n23, 166n46; *Bump!* (travel program) and, 102; civic engagement and, 153, 154; database design and, 47, 140, 141, 142–148, 151, 159–161; desire and, 140–142, 143, 145–146, 147, 149, 150–151, 153–155, 157, 159–162; deterritorialization and, 142–143; digital facial image (DFI) and, 144, 145; ethnicity and, 148, 149, 155, 165n33; face pics and, 144–145, 164n20, 165n28; functionalized interfaces and, 144, 145–146, 146–154; gay sex bifurcation and, 164n16; gender and, 151, 161, 168n70; genres and, 47, 154, 163n11, 164n14; HIV/AIDS and, 148, 149, 165n36; human-computer interface (HCI), 144; identity and, 144, 146, 147–148, 150, 151,

153–154, 155; marketing discourses and, 141–143, 149–150, 151, 154, 161; memes and, 140, 142, 162n1, 162n2; mobile media companies and, 141–142, 149–150, 153, 154, 161; race and, 148, 155–156, 165n33; romance and, 142, 149–150, 152, 161–162; sexual minorities and, 17–18, 47, 149–150, 161; sexual politics and, 142; speculative pragmatism and, 163n12; territorialization and, 142–143; virtual intimacies and, 162n2. *See also individual apps*

Ariztical Entertainment, 59

Asian men, 40, 155, 156

Aslinger, Ben, 84, 98

Banet-Weiser, Sarah, 21n36, 85, 106n5

Barthes, Roland, 158

bear subculture, 46, 92, 116, 147

Becker, Ron, 115–116, 119, 122, 135n17, 135n18

Behind the Shoot (video series), 96

Belge, Kathy, 100

Bellini, Jason, 86–87, 107n22

Bench (bar), 36

Benson-Allott, Caetlin, 61

Bent (podcast), 93

Berlant, Lauren: citizenship and, 18n5, 67; conventionality and, 72, 73; desire and, 128, 155; *The Female Complaint: The Unfinished Business of Sentimentality in American Culture*, 9–10; genres and, 164n14; the National Symbolic and, 54, 67, 71; normativity and, 122; race and, 78n1

Big Chicks (Chicago), 39

BitTorrent, 133

black men, 32, 34, 35, 51n32, 62, 65, 155, 156, 167n62

blog posts, 143, 155, 156

bodies, 144–146, 149, 150–151, 157, 164n23, 166n46

Bordwell, David, 63

Boyd, Nan Alamilla, 35

Brinkema, Eugenie, 11, 21n30, 21n33

Bump! (travel program), 98, 102–104, 111n83
business models, 83, 86, 90–92, 94–95, 104, 108n33, 116, 122
businesses, 37–39, 42, 44–45, 47. *See also* commerce; marketplace; media commerce

cable TV, 82–106; aesthetic value and, 129; aggregation and, 42; business models and, 86, 90–92, 94, 104, 108n33; capital and, 84, 105; centrism and, 84, 90–91; commodity activism and, 82–84, 85–86, 103, 105, 106; digital technologies and, 83, 86, 107n20, 108n35; funding models and, 83; genres and, 47; identity politics and, 84; marketplace and, 44, 105–106; multiple publics and, 42; network television and, 135n17; politics and, 17, 82, 84, 85, 98, 105; scholarship and, 105–106; sexual minorities and, 84–85, 86, 89, 105, 108n33; travel programs, 42, 98–104; viewer interactivity and, 83, 86, 107n20. *See also* news programs; television; *individual networks; individual programs*
Caldwell, John Thornton, 107n20, 122–123
camera shots, 56, 63–67, *64*, 68–69, 72, 74–75
capital: affective value and, 16; cable TV and, 84, 105; digital media and, 172; *East Side Story* (2006) and, 70; gay and lesbian media and, 24; identity and, 171; *Julie Johnson* (2002) and, 72; media and, 13; queer sociality and, 27; *Shelter* (2007) and, 73; special case and, 14; television and, 113–114, 128, 129, 130, 131, 133, 134
capitalism, 11, 66–67, 73, 77, 114, 115, 130, 162n4. *See also* consumer capitalism
Case, Paul, 93
Castro neighborhood (San Francisco), 35–36
Cat Club (San Francisco), 39
CBS News, 86–88, 95
CBS News on Logo, 86–87
centrism, 4, 84, 90–91
Charlie's (bar), 37, *38*
Chauncey, George, 32, 49n7
Chavez, J. C., 93
Chelsea neighborhood (New York), 30
Chicago, 25, 28, 34–35, 37, 39, 42, 43, 44. *See also Gay Chicago Magazine*
Cinema 1 (Deleuze), 145
citizen-consumers. *See* consumer citizenship
citizenship, 5, 6–7, 8, 14, 18n5, 27, *64*, 66–67, 73
city iconography, 68–73, 77, 80n32, 80n36. *See also* urban signifiers

civic engagement, 153, 154
Clarke, Eric, 21n37
class: Chauncey, George and, 49n7; continuity editing and, 72; digital media and, 37; *East Side Story* (2006) and, 69; gay and lesbian cinema and, 54, 76; gay and lesbian media and, 11; gentrification and, 31–32; Henderson, Lisa and, 76; *Julie Johnson* (2002) and, 72; magazines and, 28; network television and, 115, 119, 121; romance of community and, 15; sexual minority publics and, 24, 28; *Shelter* (2007) and, 73; urbanization and, 26; Villarejo, Amy and, 14
Clinton, Hillary, 86–87
Club Escape (venue), 35
Colichmann, Paul, 92, 104–105
commerce, 29, 31, 39, 42, 49n6, 84. *See also* media commerce
commodity activism, 82–84, 85–86, 89, 91, 97, 103, 105, 106
conservatism, 57, 67
consumer capitalism, 4, 75
consumer citizenship, 5, 12, 21n36, 27, 83, 89, 106n5
consumer taste, 116, 117, 118, 120, 121, 122, 126
consumers, 4, 5, 12, 16–17, 22n41, 23, 27, 75, 83–84
continuity editing, 61–75; camera shots and, 63–67, *64*, 68, 72, 74–75; capitalism and, 73; city iconography and, 68–73, 77; class and, 72; definition of, 62; distribution companies and, 63; *Dorian Blues* (2004) and, 65, 66, 68; *East Side Story* (2006) and, 68–70, 73; ethnicity and, 69–70, 74; *Gypsy 83* (2001) and, 62–63, 66, 68; Hollywood and, 63; intensified continuity and, 63; *Julie Johnson* (2002) and, 70–72, 73; *Latter Days* (2003) and, 63, 68, 74; *Leave It on the Floor* (2011) and, 62, 68, 74; metronormativity and, 66; *Molly's Girl* (2012) and, 66, 74; sexual identity and, 73; sexual minorities and, 70, 73; *Shelter* (2007) and, 72–73; *The Skinny* (2012) and, 66, 68, 74; *And Then Came Lola* (2009) and, 65–66; urban settings and, 63–75
convergence, 23, 25, 28, 29, 47–48, 48n1
counterpublics, 49n10
criminal intimacy, 8
Crystal, Billy, 132
Cummiskey, Coley, 150–151
Curve (magazine), 100
cybernetics, 11–12

Daatch/HER, 151
Daggett, Gina, 100
Daley, Richard, 34
database design (apps), 47, 140, 141, 142–148, 151, 159–161
David, Charlie, 103–104
Davis, Nick, 76–77, 78n6
DeGeneres, Ellen, 117, 124
Delany, Samuel, 31–32
Deleuze, Gilles, 19n8, 144, 145
delivery platforms. *See* platforms
delivery technologies, 59, 61, 133
D'Emilio, John, 26, 49n13
desire: affective value and, 14; apps and, 140–142, 143, 145–146, 147, 149, 150–151, 153–155, 157, 159–162; Berlant, Lauren and, 128; commerce and, 5; gay and lesbian media and, 1; heteronormative culture and, 1; #LoveWins and, 169; modernity and, 5
deterritorialization, 142–143
digital facial image (DFI), 144, 145
digital media: aggregation and, 42; capital and, 172; class and, 37; convergence and, 23; Farman, Jason and, 48n4; gay and lesbian cinema and, 17; gender and, 37; genres and, 47; homonormativity and, 4–5; magazines and, 25, 48; media commerce and, 18, 23; media impact and, 5; modernity and, 5, 17; race and, 37; representations and, 37; urban centers and, 25, 172; urbanization and, 23, 48
digital technologies, 83, 86, 98, 107n20, 108n35
direct-to-video cinema, 79n19
dispersal/concentration, 23, 24, 29–37, 42, 47
distribution companies, 59–61, 63, 75
diversity, 37, 39, 42, 69–70
DNA Lounge (San Francisco), 39
Dorian Blues (2004), 65, 66, 68
Douchebags of Grindr, 155–156
Duggan, Lisa, 4
Dugout (venue), 34

East Side Story (2006), 68–70, 73
Eastern Bloc (bar), 32, 33
Eastwood, Chrisanne, 91
Ellen, 123, 124, 130, 132, 137n43
Ellen Show, The, 112, 113, 115, 117–119, 122, 123, 124, 125–126, 130, 132
emotion. *See* feeling/emotion/affect
employment protections, 3–4
EndUp (San Francisco), 40

Escalante, Isaac, 101–102
Escapades (venue), 35
Escuelita (New York), 40, *41*
ethnicity: aggregation and, 39–40; apps and, 148, 149, 155, 165n33; *Bump!* (travel program) and, 103; Chicago and, 35; continuity editing and, 69–70, 74; *East Side Story* (2006) and, 69; gentrification and, 31; New Jersey and, 34; New York and, 32, 34; Oakland (California) and, 36; queer sociality and, 49n7; television and, 121
evolutionary economics, 42

face pics, 144–145, 157, 164n20, 165n28
Facts of Life, The, 131
Farman, Jason, 48n4
Fatal Attraction (1987), 159, *160*
feeling normal, 1, 3, 6, 13, 172
feeling/emotion/affect, 3, 5, 11, 13, 16, 19n8, 171, 172
Female Complaint: The Unfinished Business of Sentimentality in American Culture, The (Berlant), 9–10
file sharing, 133
For & Against, 96
Forbidden Love (1992), 22n45
Freedman, Eric, 147
Freitas, Anthony, 84, 98
functionalized interfaces (apps), 144, 145–146, 146–154

gay and lesbian audiences, 5, 11, 47–48, 90, 95–96, 97
gay and lesbian cable networks. *See* cable TV
gay and lesbian cinema, 53–77; American Dream and, 76; American nation-state and, 77; capitalism and, 73, 75, 77; citizenship and, 67, 73; city iconography and, 68–73; class and, 54, 76; as cultural form, 60; delivery technologies and, 59; distribution companies and, 59–61; identity and, 53–54; lesbians and, 58; New Queer Cinema, 57–61; politics and, 53–54, 58, 60–61, 63, 74–75; race and, 54; Rich, B. Ruby and, 57, 58, 60; sexual identity and, 54, 62, 73, 77; viewing platforms and, 61. *See also* continuity editing; *individual films*
gay and lesbian media: affect and, 10, 19n9; American Dream and, 5; assessments of, 2; capital and, 11, 24; centrism and, 4; citizenship and, 5, 6–7, 14, 27; class and, 11; consumer capitalism and, 4; consumption

gay and lesbian media (cont.)
and, 14; feeling/emotion/affect and, 3, 13, 172;
gay and lesbian cinema and, 17; gender and,
11; genres and, 47; homonormativity and,
4–5; identity and, 1–2; individual happiness
narratives and, 2; as juxtapolitical, 10;
narrative formulas and, 10; nation-states
and, 11; normativity and, 2; norms and, 173;
politics and, 4, 12; queer critique and, 170;
race and, 11; sexual politics and, 2; sexuality
and, 11; urban centers and, 24
Gay Chicago Magazine, 25, 27, 28, 35, 38, 39,
43, 48
gay marriage. *See* same-sex marriage
Gay Pride celebrations, 31, 44, 91
gender: aggregation and, 39; apps and, 151,
161, 168n70; Chicago and, 34, 35; Davis,
Nick and, 78n6; digital media and, 37; gay
and lesbian media and, 11; *Gay Chicago
Magazine* and, 39; *Julie Johnson* (2002) and,
71; magazines and, 28; *Next*'s map and, 34;
Nightspots (Chicago) and, 39; romance of
community and, 15; sexual minority publics
and, 24, 28; television and, 129; urbanization
and, 26
genres, 24, 44–47, 52n46, 52n47, 154, 163n11,
164n14
gentrification, 28, 31–32, 68, 69, 80n41
geosocial networking applications. *See* apps
Girls on Girls (podcast), 93–94
Gloss (San Francisco), 25, 27, 28, 29, 36, 40
Good Morning Gay America, 91
Goodman, John, 116, 117
governance acts, 31–32, 34
Greenwich Village, 30, 31–32, 34
Grindr, 140, 141, 147, 150, 151–153, 155–156,
157–160, 160, 167n54
Grindr Guide, The, 157–158
Growlr, 147, 150, 153
Guattari, Felix, 19n8, 144
Guerrilla Gay Bar, 46
Gypsy 83 (2001), 62–63, 66, 68

Halberstam, Jack, 26, 66
Halperin, David, 18n1
Hamburger Mary's (Chicago), 37, 39
Hansen, Mark, 144–145, 146
Harlem, 32, 34
Hell's Kitchen (New York), 30, 32
Henderson, Lisa, 22n42, 76
HER, 151

Here TV, 82–83, 85–86, 92–94, 96–98, 102,
104–105
Here with Josh and Sara (podcast), 92–93
heteronormative culture, 1, 3
Hideaway, The (Chicago), 39
Hilderbrand, Lucas, 61
Himberg, Julia, 108n33, 108n35
HIV/AIDS, 7, 8, 28, 29, 35–36, 55–57, 96, 148,
149, 165n36
Hollywood, 54, 58, 59, 63. *See also* gay and
lesbian cinema
homo/hetero binary, 119–120
homonationalism, 20n27
homonormativity, 4–5. *See also* normativity
homophobia, 3, 7, 9, 62, 63, 88, 94, 119–120, 124,
132
Hulu, 53, 59, 96, 132–133
human-computer interface (HCI), 144
HX (New York), 25, 27, 28, 31, 32, 34, 39, 43, 48

identity: affective value and, 14, 113; apps and,
144, 146, 147–148, 150, 151, 153–154, 155; capital
and, 171; checking in and, 163n6; citizenship
and, 67; city iconography and, 68; gay and
lesbian cinema and, 53–54; gay and lesbian
media and, 1–2; genres and, 24, 44–45, 46–47;
Jeffrey (film) (1995) and, 57; #LoveWins and,
169; media commerce and, 18; queer theory
and, 1; television and, 114–122, 126–128, 129,
130, 132, 134; urbanization and, 25–26;
Villarejo, Amy and, 14. *See also* sexual
identity
identity politics, 84
industrialization, 26. *See also* urbanization
InnExile (venue), 35
Instagram, 158–159
intensified continuity, 63
interfaces (apps), 144–146. *See also* affective
interfaces (apps); functionalized interfaces
(apps)
International Gay Rodeo Association, 103
Iowa, 66
It's All Relative, 112, 113, 115, 119–120, 121–122,
123, 124, 125–126, 130, 132

Jeffrey (film) (1995), 54–55, 56–59
Jeffrey (venue), 35
Jenkins, Henry, 48n1
Jett, Jack E., 91
Johnson, Victoria, 118
Jones, Jeffrey, 93

Joseph, Miranda, 15
Julie Johnson (2002), 70–72, *71*, 73, 80n45

Kaplan, Roberta, 97
Krash (New York), 39, *40*

Lakeview (Chicago), 34
Latinos, 39–40, *41*, 45, 69, 93
Latter Days (2003), 63, 68, 74
Lauderdale, Thomas, 100
Leave It on the Floor (2011), 62, 68, 74
Lefebvre, Henri, 31, 48n5
Lesarion (app), 148
lesbian documentary cinema, 13–14, 16, 22n45
lesbians: apps and, 146–147, 148, 149–150, 151;
    citizenship and, 67; *Curve* (magazine), 100;
    The Facts of Life and, 131; *Forbidden Love*
    (1992) and, 22n45; gay and lesbian cinema
    and, 58; *Girls on Girls* (podcast), 93–94;
    Hamburger Mary's and, 37; *Julie Johnson*
    (2002) and, 70–72; lesbian chronotopes and,
    80n45; magazines and, 34; maps and, 34;
    marketplace and, 42; Mesh and, 146, 151;
    Molly's Girl (2012) and, 66, 74; "A Personal
    History of Lesbian Porn" (Allison), 6; *Round
    Trip Ticket* and, 101–102; *Ellen Show* and,
    117–119; *And Then Came Lola* (2009) and,
    65–66; Wing Ma'am and, 147, 148
Levine, Elana, 129, 130
Leys, Ruth, 19n8
Living End, The (1992), 54–59
Logo network, 82–83, 84, 85–86, 86–91, 94–96,
    97, 98, 104, 105. *See also Round Trip Ticket*
Logue, Sara, 92–93
Los Angeles, 46, 68–69, 74
love, 2, 152, 158, 162
#LoveWins, 169, 170–171

Madrid (Spain), 103
magazines, 25–44; class and, 28; community
    and, 25; convergence and, 28; cultural
    membership and, 27; digital media and, 25,
    48; dispersal/concentration and, 29–37;
    gender and, 28; marketplace and, 43–44;
    promotion and, 28; public cultures and, 43;
    public service and, 28, 29; race and, 28;
    sex-related advertising and, 27; sexuality
    politics and, 50n20; urban commerce
    patterns and, 25. *See also individual
    magazines*
male/female binary, 161

maps, 29–31, *30*, 32, 34, 35
marketers, 106n3
marketing discourses, 141–143, 149–150, 151,
    154, 161
marketplace, 23–24, 42–44, 47, 105–106
marriage rights. *See* same-sex marriage
Marx, Karl, 12–13, 14
McCarthy, Anna, 123, 132, 137n43
McDonough, Shannon, 103
McGlotten, Shaka, 156, 162n2
media: affective value and, 14–15; American
    Dream and, 9; capital and, 13; consumer
    citizenship and, 5, 21n36, 106n5; convergence
    and, 23; marketplace and, 44; sexual
    minorities and, 6, 11, 172; value and, 13.
    See also gay and lesbian media
media commerce, 12, 17, 18, 22n42, 23, 161, 172
memes, 140, *141*, 142, 162n1, 162n2
Mesh, 146, 151
metronormativity, 26, 66
Mexico City, 101–102
Midnight Sun (bar), 37
Military Acceptance Project, 153
Milk, Harvey, 35–36
minorities, 8, 9, 17. *See also* ethnicity; race;
    sexual minorities
Mittell, Jason, 52n46, 129
mobile media companies, 140–142, 146–147,
    149–150, 153, 154, 161
modernity, 5, 9, 16, 17, 26, 49n13
Molly's Girl (2012), 66, 74
Monahan, Jackie, 93–94
Money Matters, 87
Monroe, Kate, 99
Monster, The (New York), 39
Morrison, Jim, 96
Morse, Margaret, 107n22
Mukherjee, Roopali, 85
multiple publics, 37–39, *38*, *40*, 42, 44
music, 45–46

Nakamura, Lisa, 165n33
"Nanny" (Steinmuller, Rose), 7–9
national culture, 5, 8, 9
national identity, 20n15
National Symbolic, 54, 67, 71, *71*, 75
nation-states, 5, 7, 11, 20n27
Neczypor, Anne, 93–94
Neighborhoods Alive, 34
neoliberalism, 53–54, 76, 85–86
Netflix, 53, 59

network television: business models and, 116, 122; class and, 115, 119, 121; commodity consumption and, 115; gay and lesbian audiences and, 5, 47; homophobia and, 132; marketplace and, 44; redundancy and, 122–123; sexual minorities and, 123–125; upscale audiences and, 115, 135n17, 135n18, 135n19. *See also* cable TV; sitcoms; television; *individual programs*

New Jersey, 34, 70–72

New Orleans Gay and Lesbian Community Center, 40

New Queer Cinema, 17, 57–61, 68, 76–77, 80n41

New York: dispersal/concentration and, 28, 30–34; *Dorian Blues* (2004) and, 66; *Gypsy 83* (2001) and, 62–63; *Julie Johnson* (2002) and, 70–72; Latino publics and, 39–40; magazines and, 25; Rich, B. Ruby on, 80n41; Rubyfruit, 42; *The Skinny* (2012) and, 65. *See also HX* (New York); *Next* (New York)

New York Times, 170

Newman, Michael, 129, 130, 133

NewNowNext website, 95–96

news programs, 86–98; business models and, 83, 86, 90–92, 94–95; commodity activism and, 83–84, 85, 86; corporate synergy and, 83, 97, 98; as genre, 47; Here TV, 82–83, 85–86, 92–94, 96–98; Logo network, 86–91, 94–96, 97, 98; podcasts and, 92–94; Q Television Network, 82–83, 85–86, 91–92, 94; viewer interactivity and, 86, 91. *See also individual programs*

Next (New York), 25, 27, 28, 30–32, *30*, 34, 39, *40*, 43–44

Ng, Eve, 84, 98

Nguyen, Tan Hoang, 156

Nickelodeon, 21n36, 106n5

Nightspots (Chicago), 25, 27, 28, 35, 39, 43

Normal, Ohio, 112, 113, 115–117, 122, 123–124, 125–126, 130, 132–133

normativity: Ahmed, Sara and, 19n10; gay and lesbian media and, 2, 171, 172; homonormativity, 4–5; metronormativity, 26, 66; sexual minorities and, 2, 53–54; Snediker, Michael and, 18n4; television and, 122, 128, 130

North End (bar), 34–35, 44

Nye, David, 20n15

Oakland (California), 36

Obama, Barack, 88–89, 93, 153

Obergefell v. Hodges (2015), 169

Okita, Teri, 87

On Q Live, 91

online communities, 24. *See also* apps

online media. *See* gay and lesbian media

online streaming, 16, 53, 59, 102, 127, 133

Opoku, Gabriel, 99

Out, 96, 97, 98

OUTtv, 102

Palombo, Ross, 87–89

Parks, Lisa, 84

Peace Point Entertainment Group, 102

Pellegrini, Ann, 105

"Personal History of Lesbian Porn, A" (Allison), 6

personal/political, 74–75, 90

Picture This! 59

Pink Triangle Press, 102

platforms, 16, 61, 163n9

podcasts, 16, 92–94, 96, 109n48

politics: cable TV and, 17, 82, 84, 85, 98, 105; citizenship and, 67, 83–84; consumer citizenship and, 12; distribution companies and, 60–61; gay and lesbian cinema and, 53–54, 58, 60–61, 63, 74–75; gay and lesbian media and, 4, 12; gentrification and, 69; homonormativity and, 4; Logo network and, 89–90; Rainbow Theory and, 21; television and, 112–113. *See also* sexual politics

Portland (Oregon), 100–101, 102

Posh (bar), 32

promotion, 28

public cultures: aggregation and, 39, 47; Chicago and, 35; commerce and, 39; counterpublics and, 49n10; dispersal/concentration and, 36–37; governance acts and, 31–32, 34; Guerrilla Gay Bar and, 46; lesbians and, 34; magazines and, 43; marketplace and, 42, 44; race and, 35, 36; San Francisco and, 35–36; sexual minorities and, 25; urban centers and, 23–24. *See also* multiple publics

public service, 28, 29, 40–42

public transportation, 34

Puerto Ricans, 40, *41*

Q on the Move, 98, 104

Q Television Network, 82–83, 85–86, 91–92, 94, 104

QTN Worldcast, 91

Queens (New York), 32

queer (as term), 4, 24, 131

queer feelings, 3, 19n10
queer readings, 128–129, 131–134
queer relay, 22n42
queer sociality, 27, 49n7
queer theory, 1, 18n4, 169

race: advertisements and, 34; aggregation and, 39–40; apps and, 148, 155–156, 165n33; Berlant, Lauren and, 78n1; Chauncey, George and, 32, 49n7; Chicago and, 35; digital media and, 37; gay and lesbian cinema and, 54; gay and lesbian media and, 11; gentrification and, 31–32; *HX* (New York) and, 34; magazines and, 28; maps and, 32, 35; *Next* (New York) and, 34; *Nightspots* (Chicago) and, 35; public cultures and, 35, 36; public transportation and, 34; romance of community and, 15; San Francisco and, 36; sexual minority publics and, 24, 28; urbanization and, 26; Villarejo, Amy and, 14
Race, Kane, 163n6, 163n12, 164n16
Rainbow Theory, 21n37
Rhodes, John David, 80n32
Rich, B. Ruby, 57, 58, 60, 68, 80n41
Richmond, Scott, 162n4
romance, 142, 149–150, 152, 161–162, 164n16
romance of community, 15, 161
Rosenzweig, Joshua, 92–93
Round Trip Ticket, 98–103, 104
Rubyfruit (New York), 42
Run Lola Run (1998), 66

same-sex marriage, 3–4, 66, 87, 95, 96, 97, 153, 161–162, 169, 170–171
San Francisco, 25, 28, 35–36, 37, 39, 65–66
Savoia, Marc, 99, 101
"Scattered Speculations on Questions of Value" (Spivak), 12–13
Schatz, Thomas, 52n47
Schleier, Merrill, 80n36
scholarship, 13, 105–106, 127–131, 133, 134, 165n25, 171, 172
Schudson, Michael, 88–89
Schultz, Jon, 100
Schumpeter, Joseph, 42
Sconce, Jeffrey, 129–130, 138n79
Screenplay, 45–46
Scruff, 147, 150, 153, 165n36
Sedgwick, Eve Kosofsky, 11–12, 19n8
Sender, Katherine, 22n41, 79n22, 79n25, 106n3
sex-related advertising, 27–28

sexual identity: as affective category, 5; city iconography and, 77; as consumer category, 17; consumer taste and, 116, 117, 118, 120–121, 122, 126; gay and lesbian cinema and, 54, 62, 73, 77; Halberstam, Jack on, 26; *Julie Johnson* (2002) and, 72; metronormativity and, 66; New Queer Cinema and, 58–59; urban centers and, 26, 66
sexual minorities: affective value and, 14–15; apps and, 17–18, 47, 149–150, 161; cable TV and, 84–85, 86, 89, 105, 108n33; camera shots and, 64; city iconography and, 69–70; as consumers, 12, 23; continuity editing and, 70, 73; distribution companies and, 59–60; enfranchisement and, 12; film delivery technologies and, 59; gentrification and, 32; Hollywood and, 54, 58, 59; marketplace and, 44–45; media and, 6, 11, 172; national culture and, 5; New Queer Cinema and, 17, 57–58; normativity and, 2, 53–54; online communities and, 24; public cultures and, 25; romance of community and, 15, 161; scholarship and, 13; sex-related advertising and, 27; television and, 17, 113, 115–116, 118, 122, 123–125, 127, 128, 130, 132, 135n21; as term, 4; travel programs and, 83; urban centers and, 24–25, 31, 47; urbanization and, 5, 17, 23; US presidential debate and, 82
sexual minority publics, 24, 28
sexual politics, 2, 15, 57, 60–61, 142, 169–170. *See also* politics
sexuality, 11, 26. *See also* sexual minorities
Shelter (2007), 72–73
Sidetrack (Chicago), 39, 43
Simkhai, Joel, 150, 167n54
Simmel, Georg, 48n2
sitcoms, 16, 47, 113, 116–117, 123, 125–127, 136n27, 137n49. *See also individual programs*
Skandros, Johnny, 150–151
Skinny, The (2012), 65, 66, 68, 74
Sleidi, Yeni, 146
Smallwood, Charlotte, 89–90
Smith-Shomade, Beretta, 84
Sneakers (venue), 34
Snediker, Michael, 18n4
Soap, 131–132
social media, 48, 143, 155, 158–159. *See also* apps; #LoveWins
Some of My Best Friends, 112, 113, 115, 119, 120–122, 125–126, 127, 130, 132
spatial practices, 31, 48n5

Spivak, Gayatri, 12–13, 14, 19n8, 139n80
Star Gaze (Chicago), 42, 43
Steamworks (sex club), 35
Steinmuller, Rose "Nanny" (great-grandmother), 7–9
Stonewall Inn, 31–32
Strand Releasing, 59
streaming, 16, 53, 59, 102, 127, 133

television, 112–134; aesthetic value and, 129–130, 139n81; affective value and, 112–113, 114, 127, 128–129, 130; apparitional television, 133–134; capital and, 113–114, 128, 129, 130, 131, 133, 134; class and, 115, 119, 121; consumer taste and, 116, 117, 118, 120–121; contextualization and, 131–132; derision and, 131; ethnicity and, 121; file sharing and, 133; gender and, 129; homo/hetero binary and, 119–120; homophobia and, 124; identity and, 114–122, 126–128, 129, 130, 132, 134; news anchors, 107n22; normativity and, 122, 128, 130; politics and, 112–113; queer readings and, 128–129, 131–134; scholarship and, 127–131, 133, 134; sexual minorities and, 17, 113, 115–116, 118, 122, 123–125, 127, 128, 130, 132, 135n21, 172; sitcoms, 16, 47, 113, 116–117, 123, 125–127, 136n27, 137n49; urban/rural geographic binaries and, 118–119; Villarejo, Amy and, 114–116, 128, 135n13, 138n70; whiteness and, 121. *See also* cable TV; network television; *individual networks*; *individual programs*
television news anchors, 107n22
territorialization, 78n6, 142–143
Thousand Plateaus, A (Deleuze and Guattari), 144, 145
365Gay News on Logo, 86, 88
365gay.com, 88, 95
Thrift, Nigel, 19n8, 48n2
TLA Releasing, 59
Tomkins, Silvan, 11–12
Trailblazers, 97
travel programs, 98–104; *Bump!* 98, 102–104, 111n83; commodity activism and, 83–84, 85; digital technologies and, 83, 98; funding models and, 83; as genre, 47; multiple publics and, 42; *Q on the Move*, 98, 104; *Round Trip Ticket*, 98–103, 104; sexual minorities and, 83
Twitter, 158–159, 169

United States v. Windsor (2013), 97
upscale audiences, 115, 135n17, 135n18, 135n19

urban centers, 8, 23–29, 42, 47–48, 48n2, 172. *See also* magazines; *individual cities*
urban development, 31–32, 34
urban settings, 63–75. *See also* city iconography
urban signifiers, 66–67, 70–71, *70, 72, 74–75, 75*, 119. *See also* city iconography
urbanization, 5, 17, 23, 25–26, 48. *See also* magazines
urban/rural geographic binaries, 118–119
US gay and lesbian rights movement, 31
US presidential debate, 82
user-generated content, 142, 143, 155, 161, 163n9

value, 12–13, 112–113, 122–123, 126–130, 133–134, 139n81
Viacom, 86, 91, 94, 96, 104
video, 57–58, 61, 79n19. *See also* delivery technologies
viewer interactivity, 83, 86, 91, 107n20
viewing platforms, 61, 163n9. *See also* delivery technologies; online streaming
Villarejo, Amy, 13–16, 22n40, 22n45, 114–116, 128, 135n13, 138n70
viral videos, 143, 155
virtual intimacies, 162n2
VJ Pro, 45

Wallace, Lee, 80n45
Wapa, 151
Warner, Michael, 21n37, 49n10
Warren, Rick, 88, 93
Water Bearer Films, 59
Wells Fargo, 96
Werner, Carsey, 132–133
White, Mimi, 87, 133
white gay men, 32–34, *33*, 36
Wikle, Will, 99, 101
Will and Grace, 122–123, 130
Willy Wonka & the Chocolate Factory (1971), 140, *141*
Windsor, Edie, 97
Windy City Media, 28
Windy City Times (Chicago), 28
Wing Ma'am, 147, 148
Withers, Scott, 91
Wolfe Video, 59
women, 39, 67, 147, 148, 151, 161. *See also* gender; lesbians
women's media culture, 9–10

YouTube, 96, 157, 163n9

F. HOLLIS GRIFFIN is Assistant Professor of Queer Studies and Communication at Denison University, where he teaches and conducts research on media studies, cultural theory, and the politics of identity and desire. He has published research in the journals *Cinema Journal, Television and New Media, Popular Communication, Quarterly Review of Film and Video,* and the *Journal of Popular Film and Television,* as well as in the anthology *The Companion to Reality Television.*

CPSIA information can be obtained
at www.ICGtesting.com
Printed in the USA
LVOW13*1509141117

556254LV00018B/323/P

9 780253 024473